ARCHAEOLOGIES OF COMPLEXITY

Archaeologies of Complexity addresses the nature of contemporary archaeology and the study of social change, and debates the transition from perceived simple, egalitarian societies to the complex power structures and divisions of our modern world.

Since the eighteenth century, archaeologists have examined complexity in terms of successive types of societies, from early bands, tribes and chiefdoms to states; through stages of social evolution, including 'savagery', 'barbarism' and 'civilization', to the present state of complexity and inequality. The book explains the often ambiguous terms of 'complexity', 'hierarchy' and 'inequality' and provides a critical account of the Anglo-American research of the last forty years which has heavily influenced the subject.

The author challenges the established arguments, supporting a radical alternative analysis of early state societies with a detailed case study of the later prehistoric societies of the western Mediterranean. He stresses the need for a more even engagement between Anglo-American and other archaeologists on issues of archaeological theory and practice. The result is a fresh and engaging look at theories of social complexity and the relevance of archaeology to modern society.

Robert Chapman is Professor of Archaeology at the University of Reading.

ARCHAEOLOGIES OF COMPLEXITY

Robert Chapman

Routledge
Taylor & Francis Group

LONDON AND NEW YORK

First published 2003
by Routledge
11 New Fetter Lane, London EC4P 4EE

Simultaneously published in the USA and Canada
by Routledge
29 West 35th Street, New York, NY 10001

Routledge is an imprint of the Taylor & Francis Group

Typeset in Garamond by RefineCatch Limited, Bungay, Suffolk
Printed and bound in Great Britain by
Biddles Ltd, Guildford and King's Lynn

British Library Cataloguing in Publication Data
A catalogue record for this book is available from the British Library

Library of Congress Cataloging in Publication Data
Chapman, Robert, 1949–
Archaeologies of complexity / Robert Chapman.
p. cm.
Includes bibliographical references (p.   ) and index.
1. Social archaeology. 2. Social change. I. Title.
CC72.4 .C47 2003
930.1 – dc21
2002031948

ISBN 0–415–27307–2 (hbk)
ISBN 0–415–27308–0 (pbk)

For Jo and Chris

CONTENTS

ILLUSTRATIONS

TABLES

PREFACE

This book addresses two main themes, the nature of contemporary archaeology and the study of social change, especially towards what is called increasing complexity. It stems from the experiences of teaching archaeology in my own country and practising archaeological research in another one. The effect of these combined experiences has been to make me think about (a) the nature of archaeological theory and its relation to practice, (b) the relevance of what I do as an archaeologist to the contemporary world, and (c) how we approach the study of past societies. Although the case study is taken from the west Mediterranean, I have tried to make clear the implications for specialists in other areas and periods. I have also adopted a style that I hope makes the book easily accessible to students who want to learn about archaeological theory and social change in an historical context. In this way, I aim to encourage a greater awareness of the more complex ways in which these subjects have been studied during the last four decades, and to escape from the 'linear evolution' model of paradigm change that has dominated archaeology. In addition, I add my voice to those who encourage a more even engagement between the Anglo-American world and 'other' archaeologies, especially those of countries in which we may practise our archaeology. The result is, I hope, both interesting and challenging to the reader.

ACKNOWLEDGEMENTS

I have written this book within two physical and intellectual contexts. First, I am grateful to my colleagues in the Department of Archaeology at the University of Reading for providing the daily environment in which to work and to think, as well as the students whom I have taught the rudiments of archaeological theory and Mediterranean prehistory. The opportunity to begin preparing and writing the book was provided by a sabbatical year in 1998–99, supported by the Research Endowment Trust Fund of the University and the strong backing of Michael Fulford. I would also like to thank Roberta Gilchrist and Heinrich Härke for relieving me of some administrative responsibilities during the completion of the book. Margaret Matthews kindly prepared the illustrations.

Second, I warmly thank all Spanish colleagues who have collaborated with me, sent me copies of their publications, shared their ideas with me and, not least, entertained me over the years. In particular I thank Pedro Castro, Trinidad Escoriza, Silvia Gili, Vicente Lull, Rafael Micó, Cristina Rihuete, Roberto Risch and María Encarna Sanahuja, not forgetting Teresa Sanz and Montserrat Menasanch, for their endless support, stimulus and friendship. Their collective spirit is a wonderful counter to the competitive individualism that pervades so much of the academic world. Following Marx's principle, each gives of his/her abilities towards each according to his/her needs. I would also like to thank the numerous specialists who have worked with the 'equipo' in the Vera Basin and whose publications are cited in this book. In particular, Jane Buikstra has been with us since the beginning of the Gatas project.

I thank Vicente Lull, Rafael Micó and Steven Mithen for reading and commenting on draft chapters. I have tried, wherever possible, to take their advice and criticism, but in some cases it would require the writing of another book! The editorial staff at Routledge has been both encouraging and patient and I thank Vicky Peters, Julene Barnes, Polly Osborn and Richard Stoneman.

Lastly I thank my family, Jan, Jo and Chris, for their support and tolerance of my interest in the past and the time investment that teaching, administration and research demands of modern academics. I dedicate this book, with love, to Jo and Chris.

1

A COMPLEX AND UNEQUAL WORLD

Knowledge, relevance and experience

We live in a complex and unequal world, a world without historical precedent. During the last two million years, successive human species have colonized the planet, and during the last five decades our species has begun the physical exploration of space. In the course of human history, the decisions which affect us have been taken at increasing distances from our daily lives: autonomy has been surrendered to, and power appropriated by, regional and national governments. Out of the first states five and a half thousand years ago grew the first empires, mobilizing and exploiting human labour and material goods across regions many times the size of the original states. From the fifteenth century AD, European colonists annexed land and peoples on other continents. As recently as the 1950s our world atlases were a collage of colours, symbolizing the empires of European nation states. The leaders of these states took political decisions affecting the lives of millions around the globe, and fought two world wars in the last century. Capitalism accentuated inequalities, both within nation states and between those states and their colonies. Although we now live, with the exception of a few enclaves, islands and promontories, in a post-colonial world, changes in technology, politics, culture and the economy mean that our lives are governed increasingly at the global scale.

The concept of globalization is the subject of much debate in the social sciences. At a cultural level, changes as diverse as mass tourism, consumerism, and modern communications based on information technology reduce diversity in the world and enhance belief in a 'global consciousness' (Turner 1994: 8–9) among dominant Western interest groups. In this new millennium it may be possible for tourists in any city in the world to eat in a McDonald's or a Pizza Hut, buy the same designer label clothes and get their CDs from a Virgin megastore. Once inside these identical microenvironments, such

1

homogenization means that these tourists could be anywhere: they can travel without travelling and continue to support Western economic interests. Such is the power of commodification that, it has been argued, the main threat to religious faiths such as Islam 'is going to be brought about by Tina Turner and Coca-Cola and not by rational arguments and rational inspection of presuppositions and the understanding of Western secularism' (Turner 1994: 9–10). The irony, of course, is that faced with this choice, many of us in the West might be tempted to reach for the Koran!

Cultural globalization supports the homogenization of behaviour and taste. Individual parts of the current world system are also linked by economic globalization, with the creation of a global financial system based on electronic money. Each day we follow the trail of such money through the East Asian, London and New York financial markets, as stocks and shares, as well as national currencies, rise and fall in relation to the confidence of such markets. Everything is interconnected (an important part of any definition of complexity). The market is one. The fall from grace of the East Asian 'Tiger' economies, followed by speculation on the state of the Chinese and Brazilian economies in 1998, sent tremors around the markets and terrified investors. This autonomous financial system, with its banks controlling Third World debt and confidence bolstered or undermined by the views of financiers and speculators, has dire consequences for the world's political order: 'the increasing powers of co-ordination lodged within the world's financial system have emerged to some degree at the expense of the power of the nation state to control capital flow and, hence, its own fiscal and monetary policy' (Harvey 1989: 165). Global capitalism has added 'money power' to the control of the means of production (Harvey 1989: 347). The worldwide domination of neo-liberal economics in the last two decades has elevated business over politics and multinational corporations over national politicians and governments: for example, of the 100 largest world economies, 51 are such corporations and 49 are nation states (Hertz 2001: 7).

Not surprisingly, the world of today is one with greater inequalities, both in the West and between it and the rest of the world. The crippling cost of Third World debt prevents much needed investment in health and education. The *United Nations Human Development Report* published in 1999 cites the case of Tanzania, where the costs of repaying such debt are nine times greater than spending on health and four times greater than spending on education (*Independent*, 12 July 1999). Companies seek to reduce labour and wage costs,

in order to maximize competitive profits. Productive labour is con-
tracted out to the Third World and poorly paid, temporary
employment ('McJobs') has increased in the West. Figures on the
world's top 100 transnational corporations from 1990 to 1997 show
that their assets have increased by a staggering 288 per cent, while
in contrast their employees have increased by less than 9 per cent
(Klein 2000: 261). The richest 1 per cent of the North American
population owns 40 per cent of the country's wealth (Hertz 2001:
45). The rise in economic inequality since the collapse of Communist states and the introduction of free market capitalism in the Soviet
Union and eastern Europe has been the fastest on record (Callinicos
2000: 2).

Since the Thatcher and Reagan years of the 1980s the Western
world has become awash with millionaires and the imbalance
between rich and poor is now the greatest in modern times. Callinicos (2000: 1) also cites the 1999 *United Nations Human Development Report* to document this disparity: the net worth of the 200
richest people in the world in 1998 equalled the income of a staggering 41 per cent of world population. The number of millionaires
in Britain rose from 6,600 in 1993 to 47,300 in 1999, and it is
predicted that there will be some 150,000 in 2002. Most of this
growth is based on the stock market, executive stock option
schemes, information technology, the media, leisure and fashion. At
the same time two out of every five children in the United Kingdom
are born into poverty, and some 400,000 people are homeless. The
estimated combined wealth of forty entertainers in the United
Kingdom is equivalent to the national debts of either Burundi or
Chad. There is also an 'embedded structure of inequality' (Callinicos
2000: 6) that serves to undermine belief in wage mobility and the
potential for economic 'advancement' based on the free market in
Western economies. One hundred and fifty years ago, Marx and
Engels condemned the 'icy water of egotistical calculation' (1998:
37) and the 'naked, shameless, direct, brutal exploitation' (1998: 38)
of nineteenth-century capitalism. These harsh judgements have lost
little of their force or relevance, in spite of changes in historical
context and scale of analysis.

Of course, if it were not for the machine, for technology, there
would be no capitalism. Digital technologies are at the heart of the
revolution in global communication, underpinning the financial
markets and enabling access to a staggering pool of worldwide
information. We live in the era of the nerd. The appallingly
rich nerds and their transnational corporations get more out of the

Internet than does the Third World. Once again, inequality rules. For postmodernists, digital technologies signify a move towards greater equality, towards 'democratization', as information becomes widely disseminated and individuals and groups possess the ability to develop alternative views. This liberating 'multivocality' (to give it its much vaunted name) 'allows special interest groups to form and create new identities and local meanings' (Hodder 1999: 151). Unfortunately for this idealistic vision, access to information technology, and hence to information, is restricted, even within the developed countries (Hodder 1999: 151–2), thus adding another inequality in the contemporary world. Although it has been estimated that some 100 million computers are linked to the Internet, they are accessible to only 2.4 per cent of the world's population (Callinicos 2000: 8). While a North American can use one month's salary to buy a computer, a Bangladeshi needs the savings from eight years' work to achieve the same aim (*United Nations Human Development Report*, cited in the *Independent*, 12 July 1999). Low levels of literacy across the planet exacerbate such inequalities.

Complexity, evolution and archaeology

How has this complex and unequal world developed? Have inequalities always existed in human societies or was there an original state of equality, natural to our species? These questions are among those that have exercised historical and social scientists since the eighteenth century. As Bruce Trigger has pointed out, the development of complexity in human societies has been tied in to the concept of evolution during modern times, given the concern of evolution with 'understanding directionality as a major characteristic of human history' (1998a: 10). Trigger goes on to argue that 'this directionality involves an overall tendency towards creating larger, more internally differentiated, and more complexly articulated structures that require greater *per capita* expenditure of energy for their operation' (1998a: 10). This link between complexity and evolution can be seen clearly in the arguments of the nineteenth-century father of modern sociology, Herbert Spencer.

> The cosmos, plant and animal life, and human society had evolved in that order from simple, homogenous beginnings into increasingly differentiated, more complexly organised, and more intricately articulated entities. . . . Societies that were more complex and better integrated were able to

prosper at the expense of less complex ones, just as human individuals and groups who were better adapted to social life supplanted those who were less well adapted.

(Trigger 1998a: 57)

Here, then, is one clear source of increasing inequalities, in the ability of the 'more complex' to dominate the 'less complex', as societies evolve from the local to the regional, continental and global levels.

The concept of social evolution through stages towards increasing complexity was present in European thought before Darwin published *The Origin of Species* in 1859: as has been pointed out often (e.g. Harris 1968), evolution was a social concept before it became a biological one. Already in the eighteenth century, Enlightenment philosophers were using the observations of missionaries and explorers to arrange non-European societies in sequences of increasing complexity. Scholars such as Montesquieu and Turgot constructed evolutionary stages from hunting, through pastoral, to agricultural societies. Others, like Miller, examined the evolution of institutions (for example, the family) rather than societies. Examples of these 'conjectural histories' became even more prominent in the nineteenth century, whether comparing whole societies, or social institutions, legal systems, kinship systems, or knowledge and belief systems (e.g. Trigger 1998a: 74–7; Burrow 1968; Harris 1968).

Underlying all of these evolutionary sequences was the Enlightenment belief in progress, with greater complexity or social evolution being equated with progress towards modernity. The clearest touchstone of increasing complexity was technology, as seen in the emerging ethnographic record, and in the distant past revealed by the new discipline of archaeology. From Thomsen's creation of the Three Age System, through the refinements and subdivisions of Lubbock, Montelius, Reinecke, Déchelette and others, technology provided the best-preserved marker of social evolution. In the hands of Lewis Henry Morgan, technology was tied into production in his three-stage evolutionary scheme, from savagery to barbarism to civilization, which became a major influence on developing Marxist thought through the work of Friedrich Engels (1972). By the 1930s Soviet scholars were using a series of evolutionary stages from pre-class to class and classless societies, although now technology was subsumed within the famous five modes of production (Bloch 1985). Another tradition of evolutionary thought, although severely ruptured in the early nineteenth century, revived in the cultural evolutionism of the 1950s and 1960s.

Technology remained a key to the capture of energy which marked the more 'successful' and complex cultures, but greater emphasis was placed upon social institutions, and especially upon the evolution of societies through stages from the 'simplest' hunters and gatherers to the more 'complex' states.

One of the great achievements of archaeology has been to construct history, and to replace conjectural history. Whatever speculations there may be about the forms taken by societies at successive stages, or periods, of their history, whatever differences of opinion there might be about any general sequence of evolution (e.g. unilinear, multilinear, convergent, divergent, parallel, etc.), and whatever the causal mechanisms championed by individual scholars, it is the archaeological record which holds the key to the study of long-term changes in complexity and inequality.

The rationality that was one basis of the Enlightenment has been put to good use to construct a human past. At the same time, this rationality has neither removed 'the irrationalities of myth, religion, superstition', nor prevented 'the arbitrary use of power' (Harvey 1989: 12). Indeed the idealistic belief in progress that was another basis of the Enlightenment has been severely dented by the experience of armed conflict and ethnic cleansing in the twentieth century. For some, such as the biologist Stephen Jay Gould, 'progress is a noxious, culturally embedded, untestable, nonoperational idea that must be replaced if we wish to understand the patterns of history' (cited in Lewin 1993: 139). For others, such as Bruce Trigger, our understanding of human societies, based on two centuries of archaeology and anthropology, has enabled us to discount the automatic association of increased complexity with general progress, and affirm that 'technological progress has sustained an extraordinary increase in human numbers and has enabled human beings – at least in the short run – to dominate and exploit the world's ecosystem' (1998a: 260). But what of the long term, which, after all, is the preserve of archaeology, and indeed, our own future as a species? Technology may support larger populations, but its appropriation has enhanced the inequalities between them.

These are serious issues that lie at the heart of the critique of modernism by postmodernists and others, for whom such notions as progress and evolution are ethnocentric: as such they mark the persistence of the intellectual legacy of racism, colonialism and imperialism and the denigration of cultural diversity. The concept of complexity has also come under close scrutiny. Michael Rowlands has argued that it is Eurocentric, and that 'the meta-narrative of simple to complex is a dominant ideology that organizes the writing of contemporary world prehistory in favour of a modernizing ethos and the primacy of the West' (1988: 36). According to Rowlands, the key traits that mark the attainment of complexity (e.g. cities, the state, writing, bureaucracy, social stratification, and long-distance trade) have been selected because of their importance in the development of European modernity (1988: 32). This simple–complex duality, a creation of modernism, underlies many other contemporary disciplines besides archaeology. For Shanks and Tilley complexity was 'ideologically loaded' (1987a: 164): the use of terms such as 'simple' and 'complex' implied 'superior' and 'inferior', the former being valued at the expense of the latter (1987a: 163–4).

But if we turn to the long-term record of archaeology, there is, I think, no doubt that the human societies which inhabit this planet have become more complex (in the sense of interconnectedness) and more unequal, both within individual societies and at the level of global relations. This is a gross trend, superimposed on shorter-term records of evolution and devolution, of 'rise' and 'fall' of more complex societies such as the earliest states, of change at different rates and scales, or to put it more grandly, of history. There have been many different forms of society, as there are today, and complexity should not be conceived as the ultimate goal of social evolution. Indeed the simple–complex duality which occupies Rowlands is itself a simplification which obscures this variety of social forms and the sequences of change visible in the archaeological record in different parts of the world. It should not be an aim of archaeologists to classify past societies as either 'simple' or 'complex'. When Anglo-American archaeologists talk of 'complex societies', they are using a kind of shorthand, a device for focusing on societies which are more like 'us'. The emergence of such societies is thought to be significant in the history of our species. Rather than a discredited piece of modernism, is it not inevitable that we look to identify and understand such major social changes in our past?

Of course, the criteria that we use to identify changes – such as the emergence of complex societies – in the past are chosen in the present, in historically determined contexts. The term 'complex' may be defined in different ways, and the criteria by which complexity can be materialized may differ between societies. This is not to advocate relativism, but to recognize the divergence of world archaeology as practised today, and our greater understanding of the use of material culture in everyday social practices.

Contemporary studies of complexity are, then, the latest in a long line of such studies, beginning with the conjectural histories of the eighteenth and nineteenth centuries. Unlike these predecessors, we are dealing with an empirical record, that of archaeology, and can trace sequences, traditions, different social forms and different materializations of complexity and inequality. The record of complexity has become more complex! It also permeates disciplines such as ecology and biology. Across the disciplines there is much talk of 'complex systems' (e.g. McGlade and van der Leeuw 1997), and of 'Complexity Theory', which, it is claimed, can unify the human and natural sciences, and which also makes use of archaeological data (Lewin 1993). In this sense, archaeology is argued to be making a significant contribution to the understanding of all living systems.

Knowledge and relevance

But what does it matter that archaeologists and other researchers are studying complexity in such systems? Surely, one might argue, an understanding of the archaeological record is not going to change the world? Despite the idealistic commitment of some (e.g. Shanks and Tilley 1987a), is not change in the 'real' world in the hands of the financiers, the entrepreneurs, the military-industrial complex, and the transnational corporations? Is not the message of globalization one of despair and hopelessness? While the intellectual talks of knowledge and truth, power in the real world is surely based on the maxim of the former American Secretary of State, Alexander Haig: 'if you've got them by the balls, their hearts and minds will follow'?! We are aware, as Marx intended, that capitalism is a product of history, but this knowledge has not removed capitalism and all its inequalities. Is not knowledge powerless?

A cynic (perhaps self-defined as a 'realist') would answer 'yes' to most of these questions. For him/her, archaeology is a pastime, a personal, sometimes romantic, voyage of discovery, a way of satisfying curiosity about one's ancestors, but in no way a means for action in the present. And yet knowledge can be a source of power. Why else have dictators and despots tried to control knowledge by imprisoning and exiling academics and teachers (as in the Chinese cultural revolution of the 1960s), or by burning books (as in Nazi Germany)? Is not a sound knowledge of the history of our species an effective counter both to creationism and fundamentalism, let alone to racial or ethnic prejudice? To understand that ethnicity is not inherent in human nature, nor unchanging through time, is a knowledge which is lacking in many areas of the world today, at the cost of thousands of lives. To understand how inequality is created and maintained is a basis for critical thought and action. To understand that there are 'other' ways of organizing society and life, and that gross inequality and exploitation are not part of some 'natural order', can provide the basis for political action and personal empowerment in daily life.

The past as 'the heritage' is already appropriated and funded by governments, and by cultural and ethnic minorities, to express unity and difference (see Hodder 1999: 159). It is appropriated by all manner of 'alternative' voices, including ecofeminist goddess worshippers and New Age groups (see Hodder 1999; Meskell 1998). Indeed, one of the fascinating things about archaeology is that each year another group or individual with no training in, or critical knowledge of, the discipline feels free to voice opinions which make popular television programmes but outrage and dismay professional archaeologists. We would not dream of marching into engineering or neuro-surgery and claiming to have discovered the solution to problems that puzzle practitioners of these disciplines. Books on lost continents, on Atlantis, on prehistoric goddess worship, reach wider markets than anything published by professional archaeologists. The past is appropriated, whether we like it or not, and we should stand up for rationality, and for what we know and can demonstrate about the past. We cannot transform contemporary power relations and inequalities by archaeology alone, but we must not stand apart from the real world and allow the appropriation of pasts that are just plain wrong.

This book as experience

If we accept that complexity and inequalities of all kinds (racial, ethnic, gender, class, etc.) are critical problems in the world today, and that the past offers one avenue for their understanding, then there is a basis for relevant archaeological research. Complexity and inequality have been studied in both prehistoric and historic periods of the past; their material manifestations, whether in the form of impressive monuments or rich burials, have played a prominent role in the history of archaeology, and attract great public interest. What has changed in the last four decades is the conception of both complexity and inequality, as archaeologists have become more interested in theoretical approaches; the latter determine the concepts they use, how to give them meaning through archaeological data and how to evaluate our ideas using this unique record.

My concern in this book is with issues of theory and practice and their articulation in the study of early complex societies, as well as with the complexity of contemporary archaeology. The link here is provided by my own experience. During the last three decades my research in the west Mediterranean has brought me into contact with non-Anglo-American traditions of thought in the social and historical sciences. The subject of research, much of it collaborative, has been the development of inequalities in Copper and Bronze Age societies, especially in south-east Spain. The archaeological record of this region is widely recognized in Europe and has also been included in comparative syntheses and edited volumes on emerging complexity in both the Old and New Worlds (e.g. Earle 1991b; Price and Feinman 1995; Arnold 1996c).

My experience has been one of an 'outsider'. I first arrived in Spain with processualism, literally, as I was carrying a new copy of Lewis Binford's *An Archaeological Perspective* (1972) on my first visit to the south-east. I was the latest member of the Cambridge archaeological diaspora, leaving behind the archaeological record of my own country and bringing 'The Word' to more distant (and less 'developed') regions. This self-confident intellectual colonialism kept me going for a decade. But it was only when I entered into collaboration with Vicente Lull and his colleagues and students on the Gatas project that I began to see the archaeology, especially the theory and methodology, of the Anglo-American world, more as an outsider. Both processual and postprocessual archaeologies were subjected locally to critical review, as their essential texts became available in Spain. A strongly independent attitude was created: these Spaniards did not lie back and think of Cambridge! Armed with the perspective of historical materialism, they proposed a theory of social practices, and they followed through the implications of such a general theory for units of analysis, whether these are artefacts, excavation units or regional groups. Above all, there was a commitment to the relationship between theory and practice, as was developed in our fieldwork on the Gatas project. Suddenly aspects of the ongoing processual–postprocessual debate seemed both distant and parochial.

At the same time, archaeological research on social change in the west Mediterranean began to cause me concern. I noticed that terms like 'complexity', 'hierarchy' and 'inequality' were used interchangeably, or ambiguously. Concepts like 'complex society' were used without definition, or based on different categories of material evidence. 'Complexity' was opposed to 'lack of complexity'. Clearly there were problems in the ways in which society and social change were being conceived and measured. How could we compare and contrast the historical sequences in different regions if these problems were not addressed?

In the chapters that follow, I will attempt to discuss these problems, within the context of archaeological theory and practice, using the archaeological record of south-east Spain as my main example. My concern is with disentangling concepts and ideas, with highlighting ambiguity, and with examining how archaeologists work on specific problems, rather than with more abstract modelling of changes in complexity. I begin by taking a critical look at contemporary archaeology, with an 'outsider's' view of Anglo-American archaeology, and an examination of the Spanish experience of archaeological theory and practice in the last three decades. In Chapter 3 I introduce the reader to different traditions of study of society and social change during the last four decades in the Anglo-American world. This is followed, in Chapter 4, by scrutiny of the definition and use of concepts such as 'egalitarian', 'inequality', 'hierarchy' and 'complexity' in Anglo-American archaeology. In both of these chapters, the view is now that of an 'insider'. The substantial case study of early complexity, as seen through projects relating theory to practice in south-east Spain, is presented in Chapter 5. The implications of Chapters 3–5 for other areas of the west Mediterranean are examined in Chapter 6 while Chapter 7 draws together the main arguments and suggests some wider implications for archaeology in the twenty-first century.

2

⅂AEOLOGICAL THEORY AND PRACTICE

From the outside looking in

It is hardly a novel insight that archaeologists disagree with each other about matters of theory and methodology. What marks out the last three decades in Anglo-American archaeology is the antagonistic nature of debate, and the time and space it has taken up in conferences and publications. Much of this debate has been welcome and essential to the growth of our discipline. Even those who do not regard themselves as 'theoretical archaeologists' recognize the role that theory has to play in structuring our thoughts and practice, as well as in defining data relevant to the problems that we study.

Isms, insiders and typologies

Different theories and schools, usually with names ending in 'ism', have been recognized in the social and historical sciences since the nineteenth century: functionalism, evolutionism, Marxism and idealism were all keenly debated at this time. Other isms (e.g. structuralism) have emerged in the twentieth century. Interest in these theoretical approaches has ebbed and flowed in different regional traditions: evolutionism declined in popularity in the early part of the last century and then underwent a resurgence of activity in the 1950s and 1960s; Marxism maintained itself as an intellectual tradition in Europe (although the number of Marxist archaeologists only increased significantly in the last two decades) while being virtually prohibited in North America (Bloch 1985). It is the nature of the social and historical sciences that such isms do not succeed each other in a linear sequence, each restricted to its time. They are traditions of thought, subject to internal debate, defining their existence by their content and by their opposition to other such traditions.

A lot of the variation that characterizes activity in different schools of archaeology has been subsumed, and as a consequence ignored, in the last three decades. First we went through a phase of 'processualism' versus 'traditionalism' from the mid-1960s to the late 1970s; this was followed by 'processualism' vs 'postprocessualism' (or 'interpretive' archaeology). I do not propose to go through the detailed histories of these conflicts, let alone the rhetoric and argument by caricature used by proponents. The founding texts of New/Processual archaeology (hereafter PA) were published from 1968 to 1972 (Binford and Binford 1968; Clarke 1968; Binford 1972; Clarke 1972; Renfrew 1972), while those of Postprocessual archaeology (PPA) appeared from 1981 to 1987 (Hodder 1982a, 1982b; Shanks and Tilley 1987a, 1987b). Positions were defined by opposition, debates took place in the public arena (e.g. at meetings of the Society for American Archaeology, or the Theoretical Archaeology Group in Britain), and barriers to communication were erected. As Hodder has written recently, 'theoretical debate has become factional and divisive and exclusionary' (1999: 12) and 'archaeological theorists are trapped in separate non-communicating discourses' (2001: 10–11).

The act of definition of these archaeologies was in some respects analogous to that of ethnic group differentiation. At a more basic level, it was, and remains, an act of classification. The typologies of artefacts which were so roundly condemned in 'traditional' archaeology (not to mention the evolutionary 'types' of societies used by processual archaeologists) have now been replaced by typologies of archaeologists (see Thomas 1995: 349–50 for archaeologists employed in British universities). Assumptions are made that all individuals share all of the traits which define the group, or type, that they continue to share those traits, and that internal variation is less important than boundary definition.

Internal variation was visible within PA from a very early stage. For example, Lewis Binford (1972) made a specific point of criticizing David Clarke's *Analytical Archaeology* (1968), while Clarke (1973) and Flannery (1973) launched critiques of Hempelian positivism and laws of human behaviour in the same year. Changes in Binford's position on these issues were apparent soon after (1977), as were his disagreements with Michael Schiffer (Binford 1981). The differences between Old and New World variations of PA were also apparent in Whallon's (1982) comments on archaeological explanation.

Preucel (1995: 147) has argued recently that 'postprocessual archaeology is a label that actively resists definition . . . not a unified program but . . . a collection of widely divergent and often contradictory research interests' (cf. Coudart 1999: 163). A single typology is insufficient to bring out this variation. Likewise Hodder acknowledges that 'there is as much or more variation within post-processual archaeology as there is between it and processual archae-ology' (1991b: 37); for him the very diversity of theoretical approaches is one of the key defining features of PPA. While uphold-ing its distinctiveness as a school of thought (a claim that is difficult to sustain in typological terms, given his definition of PPA cited above), Hodder proposes that PPA is 'less a movement and more a phase in the development of the discipline' (1991b: 37), and more recently that PA and PPA are 'not contradictory but complementary' (1999: 12). Thomas (2000: 2) recognizes the diversity of research activity within PPA, which he describes as 'a non-existent school of thought' (cf. Tilley 2000: 73), and follows Hodder in referring to a 'post processual era' (2000: 18).

The nature of academic debate is such that variation within schools of thought is often ignored by their proponents or critics (e.g. see Shanks and Tilley's 1987b critique of PA); and yet this variation is the key to a more nuanced understanding of theoretical debate and disciplinary change. For a Darwinist, selection could be seen to act on this variation in the course of disciplinary evolution, while a Marxist would no doubt focus attention on the contradic-tions, within any such ism, which led to its transformation. It seems to me strange that the role of agency in social change is widely proclaimed in PPA, with stress placed on the activities of 'know-ledgeable actors', and yet such freedom of thought and action is denied to individual archaeologists.

This judgement may be a little harsh, given recent arguments for compatibility between some aspects of PA and PPA (e.g. Earle 1991a; Hodder 1991b; Preucel 1991a; Preucel 1995), of their com-mon status as science (VanPool and VanPool 1999), and of their common use of middle-range methodologies (Tschauner 1996). But to reduce disciplinary change to a simple succession of hermetically sealed Kuhnian paradigms does little service to reality; the same applies to the simplistic attribution of labels like 'processualist' and 'postprocessualist'. Definition of these schools is now part of the history of archaeology, and yet discussion is still framed in terms of such definition. For example, while I can recognize some of the same variation as Thomas (1995) in theoretical positions adopted by uni-versity-based archaeologists in the United Kingdom, his definition of PA as opposed to PPA is over-restrictive because it is historically situated in the latter's opposition to the former in the 1980s. To merge together those influenced by the American New Archaeology with the Cambridge palaeoeconomy school combines individuals who had little in common with each other when terms like PA were coined.

These problems with typologies of archaeologies and archaeologists should focus our attention on a more subtle analysis of theoretical positions within Anglo-American archaeology, and on similarities as well as differences. This may not help those whose political strategies within the discipline favour exclusion and restriction, or those who feel the need to claim identity through inclusion within a particular, mode-ish (or post-mode-ish) group. Moving beyond such tribalism will, I think, enhance our internal debates, as they respond to, and incorporate, the outcome of practice by individual archaeologists and archaeological projects. There is also something to be learnt from the reaction of 'outsiders' to such debates within Anglo-American archaeology; our prime concerns are not necessarily theirs, as we shall see in the next section.

Isms and outsiders: a world archaeology?

Reading through the papers in Hodder's (1991a) edited book on archaeological theory in Europe, it is striking how uneven, selective or marginal the impact of PA and PPA has been. Long traditions of environmental and ecological approaches, tied into the study of settlement patterns and landscapes, ensured that Scandinavia and Holland were the most receptive areas. Scientific interaction and collaboration existed between these countries and the United Kingdom from the 1930s. But beyond this north-west European network, different intellectual traditions and institutional structures have combined to restrict the adoption of Anglo-American theoretical approaches.

Within the former eastern bloc, Marxist state ideologies combined with the isolation of scientific communities to limit knowledge and discussion of both PA and PPA (e.g. Kobylinski 1991). In Greece, the expansion of interest in archaeological theory was due to the influence of French structural Marxism from the late 1970s, while PA was valued primarily for its materialist methodology (Kotsakis 1991). The situation in Italy seems more complex: the impact (much of it methodological) of PA was evident mostly in the 1980s, but its anthropological approach was countered by the historical strength of the indigenous classical tradition and, to a lesser extent, by the Marxist research of scholars such as Peroni, Puglisi, Carandini and Tosi, while PPA's espousal of idealism (through Collingwood) was thought to be unoriginal, and even reactionary, in the land of Croce (Guidi 1988, 1996). Even in France, there was no widespread adoption and discussion of PA, in spite of the famous Binford–Bordes debate on the meaning of Middle Palaeolithic variability, while postmodernist writings have had minimal impact on French archaeologists, let alone other humanities and social sciences there (Coudart 1999: 162).

Olivier and Coudart argue that the need for both scientific explanation and historical understanding, as perceived in France, makes PA and PPA 'two different expressions of the same thing' (1995: 365); more recently Coudart has argued that 'the majority of French archaeologists typically use the term "theoretical archaeology" to designate both approaches together' (1999: 166–7). This perception may also account for the highly selective approach to Anglo-American archaeological theory in countries such as Greece (see above) and Portugal (Jorge and Oliveira Jorge 1995). Such oppositions as explanation/understanding, and objectivity/subjectivity, which seem to form major stumbling blocks to communication between PA and PPA, are also played down within Marxist thought (McGuire 1992).

Where there has been communication on issues of theory and methodology, it has been characterized by a marked time lag. Key texts or journals have been unavailable because of poor library facilities, financial difficulties, political constraints, and the lack of English translations. But in all cases I would argue that communication has been predominantly in one direction: how many foreign works on archaeological theory and practice have been translated into English, thus exposing the Anglo-American world to ideas from outside? The history of translation of the seminal works of the French prehistorian André Leroi-Gourhan on ethnographic analogy and prehistoric archaeology (the most famous book taking thirty years to appear in English) provides a good example of communication hindered by language (Scarre 1999: 157). In this context, I wonder whether some Anglo-American 'theoretical archaeologists' have read far more in translation of continental European philosophers and social theorists than they have of European archaeologists and their current research. Even with such a lingua franca, increased communication via the journal and meetings of the European Association of Archaeologists, and via the Internet, we still have to confront the subtleties of meaning and the logic and concepts that are central to thought in different languages.

The existence of different intellectual traditions, institutional structures and political contexts, as well as linguistic and other barriers to communication, have all combined to create a rather eclectic approach to PA and PPA within European archaeology. We are not dealing with the all-conquering 'types' of archaeology perceived within the Anglo-American world. In contrast, the degree of adoption of Anglo-American ideas on theory and methodology depends on context, hence its eclectic nature. Communication has tended to be in one direction only, enhanced by the use of English as the lingua franca. Although PPA may be defined as a phase in the discipline's evolution (Hodder 1991b: 37), this seems hard to support in a European context unless PPA is conceived of in its broadest sense, as 'simply "post-", without offering a new unity' (Hodder 1991b: 37). However, this defines PPA by opposition, or contrast, rather than by content, and fails to contend with the accusation of Anglo-American 'hegemony', by which the agenda for theoretical debate is set within the main English-speaking nations. According to the Norwegian Bjorner Olsen, such hegemony is dangerous for the discipline as a whole: 'we have to avoid centring and unifying any discourse as processual or postprocessual; such a position can only lead to orthodoxy, repression and exclusion' (1991: 224). The French archaeologist Laurent Olivier refers to the perception of PPA in continental Europe as 'an intellectualized European version of American globalization' (1999: 176). Most recently, Cornelius Holtorf and Håkan Karlsson (2000: 8) have asserted the need for non-Anglo-American archaeologists to play more central roles in debates on archaeological theory.

Many of the same observations on the impact of Anglo-American archaeology can be made for areas of the world outside Europe (Ucko 1995). Much again depends on context, intellectual traditions and networks, political contraints, language and availability of texts in translation. Time lag again characterizes the reception of ideas from Anglo-American archaeological theory. In addition, we have to understand the legacy of colonialism: in some countries, European 'schools' of archaeology are still active, while in others the influence of the archaeology of colonial powers is still evident (e.g. Kinehan 1995, on German influence in Namibia). Post-colonial independence is also seen in an intellectual form, as local traditions of archaeological practice assert themselves: in Africa, for example, it has been argued that European archaeological influences 'have at best constrained rather than aided or facilitated a proper understanding of African cultural history' (Andah 1995: 96). If, as this argument continues, 'archaeologists, anthropologists and historians start out from European concepts and standards, not those of African society' (Andah 1995: 98; cf. Schmidt 1983), it is not surprising that attempts to set the archaeological agenda are being actively resisted.

The case of South America provides a range of examples of the development of local archaeologies in the context of colonialism, nationalism and political instability (Politis 1995; Funari 1995). While experience varied from country to country, American and European influences account for training in basic archaeological methods and for the introduction of theoretical frameworks (e.g. evolutionism, diffusionism, Marxism). For example, Funari (1999) documents the influence of the north American ecological approach through archaeologists such as Meggers in Brazil, while López Mazz (1999) shows the traditional influence of French techniques, analytical methods and theoretical approaches on archaeological fieldwork, lithic typologies and rock art studies in Uruguay and Brazil. The influence of PA was most noticeable in the 1980s, although its reception was far from uniform. The reading, discussion and citation of key texts in countries like Chile and Argentina (under conditions of political dictatorship in which Marxism became the ideology of resistance) was not matched in Mexico (see Bate 1998), where Marxist debate flourished. Currently PPA is beginning to be discussed in countries such as Brazil (Funari 1995) and Mexico (Bate 1998), where positivism has already been criticized, along with the perceived lack of theory on social change in PA, and the nature of archaeological knowledge.

As with the European countries discussed above, both PA and PPA have been of marginal importance to large parts of South America. But Politis (1995: 227) argues that 'so far in the history of South America, there has been no such thing as a school of "indigenous archaeology", if that implies a way of thinking and practising archaeology which has not been derived from Western archaeology'. Does this imply that the influence of PPA in particular will continue to grow across the continent? I think it highly unlikely. While Politis's view of the relations of dependence between South American and Western archaeologists will continue at the level of technical resources and infrastructure, I see strong evidence of intellectual independence, for example, in the work of the Grupo Oaxtepec (see McGuire 1992: 67–8), with their rejection of French structural Marxism, as well as of polar oppositions such as subjectivity/objectivity.

The Mexican Manuel Gándara studied at the University of Michigan at the turn of the 1980s, and then produced what must be one of the most detailed, well-argued and balanced critiques of processual archaeology published anywhere (1982). He recognized the differences, and changes, of opinion among proponents of PA, as well as its positive contributions, and, using the concept of a 'theoretical position', rather than Kuhn's 'paradigm', analysed the degree to which PA was internally coherent. Interestingly, Gándara also anticipated the relativist critique of PPA by pointing out that 'if there is no way of evaluating our propositions (on the past), and "all science is ideology" is a proposition, then there is no means of evaluating it' (1982: 154).

Vargas Arenas and Sanoja (1999) provide an excellent example of the history and development of what is called 'Latin American social archaeology', for which Gordon Childe and Marx and Engels are the central intellectual ancestors. Reacting against what is seen as the use of Latin America to test 'First World' theories, archaeology is employed as 'a starting point in explaining the ulterior historical processes that led to the emergence of nations, national states, social classes, and cultural and national identities' (Vargas Arenas and Sanoja 1999: 59–60). In this way local history is ultimately asserted, in the face of the external cultural and economic pressures of globalization. As we shall see in Spain, an archaeological methodology is developed, in this case using such concepts as socio-economic formation, domestic space, mode of life and mode of work, from the classic texts of historical materialism.

The writings of these, and other, Marxists of the Grupo Oaxtepec (see McGuire 1992: 67–8) have been fiercely independent of Anglo-American archaeology in attempting to develop local theoretical structures. This does not mean that they have ignored the work of Anglo-Americans: their publications are cited, especially on topics such as settlement analyses, spatial archaeology, formation processes and analytical techniques. Similarly they have rejected French structural Marxism in favour of a 'back to basics' development of the writings of Marx and Engels. Competing theoretical positions (to use Gándara's concept) are recognized and accepted, rather than adhering to a model of linear succession (as in 'traditional' followed by 'processual' and then 'postprocessual' archaeologies). Such theoretical positions develop knowledge through practice, as links are established between general theories and what are called 'observational' or 'mediating' theories, which tie in to the empirical world and enable the study of aspects of relevance to the general theories.

The most recent, detailed statement of many of these issues is given by Bate (1998).

Perhaps the main observation that can be made about world archaeology is that it consists of shared methods and techniques within networks of theoretically divergent traditions. The theories vary on a spectrum from deterministic materialism to relativist idealism. We are dealing with a world of pluralism. In spite of the perceived hegemony of Anglo-American archaeology, both PA and PPA have been adopted in an uneven and eclectic manner. The major theoretical schools defined in Anglo-American archaeological theory since the 1960s have been of marginal relevance to the experience of archaeologists in much larger areas of the world. And yet 'we' still try to set the agenda, or imagine that 'our' concerns are 'their' concerns. In addition to the need for greater humility, I also argue that we need to look closely at other regional traditions to see what we can learn from their experiences and practices. With this in mind, let us now look at the history of Spanish archaeology during the last three decades.

Pensamiento Crítico: Spanish archaeology

Spanish archaeology is not a unified tradition, or school of thought, any more than is the archaeology of other major European countries (cf. Scarre 1999 on France). It shares a recent history of isolationism and centralization, as well as a prevailing philosophy of cultural history and idealism, under the dictatorship of Franco. Since his death in 1975, democratic government has been combined with decentralization (the creation of the autonomous, regional governments in 1978), the opening up of political, economic and cultural ties with other countries, and the end of repression of left-wing ideologies. Within this context, Spanish archaeologists have studied overseas (mainly since 1990), in countries such as North America and Britain, as well as engaging in collaborative projects and exchanges (both personnel and books/periodicals) with foreign institutions. This has exposed them to the theoretical debates of the Anglo-American world, as well as to the rich continental European tradition of the social sciences, and reaction has varied from the rejection of theory to the embracing of different theoretical positions. Rather than present a detailed history of such reactions (for which the reader is directed to Lull 1991; Vázquez Varela and Risch 1991), my aim here is to examine such reactions in the context of a predominantly materialist approach in which stress is placed upon the relationship between theory and practice.

There has been no processual or postprocessual phase of development within Spanish archaeology. The publications of PA which began to be cited, translated and discussed in Spain from the mid-1970s raised awareness of the lack of theory, as expressed by a small number of 'voices in the wilderness' (e.g. Gran Aymerich, Rivera, Alcina, see Martínez Navarrete 1989). While there were some calls for an 'anthropological' or a 'scientific' archaeology, there was no widespread adoption, or school, of PA. Instead it was the methods associated with PA, or what was seen as PA, which more readily passed into practice: the importance of all kinds of scientific methods (for which a local infrastructure did not yet exist) was recognized, especially in relation to environmental reconstruction, settlement patterns, prehistoric territories and the importance of landscape surveys. For example, Ruiz *et al.* (1986: 41–2) contrasted the advances in methods of PA with its failure to consider social relations as more than the epiphenomena of technological change and environmental adaptation. This emphasis on methods rather than theory characterizes a large sector of Spanish archaeology.

The theoretical bases of PA were criticized in the 1980s, as Spanish archaeology expanded within the university sector and the first conferences on theory and methodology were held. Strong criticism was made of such key issues as the hypothetico-deductive method, laws of human behaviour that were timeless and spaceless, cultural adaptation, and external causality. Such criticisms find a common ground with those published in the 1980s within postprocessual archaeology in Britain, but they did not stem from this external tradition (as we shall see below). The PPA school in itself was also subjected to critique by Spanish archaeologists, who attacked its relativism, particularism and idealism, as well as its perceived lack of a coherent theory (e.g. Ruiz *et al.* 1988; Lull *et al.* 1990). The embracing of Critical Theory from the Frankfurt School by Juan Vicent did not prevent him from launching a critique of PPA (1991). Indeed, if I were to attempt a typology of Spanish archaeologists and their theoretical stances over the last decade, I doubt whether I could name more than a handful who might be described as postprocessual archaeologists: Felipe Criado is one of the best known of these, while Martín de Guzman adopted a structuralist approach independently of PPA.

How did this situation come about? The answer lies in the spread of historical materialism in the social and historical sciences in post-Franco Spain, as Marxism re-emerged as a political philosophy. In Cataluña especially, historical materialism was known and discussed in intellectual circles (e.g. in studies of modern history) in the Franco years. It was in the years immediately following Franco's death that the form of the transition to democracy was debated, along with the role of a variety of left-wing political groups. This ferment was at its most active in Barcelona, where different models of Marxism (e.g. Gramsci, Althusser), along with the works of postmodernists such as Foucault and Derrida, were the focus of detailed and intense argument (Vicente Lull, personal communication). In the archaeology of the 1980s, citation of the sources of classical and structural Marxism, along with reference to the works of Marxist archaeologists such as Childe and Carandini, began to appear in publications (e.g. Lull 1983; Ruiz *et al.* 1986). Martínez Navarrete (1989: 73) included historical materialism as one of the four alternative approaches to the crisis in theory and methodology in Spanish archaeology (the others being derived from PA, structuralist anthropology and the philosophy of science). From the earliest centres in Barcelona and Jaén, the influence of historical materialism has spread more widely in Spanish archaeology during the 1990s, although this is often more evident in the citation of sources than in any coherent analyses.

Within the last decade Spanish archaeologists have become more aware of the historical materialist tradition exemplified in Latin American social archaeology. Books published in the 1970s by the exiled Chileans Bate (1977, 1978) and Montané (1980) and the Peruvian Lumbreras (1974) began to be circulated in Spain, along with papers in journals such as *the Boletín de Antropología Americana*. Occasional citations of the publications of these authors had appeared in the mid-1980s (e.g. Ruiz *et al.* 1986 cited Bate 1977), but it was not until 1989 that Latin American social archaeology was widely cited in a general book on archaeology (Alcina Franch 1989). In 1992–3 personal ties were established through invitations to Latin Americans to give papers in Barcelona and attend a conference in Huelva. This provided the opportunity to explore areas of agreement and disagreement on issues of ontology and epistemology (Vicente Lull, personal communication).

As in Latin America, independence of thought, in the context of critique, has been visible within Spanish historical materialism. Similarities in the state of archaeology with the Anglo-American world (e.g. absence of theory, emphasis on culture history and idealism, lack of focus on social relations, lack of methodological rigour, emphasis on archaeology as technique – see Estévez *et al.* 1984) were noted as soon as the works of PA became more widely available in Spain. In some cases the range of positions within PA, as well as changes of opinion, were ignored by its critics (e.g. Ruiz *et al.* 1986). But this critique, in its broader intellectual milieu, aimed at creating a different archaeological theory and practice: 'Spanish, and more widely Mediterranean ... and Latin American social thought has produced a ... critical tradition sufficient to develop its own approaches, rather than just reproduce out of context the models of the English-speaking world which are now so much in fashion' (Risch, in Vázquez Varela and Risch 1991: 46).

The active construction of archaeological theory and practice in Spain, as in Latin America, has been fuelled by historical materialism, with an explicit rejection of idealism (e.g. Ruiz and Nocete 1990: 105); priority is given to the material conditions of life, with emphasis on factors of production and reproduction. This not only reflects the theoretical basis of materialism (and here archaeologists such as the members of the Barcelona group – see Vázquez Varela and Risch 1991: 36 – have gone right back to basics, in the same way as their Latin American colleagues, in rebuilding theory from the original works of Marx and Engels), but also a strategy for establishing priorities in archaeological research. As González-Marcén and Risch have argued, materialism 'does not mean that other aspects such as politics, ideology, aesthetics, etc. are irrelevant for the understanding of concrete historical processes, but that in order to locate them, it is first necessary to establish the material conditions in which they develop' (1990: 99).

This materialism is allied to belief in a 'real' world of experience, against which our ideas can be evaluated. According to this, it is argued that 'reality exists, or existed, that it is or has been out there, outside of the observer'. This realism 'implies that (archaeological) remains are observable, discernible, measurable and experimental and are, or have been, materials in transformation' (Lull 1988: 72, my translation). These archaeological 'facts' do not speak for themselves; they are given meaning within a theoretical framework, which itself provides the means for evaluating ideas through 'empirical tests' (e.g. excavations). As Lull says, 'a theory which does not propose a methodology for empirical evaluation is only speculation' (1988: 70; cf. Audouze 1999: 168, note 1). This anti-relativist stance, by which different 'representations' (rather than 'reconstructions' – Lull 1988: 71) of the past are subjected to testing (the success of this being judged by criteria such as the degree of empirical support, and the methodological coherence of the theory) avoids the reduction of scientific debate to a matter of political opinion. Social science is seen as neither value-free nor politically determined.

The question of the relationship between theory and practice has been central to historical materialism in Spain since the first discussions of theory in the late 1970s and early 1980s. Here dialectic supplants dichotomy; it makes no sense to a Marxist to develop theory without practice, or vice versa. A purely 'theoretical' archaeologist is like a driver without a car. One of the first objects of criticism in Spain by the Barcelona group was the adoption of fieldwork and analytical techniques without thought as to the new practices that might be required by different theoretical arguments. Like their Latin American colleagues, they have proposed that general theory be linked by relevant operational concepts and units of analysis to the archaeological record (a proposal which finds clear comparison with 'top down' approaches to theory and practice in PA, as seen, for example, in Whallon 1982, and Raab and Goodyear 1984 on the use of 'middle-range theory' to derive more directly testable, lower-level propositions or hypotheses from the high-level theories such as Marxism or Darwinism). This approach stems from the belief that Marxist archaeology must use the principles of historical materialism to develop analytical procedures for the study of the archaeological record.

> If we take the concept of exploitation as a central category on which the general categories   acquire their specific content, its analysis must be linked to production, distribution and   consumption. Therefore one of the principal aims of Marxist archaeological research is to   elaborate analytical procedures that allow one to infer the processes of production and their organisation through archaeological indicators.
>
> (González-Marcén and Risch 1990: 99)

As in Latin America, the Barcelona group has attempted to develop a materialist theory of human societies (a 'theory of the production of social life' – see Castro *et al.* 1998a) based on the work of Marx (principally using *Das Capital* and *Grundrisse*). Central to this process have been the redefinition of types of social production, and an analysis of exploitation in relation to the concepts of class, surplus and property. As we shall see later, this has important implications for the analysis of the concept of complexity, and particularly for the identification of state societies (Lull and Risch 1996; see also Nocete 1994).

How do general concepts such as social production and exploita-tion find expression in the archaeological record? The first step is to define a theory of 'social practices', by which social production is manifested in the course of everyday activities (Castro *et al.* 1996a). The principal focus is on the 'materialization' of these activities and practices, through the use of the material culture that is so visible in the archaeological record. The theory of 'archaeological objects' thus provides a link between social production and material culture (Lull 1988). These two theories provide the key link between high-level Marxist theory and the activity of the archaeologist.

But we still require the definition of relevant units of analysis by which the archaeological record can be studied. A change of theory is insufficient without a change in practice (a criticism which some Spanish archaeologists make of both PA and PPA). It is argued that excavation methods and recording units ought not to be based on the assumption that objective description will precede such inter-pretation; description and interpretation are not mutually exclusive in practice. But the use of the Harris system, by which the context is the main stratigraphic and recording unit (Harris 1989), and the grouping of contexts as the basis of interpretation occurs after the excavation, elevates description over historical interpretation. In contrast it is argued that the basic units of analysis ought to have both natural and social meaning: 'natural', given the post-depositional processes which take place on archaeological sites (Castro *et al.* 1993), and 'social' given the social practices which have contributed to the material patterning. The unit of analysis here is the *conjunto* (or 'whole', 'ensemble'), which might be, for example, a complete structure, or house, at different phases of its occupation and use; a *conjunto* is a hypothesis, a proposal made during the course of excavation which compels excavators to make explicit their inter-pretations as fieldwork proceeds. All finds, samples and so on are also labelled according to these *conjuntos*, grouping together material which resulted from social or natural practices in that same unit of analysis. The first use of the *conjunto* was in the excavations of the Talayotic settlement at Son Fornés in Mallorca (Gasull, Lull and Sanahuja 1984: 6–10), and more recently it has been used on the Bronze Age settlement of Gatas in south-east Spain (Castro *et al.* 1999a).

It is interesting to note that, in spite of developing in a different tradition, this approach to excavation is echoed by later develop-ments within PPA: Hodder's conception of interpretation occurring 'at the trowel's edge' (1997: 693), and Richards's view of excavation 'as interpretive practice, as opposed to neutral observation' (1995: 218) mirror the view of the Barcelona group. Hodder's (1999) discussion of what he calls a 'reflexive method' and his critique of Harris matrices examines the stratigraphic integrity of 'primary recording units', without discussing what these units are, and how and why they are selected prior to excavation. But given his argument that observation and interpretation are not rigidly separated during excavation, it is a logical step to argue that the choice of such 'primary recording units' would relate to the problems under study. In his discussion of archaeological reasoning, Hodder lists nine characteristics of such reasoning in the field (1999: 33–62). His third characteristic is that such reasoning depends upon 'pre-understandings', which seem to include the existing state of knowledge of the types of site under study. According to the system developed by the Barcelona group, such knowledge is essential for the definition of *conjuntos* in the field, as structures, floors, phases of deposition and collapse are recognized during excavations and decisions made about sampling and detailed recording. The level of 'interpretation at the trowel's edge' here extends to the definition of the 'basic' units of analysis.

Taken as a whole, the Spanish experience of archaeological theory during the last two decades usefully counters the notion that innovation centres on the Anglo-American world. If nothing else, this should instil some humility in English-speaking archaeologists: we should avoid looking down from our peripheral island on theoretical debate in eastern and southern Europe as 'less well developed' (Pluciennik 1999: 659). We should also think carefully about two related issues: (1) the comparability and compatibility of different theories, and (2) the advantages of a materialist approach to archaeology.

Conflicting theories?

The thesis that the evolution of any discipline is marked by a succession of mutually exclusive theories, or paradigms, or isms, is superficially attractive, at least to the proponents of the latest approach! But we should ask ourselves two questions:

1   Is there such a neat, evolutionary sequence, which conforms to the influential, discontinuous model of disciplinary change advanced by Thomas Kuhn (1962)?
2   Are these theories or schools really mutually exclusive?

It has been argued (Bunge 1996: 190) that Kuhn's idea of 'mono-paradigmatic' normal science is only really applicable to the seventeenth and eighteenth centuries. If we take the history of archaeology and anthropology, there is sufficient evidence to support the claim that theories may have varied in popularity during the last two centuries, but continued to co-exist, mainly between, but also within, regional traditions. Thus, for example, evolutionism domin-ated mid-nineteenth-century thought, but declined in popularity in the Anglo-American world during the first half of the twentieth century, overtaken by cultural approaches in North America and functionalism in Britain. At the same time, evolution (e.g. in the form of the five modes of production, see Bloch 1985) provided the basis of both anthropology and archaeology as practised in the Soviet Union and, after the Second World War, in eastern Europe. But evolutionary approaches returned to the fore in North America in the 1950s, moving from the cultural ecology of Leslie White (an isolated figure in the 1930s and 1940s) and Julian Steward through to the development of processual archaeology. It continues to main-tain a strong presence there, not only in terms of cultural ecology, but also in an approach rooted in Darwinism and called 'evolution-ary archaeology' (e.g. Dunnell 1980; Boone and Alden Smith 1998).

The expansion of theoretical debate within archaeology, as well as the breakdown of state-imposed theoretical structures in the former Soviet Union and eastern block countries in Europe, has encouraged the proliferation of different theories. What appears to be different now is that such theories co-exist more markedly within, rather than simply between, regional traditions. Within the Anglo-American world, the expansion of publishing outlets, along with international conferences, journals, and the Internet, have combined to accentuate this trend. We can, of course, look on this as being the result of the triumph of postprocessual archaeology, an archaeology of its time, which shows the Kuhnian model in action. Alternatively we can take the proponents of PPA at their word (see above) and recognize a period of theoretical fragmentation in which the nature of archaeo-logical knowledge and practice, as well as of social change, are all debated from such initially diverse positions that any definition of a dominant paradigm is impossible.

I have used the phrase 'initially diverse' to describe different the-ories, because of the evidence from the history of archaeology for changes of position as the proponents of such theories recognize the existence of common ground. This should not happen if the theories are mutually exclusive. According to what is called the 'incommensurability thesis' in the philosophy of science 'two bodies of discourse – whether theories, world views, paradigms or what have you – are incommensurable if the assertions made in one body of discourse are unintelligible to those utilizing the other' (Laudan 1990: 121). Different theories are supposed to look at the world in different ways; observations and interpretations depend on theory, so major theory shifts require us to look at the empirical world in totally different ways. This is the essence of the model proposed by Kuhn (1962) and embraced by processual archaeology (e.g. Sterud 1973).

And yet theories and isms in archaeology (let alone other social sciences) do not exist in isolation. For all their differences in conceptions of society (e.g. based on conflict vs consensus), social change (e.g. internal vs external causality) and the nature of archaeology (e.g. politically committed vs neutral), these theories show histories of development through overlap and interaction. For example, Marxism and processualism share a materialist approach and an opposition to idealism. An interest in social evolution finds a common ancestor in Lewis Henry Morgan (Bloch 1985), through the cultural ecology of Leslie White and the cultural materialism of Marvin Harris. This influence of Marxism, however diluted, on early processual archaeology, has been acknowledged at the same time as its influence on postprocessual archaeology (McGuire 1993: 132). Both Trigger (1989: 326) and Klejn (1977: 13) have stressed the similarities in theory between processual archaeology and Soviet archaeology in the 1930s, while Dolukhanov argues more strongly that they can be 'viewed as a single paradigm' (1995: 333). More recently Gilman has pointed out examples of processualists who have begun to study property in the archaeological record (1998: 911); he has argued that 'the work of many of the more sophisticated practitioners of cultural ecology is fully compatible with Marxist approaches to analogous problems' (1989: 72) and that 'the closeness between Marxism and the mainstream of American archaeological research is particularly striking at the level of practice' (1989: 72).

Similarity is not, of course, identity: individual theories retain sufficient identity to make them distinct from other theories. Working with different theories in the study of the past, finding areas of convergence and conflict (Hodder's 'productive tensions', 1999: 58) is, it seems to me, part of 'normal' archaeology. The relative popularity of such theories may be attributed to internal factors, such as their internal coherence (e.g. between high- , middle- and low-level theory, see above; or between factors such as the ontology and methodology of the theory, see Bate 1998: 28–9 citing the work of Gándara), and external factors such as their fashionability in the academy (whether from peer pressure or perceived job opportunities!). Proponents may work to gain a mutual understanding, a position advocated by Kuhn himself, and by Binford, who recommended the adoption of a different paradigm as a means to 'view experience' in a different way (1989: 486, see Wylie 1992: 282). Such a viewpoint recognizes the value of different theories, as well as the complexity of both the archaeological record and human behaviour.

If theories or isms were irreconcilably theory-laden and incompatible with each other, the whole world of knowledge would change with each change of theory. But proponents of one theory make use of the data produced from the fieldwork generated, sometimes over generations, by different theories (e.g. the search for symbolism in Breton megaliths by Kirk 1991, 1993; Thomas and Tilley 1993). This is often observed in the initial stages of a theory's development, as proponents seek to show how the same data can be interpreted in novel ways. Knowledge is shared between different theories (Wylie 1992), such that these theories may start their quest for understanding based on widely recognized patterning in the archaeological record. It is also accepted that archaeologists collect data that may be relevant to more than one theory. From this perspective, the internal dynamics of archaeological theory and practice are infinitely more complicated than a simple paradigm replacement model.

A materialist approach

Much of postprocessual archaeology (at least its poststructuralist branch), as well as European social thought, is permeated by idealism; ideas are claimed to exist independently of matter. People's actions are determined by their interpretation of other people's actions. The central concept here is 'meaning': people respond to symbols, they give meaning to them (which may not be the meaning given by other people), and they act according to their perception of these meanings. The task of interpretation has become analogous to that of giving meaning to 'texts', as in hermeneutics. Once we were archaeologists, but now we are all literary critics! What is more, Ricoeur and others argue that 'reality' has no existence independent of the meanings which people give to symbols and signs; reality is constructed, according to scholars such as Kuhn and Feyerabend. Ideas cannot be evaluated against an exterior world of experience, as required by the scientific method; indeed science itself, like technology, is frowned upon, as being a tool of capitalism.

This perspective is both subjective ('the philosophical view that the world, far from existing independently, is a creation of the knower', Bunge 1996: 330) and relativist ('facts' are created by different different theories, or paradigms, which are incommensurable). The view that material objects are independent of our perceptions is termed realism ('the epistemology that all of us adopt tacitly when not under the influence of narcotics or anti-scientific philosophies', Bunge 1996: 335), and is upheld here. In contrast to idealism, materialism proposes that 'everything in the world is material or concrete, ideas being bodily (brain) processes' (Bunge 1996: 282). Of course, human beings make use of symbols, in a manner that is unparalleled in the animal kingdom, and the fact that these symbols are visual means that they can play an important role in social interaction. But this process of giving 'meaning' occurs within the context of material constraints; any such meaning is, in itself, not an interpretation, but an hypothesis which requires evaluation in the material world (Bunge 1996: 291).

The idea of archaeology as text, with its talk of 'reading' the past, meets its first obstacle in the acknowledged disagreement over the meaning of the 'text' in itself (Buchli 1995: 183). In literary criticism there are individual authors of individual texts. The archaeological record, in contrast, was created, both intentionally and unintentionally, by multiple 'authors' (see Preucel 1991b: 23), acting under the constraints of the material world and social structure, let alone subsequent processes of human and natural transformation. That record is what exists now. No one would propose that individuals in the past thought about 'creating' the archaeological record. This criticism could be accepted (in which case it leaves the problem as to how this record is studied and given meaning) but the textual metaphor maintained for human action in the past. Given the nature of our data, it would seem that the study of individual attribution of meaning would be better carried out within the context of historical or living societies (see Trigger 1989: 30–1; 1998b: 18; cf. Meskell 1999: 34 on the more 'fruitful' study of individuals in historical contexts). We may refer to this as the 'horses for courses' model of archaeological enquiry.

The material world may be viewed through meaning, but it is created through action; symbols and ideas are undoubtedly part of that meaning and action. People perceive the world around them, but as Trigger, citing Childe, has pointed out, 'humans adapt to a symbolic world rather than to a real one ... (but) this symbolic world has to correspond to the real one to a very considerable degree if a society was to survive' (1998b: 8). This leads Trigger to stress the importance of a materialist approach which does not neglect symbolism and cognition: 'the archaeological record is a product of human behavior that was shaped with varying degrees of directness by material constraints, as these were comprehended in terms of culturally conditioned understandings of reality' (1998b: 12).

To argue for a materialist approach to archaeology does not mean that ideas are neglected (as was mentioned above with regard to the work of the Barcelona group). It is always a challenge to see if new ways can be developed to find out about different aspects of past human behaviour, whether economic, social, political or cognitive. But examples of idealist approaches often leave symbols and ideas floating in isolation, with no consideration of productive factors and no testable hypotheses. For example, Hodder's presentation of material culture as text (1988) used the example of the development of Neolithic enclosures in central and north-west Europe from non-domestic to domestic use to propose that 'it is possible to argue that the text for the formation of defended settlement enclosures was initially written in a non-domestic, and often ritual context' (1988: 70). For southern Scandinavia Hodder proposed that 'the idea of settlement agglomeration and communal centres first came about in a ritual context', and that 'later practical activity could build on the initial statement' of ritual activity (1988: 71). But how did settlement agglomeration come about? How did production support this? Must we imagine Neolithic populations blindly following an 'idea', an 'initial text', rather like the crowd chasing Monty Python's Brian, holding aloft his sandal as a sign? And can we really oppose 'ritual' and 'practical' activity in this polarized way? The same criticisms are provoked by another of Hodder's examples, the change from initially individual to later communal earthen and stone tombs in the southern Scandinavian Neolithic. The initial tombs may very well have created 'the potential for the idea of a descent group linked to a common ancestor' (1988: 71–2), but what activates that potential, and how is it embedded in the social relations of production?

Conclusions

The arguments proposed in this chapter are the basis for what follows in the rest of this book. The approach taken is materialist and realist. It accepts the plurality of positions on theory and method-ology that have been taken, and are being taken, within archaeology. The history of archaeology cannot be reduced to a simple, linear sequence of grand theories or isms; competing theories are accepted, and unavoidable, given the complexity of human behaviour and the archaeological record.

Archaeology is now a world discipline, with different regional traditions evolving in response to local histories and needs. While they may share common methods of 'doing' archaeology (put a Marxist, a structuralist and a positivist in the same trench and they will not hold their trowels or physically dig any differently!), they do not, and will not, blindly follow the latest trends of the Anglo-American world. When faced with these different traditions, we would do well to show a little humility, and see what we can learn from them. How do they conceive of archaeology as a discipline? What contribution can they make to debates on the strengths of materialism or idealism as strategies for learning? How do they go about relating theory to practice and developing theoretical con-cepts? Do these concepts allow them to see and study the past in new and productive ways? Answers to these questions have been suggested in this chapter in relation to parts of the Spanish-speaking world, and they will be developed further in relation to the study of society and social change in the past. But before we move on to these issues, we need to examine how they have been studied in the Anglo-American world since the 1960s. This is the subject of Chap-ter 3, in which I adopt a critical insider's view of the ways in which the theory and practice of social analysis in archaeology have changed in the last four decades.

3

MODELS OF SOCIETY AND SOCIAL CHANGE

From the inside looking out

In Chapter 1, I pointed out that the idea of social evolution has been an integral part of Western thinking since the eighteenth century. Different criteria (whether material or not) have been used to divide human societies into successive types, or stages, in the evolution from 'simple' to 'complex' societies. The early practitioners of archaeology and anthropology used technology as a direct measure of the evolution of societies. Although the proto-anthropologists were studying non-Western societies such as the Bushmen, the Australian Aborigines and the Indians of the American north-west coast, their view of them was as survivors, as fossils from earlier stages of evolution (e.g. Sollas 1911). This present was their past. During the first half of the twentieth century, the interests of the two disciplines diverged, as anthropologists rejected what they viewed as 'conjectural history' in favour of fieldwork-based studies of these societies as they are now. Archaeology continued to focus on technology and subsistence as criteria for defining successive stages of social evolution, most notably in the work of Gordon Childe (1936, 1942 and 1951). But the direct inference of past social organization remained a minority activity among archaeologists, located on a higher rung of the ladder of archaeological inference (Hawkes 1954).

The re-birth of social evolution within North American anthropology in the 1950s also renewed the links between the study of the present and of the past. From the perspective of archaeology, ethnographic analogy and the direct inference of social organization from material traces of the past were two of the central activities of North American processual archaeology (e.g. Binford and Binford 1968). Although this impact of neo-evolutionism in anthropology upon archaeology now seems a long time ago, part of the history of our discipline, it is still the important starting point for the topic of this book. The concepts of neo-evolutionism permeate archaeological thought in the English-speaking world. Whether one agrees with them or not, they have formed the basis of much archaeological practice during the last four decades. During the course of this chapter I will trace changes in neo-evolutionary thinking, as well as the effects of critiques from historical materialism and practice theory. My aim is to show how our concepts of society and social change vary, and have varied, along with ideas as to the appropriate units and scales of analysis for their study. A secondary aim is to place these changes within the broader context of the approaches to archaeology discussed in Chapter 2. My focus throughout is on Anglo-American archaeology: unlike Chapter 2, I am now on the inside looking out.

Introducing the fall guys

Although North American neo-evolutionism began with the work of Leslie White and Julian Steward (for discussion see Trigger 1989: 289–94), I want to focus attention here on two of the books most cited by archaeologists: Elman Service's *Primitive Social Organisation* (1962) and Morton Fried's The *Evolution of Political Society* (1967).

For Service, social organization comprised the structure of a society (its constituent groups, whether residential or non-residential) and the network of interpersonal relations which were 'regulated' or 'influenced' by statuses ('recognised social positions' which were achieved or ascribed) held by individuals. Each of these statuses was associated with what was regarded as 'appropriate' behaviour, or a role. After speculating on the origins of social organization, Service used the ethnographic record to define four types of society, presented in order of their evolution, from hunting and gathering bands, through agricultural tribes and chiefdoms to states.

Band societies were defined on the basis of kinship, and particularly the nuclear family, which was the basic unit for any division of labour, and by the absence of any separate political, legal or religious groups: for example, the economy 'is not separately institutionalised, but remains merely an aspect of kinship organisation' (Service 1962: 108). The number of people in a band ranged from thirty to one hundred or more, with an average density of one person or fewer per square mile, although such densities would vary according to the seasonal availability of food. Service recognized some variation among band societies, such as his distinction between patrilocal and composite bands, and he speculated that the patrilocal band occurred earliest in human evolution, given that it had a simpler social structure. The exceptional nature of hunter-gatherer groups such as those on the north-west coast of America suggested to Service that the band level of social organization might not have been universal during the Palaeolithic.

'A band is only an association, more or less residential, of nuclear families, ordinarily numbering 30–100 people, with affinal ties loosely allying it with one or a few other bands. A tribe is an association of a much larger number of kinship segments that are each composed of families. They are tied more firmly together than are the bands, which use mostly marriage ties alone . . . the few inter-marrying multifamily local groups that were the *whole* of band society are now only a *part* or aspect of tribal society' (Service 1962: 111). Such larger population aggregations owed much to the adoption of an agricultural subsistence and increased sedentism, and in turn required more non-residential groups (e.g. clans, lineages, secret societies) to hold tribal societies together. Such groups made use of ancestry, ritual and mythology to achieve this goal. Egalitarianism and the absence of political hierarchies, with situational leadership based on personal qualities, were characteristics shared with band societies. Residential groups were economically self-sufficient. Once again, Service recognized variation in the ethnographic record, and distinguished two 'highly generalised polar types of social structure', namely lineal and composite tribes (Service 1962: 118).

As with the relationship between bands and tribes, there was usually a further increase in population density between tribes and chiefdom societies. The size of the individual residence groups increased, and the greater density as a whole was underwritten by greater productivity. The chiefdom was, in Service's own words, a more 'complex' and 'organized' type of society, with economic, social and religious activities being centrally controlled. Regional or ecologically based specialization and redistribution of produce were both under central control and, according to Service, were 'selected for' by what he called the 'total environmental situation'. Centralized control was in the hands of chiefs, with ascribed statuses, rules of succession and affiliation and sumptuary rules or taboos which gave them distinctive identities (e.g. through distinctive dress or ornaments, ritual positions, etc.). Chiefs were able to mobilize human labour for a variety of public works, such as monument construction, irrigation works, etc. Within the fabric of chiefdom societies was an increase in hierarchy and inequality: 'when chieftainship becomes a permanent office in the structure of society, social inequality becomes characteristic of the society, followed finally by inequality in consumption' (Service 1962: 149).

The final stage of social evolution was reached with the emergence of the state society, which was distinguished from the chiefdom by two essential characteristics: these were the use of legitimized force to establish and maintain the authority and power of the leadership ('repressive controls based on physical force' Service 1975: xi), and the specialized, bureaucratic government which was present at the service of leaders.

Given the title of his book, it is not surprising that Morton Fried (1967) placed emphasis on the role of political factors in the evolution of society. His four-stage typology, like Service's, traced the evolutionary process from hunting and gathering to state societies, but he disagreed with Service over the intervening stages. Fried's first stage was that of egalitarian society, in which there was 'the social recognition of as many positions of valued status as there were individuals capable of filling them' (1967: 52). But whatever prestige individuals accrued as a result of their status, this did not result in the exercise of greater power. Leadership was based on authority rather than power, and was situational rather than fixed in particular individuals. Division of labour was mainly by sex. Access to basic resources was communal. Population densities were low, and the basic units were nuclear families and bands of small numbers of such families. According to the ethnographic record, egalitarian societies tended to live in marginal areas, were often mobile, and included all the hunting and gathering societies that Service called bands.

The second stage in Fried's typology was that of ranked society, and made no distinction between Service's tribes and chiefdoms. For Fried, there was no need for a tribal stage. 'Such a stage explains nothing but does divert attention from more important questions: How does ranking begin and how does it undergo adaptive radiation? How does stratification get started and how does it catalyze societies? How does it reinforce itself, and what are its effects on other societies?'(1967: 173). Some tribal societies, as studied by Service, were the result of acculturation and not representative of a past stage in political evolution. In Fried's ranked society, 'positions of valued status are somehow limited so that not all those of sufficient talent to occupy such statuses actually achieve them' (1967: 109). One means by which such ranking could occur was according to the proximity of families to a common ancestor within a descent group.

Such families could preserve or enhance their ranking by marriage alliances with other high-ranking families, and by strategies such as competitive feasting.

While high-ranking families and individuals had 'regular and repetitive' authority (1967: 134), they had little ability to enforce the obedience of their followers. Whether high-ranking or not, all members of society had equal access to basic resources, and there was only limited evidence for lesser participation in subsistence activities by high-ranking families and individuals such as chiefs. The division of labour continued to be by age and sex and craft specialization was limited. Redistribution was administered by chiefs. Residential communities were of larger size. Population densities were larger than in egalitarian societies, and generally supported by an agricultural economy. Like Service, Fried speculated on the reasons for the transition between successive social types, including such factors as ecological diversity, redistribution, the problems to communication posed by population growth, and the organization of labour for activities such as irrigation.

Fried's third stage was that of the stratified society, 'in which members of the same sex and equivalent status do not have equal access to the basic resources that sustain life' (1967: 186). Status differences are now grounded in economic differences. Such differences provide the basis for increased warfare, as compared with ranked societies. But, like Service, Fried viewed the final stage, that of state society, as marking the ultimate exercise of power. 'A state is not simply a legislative, an executive body, a judiciary system, an administrative bureaucracy, or even a government . . . a state is better viewed as the complex of institutions by means of which the power of the society is organised on a basis superior to kinship' (1967: 229). Thus state society was class society. The difference between stratified and state societies was somewhat blurred: Fried proposed that 'once stratification exists, the course of stateship is implicit and the actual formation of the state is begun' (1967: 185).

Although Service and Fried disagreed about the intermediate types of society, they were united in many of the characteristics they attributed to hunters and gatherers and early agriculturalists, as well as to state societies, they arranged societies from simple to complex and they speculated on the causes of evolution from one type of society to another. They were not the only anthropologists to engage in this neo-evolutionism. Credit must be given to Oberg (1955) for introducing the term chiefdom, and to Sahlins for his studies of tribal societies (1968) and for his proposal that tribal societies evolved into chiefdoms, based on detailed knowledge of Melanesian 'big man' and Polynesian chiefdom societies (1958): here two types defined for different parts of the Pacific region were viewed as epitomizing successive social stages.

Sahlins and Service (1960) also joined forces to edit a volume of essays on cultural evolution. They defined two forms of evolution. General evolution consisted of those processes of change towards greater capture of energy, higher levels of social integration and greater freedom from environmental constraints that are visible from the earliest societies to those of the present day. In contrast, specific evolution marks out the changes of individual cultures and regional cultural sequences, and, of special relevance here, from one stage of social evolution to another. They specified the processes of specific evolution (e.g. adaptation) as well as proposing laws which might govern the transition of societies from one evolutionary stage to the next (e.g. the law of evolutionary potential). Unwittingly, along with their fellow neo-evolutionists in anthropology, they had set an agenda for research that was to have a greater impact in archaeology than in their own discipline. Somewhat ironically Service (1967) had already accepted Fried's criticisms and discarded the terms bands and tribes (replaced by egalitarian societies), as well as chiefdoms (now hierarchical societies, including what he had previously called primitive states), before their use became widespread within archaeology.

Neo-evolutionism: setting the archaeological agenda

The concern with general evolution in the work of Leslie White and the specific evolution of Sahlins, Service and Fried, along with White's belief in the adaptive basis of culture, were embraced by Lewis Binford in what became known as new/processual archaeology. Binford (1968) argued that there were no inherent limitations on the potential for inference from the archaeological record. If we wanted to make inferences about past social organization, as well as technology and subsistence, then we just had to overcome our 'methodological naivety' (Binford 1968: 23). Neo-evolutionism, with its types of societies, each with a set of specific characteristics, helped to put social inference back on the agenda of archaeological methodology (Drennan 1992: 59). After all, stage typologies had been part of archaeology since Thomsen's Three Age system in the early nineteenth century, and archaeologists were used to thinking in this evolutionary way.

The archaeological agenda which was set by neo-evolutionism consisted of two main areas of activity: the identification and study of social organization and social types (known from ethnography) in the archaeological record, and the development of theoretical arguments to understand the process(es) of social evolution. The first of these involved archaeologists in addressing their 'methodological naivety', whether by the analysis of settlements (site hierarchies, intra-site patterning), mortuary contexts, or material culture (e.g. pottery styles). After the initial, innovative case studies (e.g. Binford and Binford 1968, in which ethnographic analogies were drawn from Sahlins 1958, and Fried offered comments) and cross-cultural analyses (e.g. Saxe 1970; Binford 1972), the inference of social type and social change became embedded within regional research projects in both the Old and New Worlds. In the process, the original types of Service and, to a lesser extent, Fried, were refined or subdivided. While Old World archaeologists, as we shall see, engaged in social inference from the archaeological record, they played less of a role in the development of neo-evolutionary theory. Taken as a whole, and whatever one thinks of it, the neo-evolutionary agenda has continued to be active in archaeology up to the present day.

It was Colin Renfrew who grasped the nettle of archaeological inference, trying to identify chiefdoms in the archaeological record of western Europe. Using Service's definition of a chiefdom, Renfrew listed twenty characteristics of this type of society (e.g. redistribution, ranking, central places, specialisation, public works, etc.) and tried to identify them in Neolithic and Early Bronze Age Wessex (1973a, 1974), Neolithic Malta (1973b, 1974) and the Early Bronze Age in the Aegean (1972, 1974). Renfrew's aims were quite clear: to focus attention on the neglected area of inference of social organization in archaeological data, and to use a concept derived from ethnography to discern new patterns in that data, and to ask new questions of that data. The chiefdom, along with ethnographic analogy in general, was a conceptual tool to be used in archaeology.

Apart from the impetus that his use of the chiefdom concept gave to the study of the archaeological records of Wessex, Malta and the Aegean, Renfrew used both the archaeological and the ethnographic records to identify two types of chiefdom. Group-oriented chiefdoms were ones in which 'personal wealth in terms of valuable possessions is not impressively documented . . . the solidarity of the social unit was expressed most effectively in communal or group activities' (1974: 74). Examples were found in Polynesian ethnography and in Late Neolithic Malta and Neolithic and Early Bronze Age Wessex (Figure 3.1). In

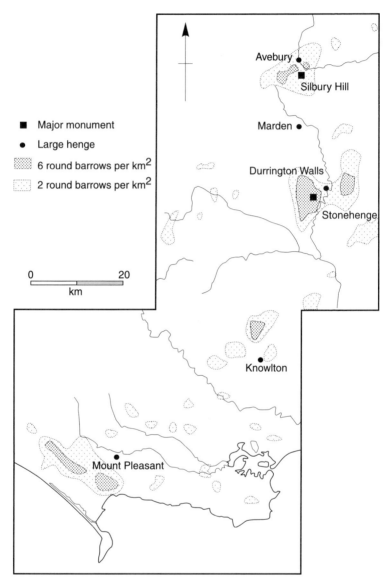

Figure 3.1 Group-oriented chiefdoms shown by the spatial concentrations of ritual monuments in Late Neolithic and Early Bronze Age Wessex (adapted from Renfrew 1973a: figure 5).

contrast, individualizing chiefdoms were 'societies where a marked disparity in personal possessions and in other material indications of prestige appears to document a salient personal ranking, yet often without evidence of large communal meetings or activities' (1974: 74). Here examples were found in the archaeological record of Bronze and Iron Age Europe. In addition to identification of these types of chiefdoms, Renfrew noted problems for future research on social change, whether in the ethnographic or archaeological records: for example, 'why do competition and competitive display become so striking a feature in certain kinds of tribal or chiefdom society?'(1974: 84).

I begin here with Renfrew's work on chiefdoms for the reasons that (1) it is clearly laid out and readily comprehensible and (2) it highlights trends in neo-evolutionism which were to remain on the archaeological agenda during the next two decades. The identification of social types, such as chiefdoms, in the archaeological record has continued in both the Old and New Worlds. Good examples are found in the work of Peebles and Kus (1977) or Creamer and Haas (1985). The definition of material correlates of chiefdoms, tribes, or states depended, of course, on what were perceived to be the defining characteristics of these social types, as seen in the ethnographic record. At the same time, the process of trying to fit these social types to the archaeological record raised problems, or drew attention to variation that departed from the ideal type. All of these changes, and examples of archaeological practice, took place in a context of debate over the extent to which social types could be discerned in the present, let alone in the past.

Rather than follow through the use of neo-evolutionism in archaeology on a chronological basis, I prefer to situate archaeological practice within the context of changing ideas and critique. In the following sections, I attempt to do this by summarizing trends in the theory and practice of the study of past societies during the last three decades. In this way, the diversity of current theory and practice is made clear.

True to type?

It has been pointed out, on more than one occasion, that social types are ideals, or generalizations, through which some order is brought to the world of empirical reality. They are attempts to represent reality, rather than reality itself (Yengoyan 1991). According to this line of argument, the typologies are heuristic devices, or concepts for use, in the way defined above by Renfrew. A lot, then, depends on

41

the criteria which are chosen to define individual types, and whether they vary continuously (that is, quantitatively) or dichotomously (that is, they are present or absent).

The ethnographic record has revealed many examples of societies that do not fit Service's social typology. For example, the Iroquoians had hereditary chiefs in what was otherwise a basically egalitarian society: the political authority of such chiefs depended on their generosity, wisdom and self-restraint, rather than on their ability to give orders (Trigger 1990). Big-man/tribal and chiefdom societies in Melanesia and Polynesia respectively are known to have traits typical of both these ideal types (Chowning 1979; Douglas 1979; Earle 1987: 282). The range of variation within Melanesian societies has been extended since Sahlins's (1958) classic work, to include 'great men' as well as 'big men' societies, thus complicating any proposed evolutionary sequence in the direction of hereditary inequalities (see Lemonnier 1991; Liep 1991). Characteristics of Hawaiian societies at the time of European contact included a lack of the monopoly of force (i.e. chiefdoms), as well as large populations and kings (i.e. states) (Cordy 1981: 28). Such examples raised questions about the definition of, and differences between, these types, as well as the range of variation that is allowed within each type.

One response to these problems is to create more types, to subdivide existing types to take into account empirical variation. We have already seen one example of this in Renfrew's (1974) distinction between group-oriented and individualizing chiefdoms. In the same year Ross Cordy (1974) published an analysis of the Hawaiian Islands, in which he defined two other types of chiefdom. Simple chiefdoms were 'societies with minimal rank, having one rank or status level and one chiefly redistributional level (the paramount)'. Populations numbered up to two thousand, and chiefs had little coercive power and were not yet removed from labour. Complex chiefdoms were 'stratified or incipiently stratified societies with two or more chiefly rank or status levels and two or more chiefly redistribution levels'. Populations were now much greater (up to one hundred thousand), chiefs had powers of coercion, there were more decision-making levels in society, and the chiefs were removed from subsistence labour. These chiefdoms were present in Hawaii at contact.

Ten years later, in an influential paper, Henry Wright (1984) defined the same types of chiefdom. More recently Nelson has proposed a division between collaborative and coercive chiefdoms (1995: 615). The prize for the most types of chiefdoms goes to

Carneiro (1998: 37, note 1), who has defined them according to local environmental/demographic conditions (impacted, dispersed, riparian and insular) and evolutionary stages (minimal, typical and maximal, as well as simple, compound and consolidated).

Types of states are more extensive, and have a longer history, than types of chiefdoms. Cherry (1978: 413) listed nearly two dozen types, including pristine, secondary, archaic, feudal, tribal, segmentary, theocratic, secular, militaristic, pre-industrial and city states. Compared with chiefdoms and states, typologies of bands and tribes are almost non-existent. This is, perhaps, recognition of the increasingly marked variation in social and political complexity, and its material expression, in chiefdoms and states. A simple typology can no longer contain all the variation seen in the empirical records of ethnography, archaeology and history.

Feinman and Neitzel (1984: 40–3) have shown how different traits have been used in the classification of human societies into types and sub-types, beginning with Lewis Henry Morgan's stages of savagery, barbarism and civilization, which were defined on the basis of their subsistence and subdivided on the basis of their technologies. Alternative schemes to those of Service and Fried for 'intermediate-level' societies have been devised on the basis of the ethnographic records of Polynesia, South and Central America, and sub-Saharan Africa. Feinman and Neitzel (1984: 42) drew attention to the classifications of Goldman and Sahlins for Polynesia. Whereas Sahlins used environment, redistribution and stratification to define four types (numbered 3, 2B, 2A and 1), Goldman used political authority and succession to define three types (traditional, open and stratified). However, as Feinman and Neitzel showed (1984: 43, table 2.2), there is no automatic correspondence between the societal types of Sahlins and Goldman when it comes to the analysis of individual Polynesian societies.

Like any exercise in classification, we choose the traits, or attributes, on which our typologies will be based. The choice of these traits, in turn, depends upon the problem(s) under study. Also we cannot assume that change in any one trait is sufficient to define the transition from one type to another, or be sufficient to identify the presence of a particular type. For example, Service placed great emphasis on the presence of redistribution in chiefdoms, arguing that such societies developed in response to ecological diversity: chiefs emerged to administer and integrate the specialized economies of different regions, so that all the population had access to subsistence goods, in spite of localized differences in production.

However, Earle's seminal study of Hawaiian chiefdoms (1978) showed the absence of such economic specialization and inter-dependence. Rather than integrate subsistence production, the chiefs pursued political strategies and competed to mobilize goods, support and labour. Altruism was not a trait of political leaders! This view of chiefs received support from elsewhere (e.g. Taylor 1975 on Africa, Helms 1979 on Panama). Clearly redistribution cannot be assumed to identify a chiefdom, or provide a mechanism for the development of this type of society.

The presence or absence of one trait that defines a type of society would be an example of a dichotomous variable. Critics of neo-evolutionism argue that the stage typologies of societies proposed by Service and Fried were examples of the use of dichotomous rather than continuous variables. The greatest support for this criticism came from the review of the ethnographic literature for North, Central and South America presented by Feinman and Neitzel (1984). Their focus was on 'middle-range' societies, omitting mobile hunters and gatherers and what they called 'bureaucratic' or 'petty' states (1984: 46), although they were not clear about the criteria by which state societies are defined. Four major attributes which have figured in ethnographic and archaeological studies of 'middle-range' societies were selected for study: the functions of leaders, social differentiation, the structure and complexity of political organization, and demography. The degree to which these attributes vary with each other was also studied.

Economic functions were not the only functions of leaders; these functions varied in number in each major area, and redistribution was not their central function. Instead redistribution increased in importance among those leaders with a larger number of functions. Feinman and Neitzel distinguished between weak and strong leaders, on the basis of the number of their functions. It is the 'strong' leaders who undertake redistribution, which, along with external trade, gives them the means to increase their power (1984: 56).

The ways in which status is marked in the ethnographic record (e.g. residence, dress, multiple wives, treatment at death, special food, servants/slaves) were shown to vary in such a continuous way that social types could not be identified and ranked and stratified societies (in the terms of Fried) could not be distinguished. There was some support for a correlation between status markings and the number of leadership functions, but this was not universal. Considerable variation was also found in patterns of succession to leadership positions.

Variation was also seen in the numbers of administrative levels in the sample of pre-state societies, which were shown to have a strong correlation with the degree of status differentiation. Surprisingly, perhaps, the numbers of administrative (or decision-making) levels correlated only weakly with the functions of leaders.

Lastly, Feinman and Neitzel studied demography by using figures for maximal community size in the Americas. A strong correlation was observed between these figures and the number of status markers of leaders, but this was not the case with the functions of leaders or the number of administrative levels. Once again, there are complex relationships between these variables, and one cannot be predicted from the others. Maximal community size was also continuously distributed. The same observations were made for total population size, which varied continuously and correlated strongly with the number of administrative levels and weakly with the functions of leaders and status differentiation.

The overall conclusion of Feinman and Neitzel was that the diversity of these four attributes of pre-state societies in the Americas 'was continuous rather than discrete and no clear societal modes or subtypes were readily apparent' (1984: 77). Other scholars (e.g. Cordy 1981) had anticipated this conclusion. Subsequently Leonard and Jones (1987: 207–10) found no support in ethnographic analyses of variation in community organization, settlement pattern and class stratification to justify the definition of Service's societal types. In his examination of South-east Asian ethnography, Hutterer (1991) also pointed out that linguistic, ethnic and other variables in this region of the world do not correlate well with each other.

These criticisms of neo-evolutionary stages of society, as well as their use, have spanned the last three decades. While the social types of Service, Fried and others were refined, subdivided or rejected, other North American archaeologists decided to rethink the theoretical basis of societies and social change. Rather than identify traits of chiefdoms or states in the archaeological record, as was attempted by Renfrew, they turned their attention to the processes of social change. Theory was used to build a comparative approach to the study of society.

Too much administration and not enough politics

It has often been observed that the processual archaeology of the 1960s was deeply rooted in cultural ecology. Both human and animal populations exchanged matter and energy with their environments. Culture, in Leslie White's famous words, was 'the extrasomatic means of adaptation' for human populations. Subsistence and the economy, mediated through technology, were the means by which cultures adapted to their environments. Following Julian Steward, social organization and ideology were relegated to the status of dependent variables in cultural change.

In an influential paper Kent Flannery (1972) argued that a successful cultural ecology had to take into account a further exchange, that of information, between populations and their environments. While an emphasis on techno-environmental factors was being reasonably successful in the study of 'simpler' cultures, such as hunter-gatherer bands, they were less successful in the explanation of early state societies. Equally unsuccessful were what Flannery called 'humanistic' studies of information exchange in such societies: these focused on art, religion, writing, and so on, but failed to consider exchanges of matter and energy (e.g. subsistence). If cultural ecology was to work, then it had to combine these approaches and examine all three kinds of exchanges with the natural and social environments.

But were exchanges of matter, energy and information of equal importance in the emergence of state societies? Flannery came to the following conclusions: 'the most striking differences between states and simpler societies lies in the realm of decision-making and its hierarchical organisation, rather than in matter and energy exchanges' (1972: 412). Human societies were one example of 'living systems' (cf. Gall and Saxe 1977), and therefore suitable for ecological analysis, but information processing assumed a greater role than in natural systems. States were political phenomena, with centralized governments, economic stratification, and professional ruling classes with a monopoly of force. Hence the study of states in these terms involved a focus on decision-making, and on the development of societies with complex structures, which were both centralized and subdivided into more parts. Decision-making hierarchies developed in response to the needs for greater information communication and regulation.

This approach was developed by Henry Wright and Greg Johnson, who defined a state as 'a society with specialized administrative activities' by which control was exercised (1975: 267). In this way politics were subsumed under administration and decision-making. Two forms of specialized decision-making/administrative activities are defined.

First there is a hierarchy of control in which the highest level involves making decisions about other, lower-order decisions rather than about any particular condition or movement of material goods or people. Any society with three or more levels of decision-making hierarchy must necessarily involve such specialization because the lowest or first-order decision-making will be directly involved in productive and transfer activities and second-order decision-making will be coordinating these and correcting their material errors. However, third-order decision-making will be concerned with coordinating and correcting these corrections.

(Wright and Johnson 1975: 267)

In addition to this hierarchy of control, with its bureaucrats perched on top of local administrators and primary producers, the actual processing of information is also specialized: 'the effectiveness of such a hierarchy of control is facilitated by the complementary specialization of information-processing activities into observing, summarizing, message-carrying, data-storing, and actual decision-making' (1975: 267). Efficient control of information processing and decision-making became the basis of state societies.

The use of information theory to formulate this decision-making approach to complex societies was further developed by Johnson (1978, 1982). He proposed a model for the development of more complex societies as a response to the needs to process more sources of information and to coordinate larger numbers of activities. Horizontal and vertical specialization in decision-making were organizational responses to these needs. Following Flannery, he argued that, rather than a continuous model of social change, there were critical thresholds in the needs for information processing (cf. Kosse 1990; Upham 1990a). These thresholds related to the scale of the social system, one measure of which was the population size of organizational units. Characteristics of more complex societies were 'selected for' as responses to such problems of information processing. The development of hierarchical structures was argued to be an exercise in 'problem-solving' (Reynolds 1984: 188).

One important threshold in social evolution was that between the chiefdom and the state. Thus chiefdoms were defined as having one level of decision-makers above the primary producers, while states, as we have seen, had two or more levels of such decision-makers. This distinction was somewhat complicated by the recognition that complex chiefdoms could have more than one level of decision-makers above the primary producers (Steponaitis 1978; Feinman and Neitzel 1984). In these societies there are higher- and lower-ranking chiefs, with political control based on tribute flows. For Wright (1977) there was a further, critical, distinction: while chiefdoms and states were both centralized decision-making organizations, chiefdoms lacked the internal administrative specialization or bureaucracy, as well as the coercive control of, state societies.

How can decision-making/administrative levels be defined in the archaeological record? The most widely used measure has been the number of size levels (normally in hectares) in a settlement hierarchy (Figure 3.2). For example, Wright (1977) defined the states of Meso-america as having large centres dominating three or more levels of a settlement hierarchy. In this case there were three levels of decision-makers over the primary producers at the bottom of the hierarchy. In a subsequent, comparative study of early state societies, Wright (1986) proposed the existence of up to five levels in the settlement

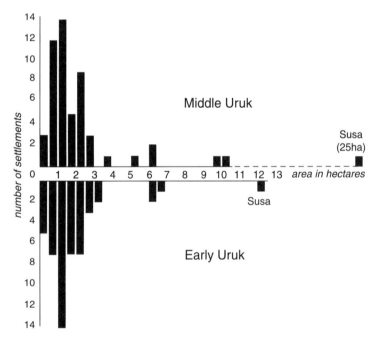

Figure 3.2 Three-level (Early Uruk) and four-level (Middle Uruk) decision-making hierarchies based on site areas in the Susiana Plain, Mesopotamia (adapted from Flannery 1999: figure 2.1).

hierarchies of Mesopotamia and of the central Andes. For chiefdoms, Peebles and Kus (1977) identified three levels of decision-making for complex chiefdoms such as Moundville (cf. Earle 1987 for a general review of chiefdoms and Steponaitis 1978 for a study of the spatial patterning of settlement hierarchies).

The sizes of settlements have often been related to the sizes of the populations inhabiting them. The relationship between the organizational complexity of a society and its size has also been the subject of debate, as population has been used as a measure of that size, and therefore become a contender for the prime mover in social evolution. Johnson's caution in taking population size as *the* measure of the scale of a society (see above) would be seem to be justified, given the varied results of work by Feinman and Neitzel (1984) (see above), Drennan (1987) and Upham (1990a) (see below).

This emphasis on decision-making enabled the redefinition of social types such as chiefdoms and states in terms of politico-administrative rather than economic features, emphasizing information processing rather than matter and energy exchanges. Organizational complexity was seen as a response to the problems posed by information processing in larger social units. Increasing levels of decision-making, efficient means of processing information and integrating social units, specialized bureaucracies were all 'selected for', in terms of their adaptive advantages. These examples of increased complexity solved problems. Political control was equated with administration, rather than with exploitation and repression. The emphasis on settlement hierarchies and the size and scale of social units found a ready field methodology in surface survey, and stimulated an interest in the role of population variables in social change. At the same time, it was difficult to identify decision-making hierarchies where there were dispersed settlement patterns (e.g. Polynesia-Cordy 1981: 35).

Given this change within neo-evolutionism, and the changing theory and practice of social inference in Anglo-American archaeology by the mid-1980s, let us now look at four conference publications from the period 1987–91. What do they tell us about changes in the archaeological analysis of past societies by this time? Were there mutually exclusive approaches to the study of society and social change? Did neo-evolutionism survive the weight of criticism within Anglo-American archaeology?

Four conferences and a funeral?

Taking the four conferences in order of evolutionary stages, we begin with Susan Gregg's *Between Bands and States*, an edited volume published in 1991 from a conference held at Southern Illinois University, Carbondale in 1988. The focus of the book was on 'sedentary, small-scale, non-hierarchical societies' or tribes. One of the main aims of the book was to use archaeological data to evaluate Morton Fried's claim that modern tribes, as studied by anthropologists, developed as a response to the impact of state societies. Thus the major period of tribal formation occurred during European colonialism and imperialism, in the last five centuries (see also Wolf 1982). According to this argument, tribes could not have existed as an evolutionary stage in the past. Case studies encompassed sedentary hunters and gatherers, as well as small-scale agriculturalists, in the Old and New Worlds. Rather than the result of acculturation, contributors argued that tribes were, in Gregg's words 'a stable and enduring sociopolitical form' (1991: xviii). Although the pressures of advancing European states did affect small-scale societies, it was argued that such similar resource and territorial pressures have occurred at other times in the past (e.g. Bentley 1991 on the Early Bronze Age in Jordan).

In addition to the characteristics of tribal societies (e.g. decision-making by consensus, extensive social networks which transmit materials and information and counter environmental risks, see Braun and Plog 1982), a number of papers focused on the means by which egalitarianism is maintained through time in hunter-gatherer and agricultural societies. Keene's study of an Israeli kibbutz raised the issue of resistance to change, inequality and social evolution. As he noted, this concept seemed to be absent from archaeological debate: 'it might be worthwhile for archaeologists to think critically about how easily prehistoric subjects are allowed to slide into ranked or stratified social formations, adopting the "benefits" of domination with no muss, no fuss, and no struggle' (1991: 390).

The theoretical focus of contributions to Gregg's book was very much based on cultural evolution and cultural ecology, with a lot of space devoted to relationships between human societies and their environments. The central importance of adaptation and selectionism was firmly advocated by Braun (1991), while Keene (1991) presented the bases of an alternative perspective.

Timothy Earle's edited book *Chiefdoms: Power, Economy and Ideology* (1991b) was the outcome of a School of American Research Seminar in Santa Fe in 1988. According to Earle, the aim of the seminar was 'to understand the processes that underlie the origins and development of complex stateless societies', or chiefdoms (1991c: 1). Elsewhere Earle referred to chiefdoms as 'intermediate-level societies, providing an evolutionary bridge between acephalous societies and bureaucratic states' (1987: 279). Clearly the chiefdom was still regarded as a concept of value for studying social evolution. But its definition now focused on power and political strategies, rather than ecology and adaptation: a chiefdom was 'a polity that organizes centrally a regional population in the thousands ... some degree of heritable social ranking and economic stratification is characteristically associated' (Earle 1991c: 1). Chiefs engaged in competitive strategies to obtain and maintain power, rather than emerging to act for the benefit of followers in solving ecological or economic problems (as was proposed by Service).

Earle proposed ten political strategies that he argued were used to create and maintain chiefdoms (1991c: 5). Strategies 1–2 focused on gaining economic power through giving, feasting and prestations, and improving the infrastructure of subsistence production. Strategies 3–6 combined internal force and external warfare to extend political power. Finally strategies 7–10 were ideological means of control, including appropriation of existing legitimacy principles or the creation or appropriation of new ones, as well as the use of long-distance wealth exchange to access the exotic symbols by which chiefly identity is created. Examples of these strategies in action were cited from the contributors' case studies on long-term change in the archaeological records of Neolithic and Bronze Age Britain, Scandinavia and Iberia, Greece from the collapse of the Mycenaean state to the emergence of the city state, pre-contact Polynesia, the Mississippian period of the south-east of North America, and the pre-Columban record of Mesoamerica, Central America and northern South America.

Differences of opinion were expressed between contributors as to the relative roles of these strategies in establishing differences of power. For example, the American pre-Columban record showed little evidence for the role of economic control (strategies 1–2). Regional polities seem to have been created, 'in part' by 'an ideology of religiously sanctioned centrality symbolized by the ceremonial constructions and exchanges in foreign objects of probable sacred significance' (Earle 1991c: 8). In contrast, Earle and Gilman argued in their papers that differences of power may be ideologically sanctioned but must have a materialist basis in 'the control over labour through control over subsistence' (Earle 1991c: 8).

This led contributors to discuss the material conditions that were deemed important in the success or failure of chiefly political strategies. Nine such conditions were natural productivity and potential for intensification, regional population density, existence of external markets, natural circumscription, concentration of productive resources, proximity to needed non-food resources, proximity to avenues of trade and communication, social circumscription, and structured preconditions of hierarchy (Earle 1991c: 10). The main focus here was on the ability of chiefs to generate and extract a surplus, the restrictions on the options of producers and how this affects the ability to mobilize a surplus and direct it towards political centres. Environmental conditions were not independent of social systems, but interacted with them in a dynamic way.

The contributors to the seminar stressed variation in chiefdoms. Differences existed, as we have seen, in the political strategies used to create and maintain regional polities, and in the material conditions in which such strategies were exercised. Differences in the types, forms, structures and evolution of chiefdoms were proposed. Earle (1991c: 3) followed Henry Wright, Vincas Steponaitis, Ross Cordy and others in distinguishing simple from complex chiefdoms, based on their regional population sizes (low thousands vs tens of thousands), levels of political hierarchy above the local community (one vs two), and the extent to which they had 'graduated ranking' as opposed to 'emergent stratification'. Feinman (1991: 230) followed Wright's definition of a chiefdom (see above), but argued that just because two societies share 'structurally similar political forms' need not imply similarity in economic organization, kinship, demography or other variables. A chiefdom was 'a sociopolitical form' and not 'a type or class of societies which (by definition) all share the same specified set of societal attributes' (1991: 230).

Kristiansen (1991: 17) subsumed chiefdoms under a more general category of tribal societies and argued that there was a major organizational difference between these as a whole and states. In tribal societies, 'economic and political processes are organized along kinship lines' and 'control, embedded in kinship, has not transformed social groups into classes' (1991: 21). Although hierarchy and exploitation may have existed (cf. Earle 1991c, Gilman 1991), this was part of a 'progression' towards their 'formalization' in state societies. Thus the more complex chiefdoms were regarded as archaic states, as were all stratified societies: structural changes such as enforced tribute/taxation and economic exploitation meant that these societies only lacked the bureaucracies of fully state societies

(1991: 18). Not only did Kristiansen differ from the other contributors in this characterization of social evolution, but also his emphasis on structural change contrasted with that on the correlation (or lack of it) between variables such as population size and levels of decision-making.

Drennan (1991: 284) contrasted the political strategies of chiefdoms in the Basin of Mexico/Oaxaca valley, where resources were mobilized for public monuments that served as communal ritual areas, and central Panama/Alto Magdalena, where mobilization was focused on status competition between chiefs. He also noted differences between areas in which the emergence of chiefdoms took the form predicted in a model of peer polity interaction, and those in which one political centre dominated. Steponaitis (1991) pointed out that Mississippian centralized chiefdoms of south-east North America AD 800–1700 had a range of different political forms, and differences in their scale and degree of centralization, as well as different regional trajectories. Kirch (1991: 144–5) contrasted the evolutionary trajectories of chiefdoms in the Marquesas Islands of east Polynesia with those which developed towards what some have argued were archaic states in Hawaii, Tonga and Tahiti: the material conditions in the latter areas were markedly higher population densities and intensified subsistence production. Once again the boundary between chiefdom and state societies becomes blurred.

Taken as a whole, the volume edited by Earle retained the concept of chiefdom, although stressing the variation in such societies in the ethnographic and archaeological records. Concepts such as chiefdoms were used as tools for thought, concepts to enable comparative analysis. They were no longer defined in Service's terms. Such societies were unstable and cyclical, they could centralize or fragment and they did not automatically evolve into states. Indeed the chiefdom/state boundary caused dissent in the real world. Chiefdoms were defined in terms of political strategies rather than ecology and adaptation, of chiefly exploitation rather than beneficial management. As Gilman put it, 'elites manage the social system in their own self-interest, not for the common good' (1991: 147). This was a world of conflict and control (either over staple production or wealth exchanges – see Earle 1987) rather than consensus. The use of ideology as a strategy of political control was discussed in terms of the creation of sacred landscapes and the use of mortuary rituals to symbolize individual positions and warrior status (cf. Earle 1987: 298–300). Debate occurred over the materialist basis of power. The scale of analysis of power was generally at the regional level.

One of the contributors to Earle's volume, Drennan, also co-edited a book on *Chiefdoms in the Americas*, the outcome of a symposium for the 45th International Congress of Americanists in Bogotá in 1985 (Drennan and Uribe 1987). The focus was on long-term sequences of change seen in the archaeological records of North, Central and South America. Several of the themes which were at the centre of Earle's book recurred here: these included the utility of the chiefdom concept, variability among societies called chiefdoms, the degree to which variation in human societies (especially in terms of increasing complexity) is continuous, the extent to which variables such as population density and organizational complexity are correlated, and the use of political strategies by chiefs.

I want to focus attention on the issues raised by the four papers in the last part of this book, grouped together under the title of 'theoretical considerations'. Drennan began by examining the relationship between population size and density on the one hand, and social, political and economic organization on the other (1987: 307–9). He came to the same conclusions as Feinman and Neitzel (1984), whose data he used, along with three archaeological sequences in Mexico and Guatemala: there was no 'tidy pattern of growing regional populations, steadily increasing population density, and greater concentration into larger and larger centers that many scholars have come to expect to correspond to sequences of developing social complexity' (1987: 319). There was marked demographic variation between chiefdoms and this 'fails to correspond neatly to various aspects of variability in complexity of organization within the chiefdom class' (1987: 319). It was the archaeological record of long-term change which offered more potential than the ethnographic record in tracing the variation in, and evolution of, the social forms grouped together as chiefdoms. For Drennan, the chiefdom concept was still of use as a starting point for description and comparative analysis of archaeological data.

Upham rejected the use of ideal types of society and followed Feinman and Neitzel (1984) in using the term middle-range society to refer to all the different forms of pre-state sedentary groups (1987: 347–9). Rather than defining traits, Upham's interest was in what he calls 'the processes involved in the development of organizational complexity' (e.g. population growth and aggregation, organization and management of labour, agricultural intensification, surplus production, development of productive specialization, etc.: 1987: 347–8). This followed in the tradition of North American archaeology in the late 1970s and early 1980s. Like Drennan, he re-analysed Feinman and Neitzel's (1984) data on demographic variables and their relationship to organizational complexity. However, he reached different conclusions to Drennan, arguing that 'the size of the total regional populations appears to be a determining factor in the organizational complexity of middle range societies' (1987: 355). Using the example of 'tribal' societies presented by Braun and Plog (1982), Upham proposed that demographic processes and adaptation to environmental risk and uncertainty were two of the more important causes of the development of organizational complexity (1987: 362). In doing so, Upham followed North American cultural ecology and moved from correlation to explanation.

In contrast to Upham, Spencer supported the use of terms like chiefdom, and argued for the cultural evolutionary sequence from bands to tribes, chiefdoms and states. One type did not evolve inevitably into the next (e.g. there are chiefdoms which do not evolve into states), but a given type evolved from its immediate predecessor (e.g. a state from a chiefdom). Such evolution was marked by a break, rather than by continuous development. The definition of a chiefdom itself has evolved from Service's focus on the economic to Wright's use of political and administrative criteria, generating specific observations (e.g. settlement hierarchies) to be searched for in the archaeological record. The key to Spencer's theoretical perspective on social change lay in selection: 'successful reproduction of the chiefly political order requires that it survive the operation of selection, which in turn demands that the elite pursue social, religious and economic strategies that are compatible with chiefly decision-making principles' (1987: 377). Such strategies included alliance formation, surplus mobilization, long-distance prestige good exchange, sanctification of authority, institutionalized social differences, etc.

Spencer's cultural evolutionism, with its emphasis on selection as the means of social reproduction, found its direct opposite in the historical materialism of Zeidler, who presented a critique of Braun and Plog's (1982) influential paper on tribal societies: essentially they denied the potential for change generated within tribes (or any other societies) by individuals and groups engaged in social production. This focus on internal causes of change in specific historical contexts tied in with Marxist criticisms of the use of biological evolutionary theory and concepts in the analysis of human societies.

The historical materialist concept of society, then, maintains a clear methodological distinction between the mechanisms of biological evolution and those of social evolution. It is argued that the complexity of human consciousness and the social learning process in human societies effectively set them apart from other biological organisms, such that their *social systems* do not necessarily evolve in accordance with strictly biological models.

(Zeidler 1987: 330)

Social transformation was argued to be qualitative and discontinuous. Zeidler addressed the criticism that a Marxist perspective cannot be operationalized in the study of past societies by proposing relevant analytical units and their material indicators (e.g. processes of production, distribution, exchange, and consumption; inferences on labour processes, the labour force, etc.) in the archaeological record (1987: 333–6). As is clear from the sources cited by Zeidler, historical materialism was the basis for influential works on archaeological theory in Central and South America (see Chapter 2).

Another School of American Research seminar, which took place in 1986, was edited for publication by Steadman Upham as *The Evolution of Political Systems* (1990b). The focus was on small-scale sedentary societies, defined by Haas as 'those societies in between the relatively simple band organisation characteristic of many known hunting and gathering societies and the centralised, hierarchical and bureaucratic state' (Upham 1990b: xvi). What Earle and others would call chiefdoms were subsumed within these so-called middle-range societies. Here we see the beginnings of political inequality when, as Hastorf (1990: 147) put it, 'certain people claim (a) power over others' decisions about labor, access to production, resources or circulation of certain goods, (b) influence on behaviors and communications between members of the group, or (c) authority over information and special knowledge.' Although such inequalities have been studied in both the archaeological and ethnographic records, the bias here was toward the time-depth offered by archaeology (cultural anthropologists are outnumbered 8:2 by archaeologists). The range of theoretical positions was slightly broader than in the Earle volume, and Marxist perspectives were more explicitly recognized in a separate section of the book.

As in the volume edited by Earle, the contributors agreed that a rigidly typological approach ignores and obscures the kinds of variations seen in present and past societies. At the same time, the focus of the conference was on societies between the levels of one type, the band, and another type, the state. Following the example of

Feinman and Neitzel (1984), some contributors tried to understand how individual variables interact with each other to define recurrent patterns and to suggest processes by which social change occurred. Upham focused on what he calls four 'axes of variability', namely demographic, economic, social and political (1990c), identifying population density thresholds which appear to be associated with major changes in the organization of societies, such as the emergence of more centralized political leadership. The search for such correlations between variables was also marked in Netting's contribution, which examined the relationships between population density, agricultural intensity and land tenure in the ethnographic record: while such relationships clearly exist (e.g. Netting 1990: 59–61), there is no automatic requirement for political centralization among societies practising intensive agriculture.

A further similarity with the Earle volume lay in the emphasis on political strategies, on control and conflict, and on the critical question as to how the autonomy of local groups and villages was given up. The extent to which political power and inequality is grounded in economic control was once again debated. Hastorf argued strongly that political and economic inequality were not necessarily associated one with another. She cited examples of societies with clear differences of wealth, but no political stratification, and proposed the 'decoupling' of political and economic inequality, at least as far as the beginnings of such inequalities were concerned.

> At this stage, leaders are more concerned with symbols of power, opinion changing, and the negotiations of their social position (often giving out as much as they take in) rather than with control of economics. That is, they are engaged in appropriating social legitimation rather than material power.
>
> (Hastorf 1990: 148)

People may, of course, resist the strategies of emerging, or even established, leaders, as was pointed out by both Trigger (1990) and Bender (1990).

Evidence of theoretical cleavage was more marked in this volume than in those of the other three conferences discussed in this section. The perspectives of Marxism and neo-Marxism intruded more forcibly, with more extensive citation of such literature in archaeology and anthropology, and even some anxiety to allay the possible fears of a North American audience over the use of the word 'communism' (Lee 1990)! This perspective formed the basis of papers by Trigger,

Bender, Lee, and Saitta and Keene (1990), while it was acknowledged and criticized by Braun, who advocated a theoretical view based on adaptation and selectionism. It is interesting to note that advocates of theoretical positions as different as those of Plog and Netting, on the one hand, and Saitta and Keene on the other used the same analytical unit, the household, as the basis for study of inequalities in production and labour organization. Although one might imagine that a different theory would dictate the use of different analytical units, this does not appear to be the case in practice here.

This observation is a good point at which to begin summing up these four conference volumes. Given that they were all conceived and published in North America, it is no surprise that cultural evolution and cultural ecology constituted the dominant theoretical approaches. Where historical materialism was introduced into the study of social evolution, it tended to be by Europeans or Latin Americans. Some archaeologists retained a belief in the existence of types of society, while recognizing variation and subdivisions within individual types, such as the chiefdom. Others rejected the existence of any social types as either useful or realistic, preferring more neutral and inclusive terms such as 'middle-range societies'. Whether evolutionists or not, there was widespread consensus that the study of such societies now had to focus on political strategies concerned with the creation and maintenance of power differences, with resistance, conflict and control, rather than simply ecological adaptation. Major differences of opinion existed over the use of biological evolution as an analogy for social change.

But, and this is a big BUT, the research on long-term change in the archaeological record, reported in these conference volumes, revealed the collection of data on variables relevant to different theoretical perspectives. These variables included agricultural production and intensification, surplus production, the organization of labour, demography, exchange and settlement hierarchies. Analytical units ranged from the small-scale, in the household, through the society or the social formation to the pan-regional world system. Neither the theoretical approaches nor the practice of archaeology could be argued to be completely exclusive, as individual archaeologists have come to grips with criticisms of their positions, as well as the implications of the data produced by their research and that of others. As far as social evolution was concerned, the world of archaeological theory and practice in the late 1980s was most certainly different from the 1960s, when cultural evolution permeated Anglo-American archaeology. Cultural evolution was not dead in the late

1980s, but the influence of historical materialism was becoming more prevalent. It is to this influence that we turn in the next section.

By the left, quick march!

Historical materialism has been a major intellectual and political force for the last one hundred and fifty years. Like other bodies of theory, its popularity has vacillated within the social sciences, as has the extent to which adherents to other theories have looked to it for inspiration. Good reviews of its practice and influence can be found for both anthropology (Bloch 1985) and archaeology (McGuire 1992). While Marx's analysis of society began with capitalism, it was always historical in character, as he attempted to show that capitalism was a product of history. But the part played by analysis of prehistoric societies was minimal, given the state of knowledge of such societies in the mid- to late nineteenth century. This did not stop the application of Marxist analyses to prehistoric societies, as we saw in Chapter 2, but this was very restricted within the Anglo-American world until the last three decades.

It is not my intention here to present a detailed exegesis of Marxist thought. The reader is best directed to any one of a series of commentaries or biographies (e.g. Berlin 1939; McLellan 1973, 1975), as well as to key publications by Marx himself (1973), Marx and Engels (1970, 1998) and Engels (1972). While scholars disagree about the interpretation of specific passages and works, and about the evolution of Marx's thought, given the piecemeal and delayed record of its publication, there are central ideas which run through it and provide the basis for the subsequent tradition of historical materialism. These begin with a materialist philosophy and methodology, which assert that the production and reproduction of life are the foundations of historical and social analysis. This materialism was developed as a counter to the Hegelian idealism that permeated nineteenth-century German philosophy. It directed attention to the analysis of production and of the organization and exploitation of surplus labour, especially by control of the means of production (as seen in capitalism). Change was generated by processes internal to society, namely contradictions between the forces and relations of production. Such contradictions and internal conflicts were central to change, as opposed to system maintenance or adaptation, and class was the key social unit of analysis. The environment constrains but does not determine. Change occurs within specific historical contexts, while the interests of the ruling class are maintained not only by physical coercion, but also by an ideology that represents its interests as those of all classes within a particular society.

With the notable exception of Gordon Childe, historical materialism played a limited role in the study of social change in Anglo-American archaeology before the 1970s. While a handful of classical Marxists looked back to original texts (as they became available in translation), it was the work of what became known as neo, structural or Western Marxist anthropologists in France which provided the decisive impetus (Bloch 1985; McGuire 1992, 1993; Trigger 1993). Scholars such as Godelier, Meillassoux, Terray and Althusser wrestled with what they perceived as the limitations of Marx and Engels's analysis for precapitalist societies, and rejected the way in which a five-stage unilineal history of society (primitive, ancient/slave, feudal, capitalist, communist) had been imposed upon Soviet anthropology and archaeology. At the same time they rejected the functionalist view of society used in British anthropology. For some, such as Terray and Althusser, the unit of analysis of precapitalist societies was the mode of production, more than one of which could be present in a society. For others, such as Rey, the concept of class was extended to apply to all societies, given the evidence for exploitation claimed to be present in non-capitalist and non-state societies (e.g. elders over juniors, men over women). The determination of the superstructure (e.g. ideology) by the economic base was also debated. Althusser gave greater weight to the social relations of production than to the forces of production, while Godelier rejected economic relations as the motor of change and argued the case for factors which would be placed in the superstructure by classical Marxists (e.g. religion, kinship, politics) as determinants of social change.

This resurgence of Marxist and Marxist-inspired thought in anthropology was by no means the result of activity by a uniform school of thought. But it was the authors mentioned above, along with the German critical theorists such as Habermas, who inspired British archaeologists in the period from the mid-1970s until the mid-1980s to draw significantly upon historical materialism (for reviews, see McGuire 1992, 1993; Trigger 1993). The centres of this activity were in University College London and Cambridge, although it was only in UCL that the label 'Marxist archaeology' was justified. Seminal papers on the importance of social relations in the development of farming by Bender (e.g. 1978, 1985) and on the epigenetic, or prestige-goods, model of social evolution by Friedman and Rowlands (1978) were widely cited and stimulated further research. For example, Kristiansen (1982) focused on contradictions between social relations and economic production from the Neolithic until the Iron Age of northern Europe. Social change was discontinuous, rather than continuous, and followed a series of evolutionary and devolutionary cycles. The scale of social reproduction was at the regional, rather than the local level, tying in with a broader interest in world systems models. Friedman and Rowlands (1978) brought together structural Marxist and other anthropologists and archaeologists for a seminar on the evolution of social systems. The first edited book on Marxist archaeology was published in 1984 (Spriggs 1984), and in the same year the themes of power and ideology were debated in another Cambridge volume (Miller and Tilley 1984).

By the mid-1980s ideas, concepts and models derived from historical materialism were diffusing widely through Anglo-American archaeology. As has been pointed out by Trigger, not all the authors who embraced this tradition were Marxists, opinion among Marxists was divided, and some wanted to dissociate themselves from the political commitment of Marxism: it is in this context that Trigger refers to 'the disembedded and free-floating nature of Marxist ideas in Western society' (1993: 174). In addition to the explicitly Marxist contributions to the four conferences held between 1985 and 1988 and discussed in the previous section, the spread of these ideas is seen in the focus on political strategies, on domination and resistance, on conflict, on ideology, and on prestige goods. If the 1970s was the decade of administrative models, the 1980s was one of political models.

The concepts of power and ideology featured prominently in such models. Miller and Tilley (1984: 5) followed Foucault rather than Marx in making their distinction between two forms of power:

> By *power to* we refer to power as an integral and recursive element in all aspects of social life. *Power over*, by contrast, can be specifically related to forms of social control. While *power to* can be logically disconnected from coercion and asymmetrical forms of social domination and does not, therefore, imply *power over*, the latter sense of the noun power must always involve *power to*.

Everyday relations were power relations: as Paynter and McGuire (1991: 13) put it, such power is 'the capacity to alter events'. This capacity may be exercised by coercion or persuasion. The principal method of persuasion discussed by theorists has been the use of ideology.

The use of ideology for domination and legitimation, for hiding the real nature of social relations, has been discussed in historical materialism since Marx and Engels's (1970) introduction of the concept of 'false consciousness'. The interests of the ruling class, those who exercise *power over*, are represented as those of all members of society. This is known as the 'dominant ideology' theory and has been subject to criticism recently. Following Abercrombie *et al.* (1980), many now argue that multiple ideologies exist in societies, and that such ideologies provide a means of resistance as well as domination.

Much of this discussion relates to the function of ideology, rather than defining what exactly it is. As much as there is any consensus in the social sciences, most authors refer to ideology in terms of the aspects of culture which are concerned with the relations of power between groups within society. Such ideology may take the form of specific ideas, or what are called 'worldviews', which are associated with particular groups or classes. But what then matters is how these worldviews are expressed and symbolized in the material world, and become the object of human action.

The extent to which these concepts of power and ideology have diffused through archaeological theory and practice may be seen by comparison of two recent books. Earle (1997) acknowledges his education in cultural ecology, and his early research would probably lead him to be classified as a processual archaeologist. But comparison of his three major field research projects in Hawaii, Denmark and Peru reveals a focus on power, including ideology. For Earle, ideology is 'a system of beliefs and ideas presented publicly in ceremonies and other occasions. It is created and manipulated strategically by social segments, most importantly the ruling elite, to establish and maintain positions of social power' (1997: 149). Earle's specific interest is in how these ideas are 'materialised', that is how they are given physical expression (cf. DeMarrais *et al.* 1996). Given Foucault's emphasis on the built environment as a means to express and contextualize power, it is not surprising that Earle examines the materialization of ideology through public ceremonies, often associated with sacred landscapes, and through artefacts symbolic of power, whether they be exotic, esoteric or coercive (i.e. weapons). Ideology is seen by Earle to have played a dominant role in the development of chiefdom societies in Denmark, whereas it was less important than physical coercion in his Peruvian study area and preceded investment in economic power in Hawaii. It is somewhat confusing for archaeological typologists (see Chapter 2) that an avowedly postprocessual book on the site of the Cahokia period societies of the Mississippi valley, from the eleventh to the thirteenth centuries AD (Emerson 1997) cites exactly the same theoretical approach to power and ideology as Earle, along with Earle's means of giving ideology material expression.

This should not, of course, suggest that all differences are merged in some kind of theoretical stew. For Hodder (1996a), the approach to ideology adopted by Earle and his co-workers (DeMarrais *et al.* 1996) elevates control of materials over that of their meanings, which can be understood in different ways, as well as manipulated according to sectional interests. How are new systems of meaning, along with new power relations, adopted? Elsewhere Hodder (1986) criticized papers by Bender, Friedman and Rowlands and others for underplaying the role of ideology, neglecting the meaning of material culture in particular historical contexts, and failing to explain the emergence of new ideologies. For Hodder, materialist is clearly not a term of endearment!

Debates also exist within Marxist anthropology and archaeology. Trigger (1993: 176–81) has grave anxieties about key tenets of neo-structural Marxism, proposing that areas of agreement between this and classical Marxism are fewer than areas of disagreement. He disputes what he sees as an overemphasis on social relations and non-economic factors in precapitalist societies, as well as the claim, propounded by Terray, that classes and exploitation exist(ed) in all societies (e.g. Saitta 1992). This runs counter to ethnographic observations on the acquisition of prestige in small-scale societies through non-accumulative strategies such as giving and feasting. Gilman (1989, 1998) shares these concerns, especially about the idealism and relativism of some avowedly Marxist authors. Both he and Trigger see a greater kinship between classical Marxism and processual archaeology than between the former and neo-structural Marxism. Trigger (no friend of processual archaeology) is led to ask: 'When does the label *Marxist* cease to have meaning? I believe that idealist explanations, and therefore much (but not all) of what passes as neo-Marxism, forfeit the right to bear that name' (1993: 186).

The final area of debate concerns the ability of historical materialists to operationalize their key concepts in the archaeological record. This criticism from non-Marxists (e.g. Wenke 1981) was addressed by Zeidler (1987, see above) with regard to production, distribution, exchange, the material forces of production (e.g. the objects of labour, the instruments of labour), etc. Other key concepts include class, exploitation (e.g. Mays 1988: 216), the organization of labour (e.g. Bernbeck 1995), and property (e.g. Hunt and Gilman 1998).

Whether formally acknowledged or not, whether explicit or implicit, there is no doubt that historical materialism has helped to raise the profile of political strategies in studies of social change in the past. As we have seen, the roles of power and ideology were widely discussed. At the same time, the relative importance of, and interaction between, social relations and economic production were bones of contention, depending on one's theoretical position. Although reference was often made to the strategies pursued by 'élites' and 'leaders', as well as to the physical and ideological resistance of followers, analysis was still very much at the level of groups within society. The main exception to this, as we have seen, was the recognition that one form of power, *power to*, existed within the context of everyday social relations. It is these kinds of relations, and the roles of individual agents within social change, that were the next objects of study by archaeologists in the 1980s.

Practice makes perfect?

A focus of social analysis on individual action and strategies, as opposed to social institutions and structure, the small scale of everyday activities as opposed to the large-scale processes which are beyond individual control, has been known in different guises as 'action', 'practice' or 'structuration' theory in the Anglo-American world. An interest in factions, individuals, the pursuit of self-interest, and the manipulation of others, whether expressed symbolically or materially, as opposed to cultural norms and structures, was a minority concern within anthropology before the 1970s. Vincent (1978) traced the roots of this approach in the work of anthropologists such as Mair, Leach and Firth, but it was only really developed, by Barth (1966), Cohen (1974), Boissevain (1964), Turner (1957) and others, within the context of what became known as political anthropology in the 1960s. Ortner (1984) provided a good synthesis of the subsequent development of this approach. However, the two scholars with whom a focus on individual action is most associated during the last two decades have been the French anthropologist Pierre Bourdieu (1977) and the British sociologist Anthony Giddens (1979). In what follows, I will focus attention on Giddens's theoretical contribution, and its effect on archaeological analysis of social change.

Giddens's structuration theory centres on the relationship between the actions of individuals and the larger-scale social structures of which they are a part. It is argued that all social actors, or agents, are knowledgeable about the social and natural worlds in which they live. This knowledgeability is not unlimited, and individuals are not necessarily able to produce the desired outcomes of their actions. There may also be unintended consequences of these actions. The character of knowledge takes different forms, depending on the degree to which individuals conceive of their actions in terms of conscious thought. These actions are carried out in the context of the everyday lives of individuals, what Giddens refers to as social practices. These practices enjoy what is called a 'recursive' relationship with social structure: that is, neither is determined by the other (e.g. structure does not determine agency), but 'the structural properties of social systems are both medium and outcome of the practices that constitute these systems' (1982: 36–7). The social system as a whole is produced and reproduced during the course of this active relationship between practice and structure. As Roscoe puts it, 'structure comprises a complex of rules and resources that shape but do not determine social action. Agents receive these rules and resources as "objective conditions", but rather than responding mechanically to them, they use them creatively to perform activities and achieve ends' (1993: 113). Social systems continue at the same time as they change.

This relationship between individual actors, social practices and the social structure (or Bourdieu's 'habitus', learnt through the process of socialization in daily life) was seized upon initially by the proponents of postprocessual archaeology in Cambridge (e.g. Hodder 1982a; Shanks and Tilley 1987a, 1987b; Johnson 1989; Yates 1989), for which the work of Giddens and Bourdieu provided an essential theoretical plank. British archaeologists who also made use of this plank, although not necessarily styling themselves 'postprocessual', include, most notably, Barrett (1988), who made the study of social practices the object of archaeological analysis (cf. Shennan 1993).

During the last decade the concepts of agency and structuration have diffused through the Anglo-American archaeological literature. Although widely cited, there is little consensus on the meaning of agency (Table 3.1), nor on the amount of change that individual action can cause in social institutions, nor on the extent to which the individual is a social product of the post-Enlightenment period. The focus on 'individual narratives of lived lives and events' (Hodder

Table 3.1 Ten meanings of 'agency'

1 Replication of unconscious cognitive structures.
2 Social reproduction of, and resistance to, system-wide power relations through cultural actions.
3 Constitution of individual subjectivity through diffuse power relations.
4 Constitution of the individual as a psychological entity.
5 The experience of individual action in creating a 'life story'.
6 The imposition of form on material via socially situated creative activity.
7 Intersubjective engagement with the material and social world.
8 The creation of formal and social distinctions through expressive activity.
9 The successful deployment of discursive and non-discursive technological knowledge and skill.
10 The strategic pursuit of intentional plans for purposive goals, especially with culturally constructed ideas of personhood, class or cosmos.

Source: Adapted from Dobres and Robb 2000: 9

2000: 22) would seem to be of limited use to archaeology, given the nature of its evidence. In some examples the works of Giddens and Bourdieu are cited, but they do not provide the basis for model building or analysis (e.g. Blanton *et al.* 1996). Discussions of emerging social complexity now include reference to practice theory, including the wider range of authors cited above, and focus on the internal generation of social change. For example, Arnold (1995: 89) advocates approaches based on power building, consultation, manipulation, calculation, negotiation and factional competition as recognition that the development of social inequality is an active, rather than a passive, process. But the opportunity to be active, to employ political strategies, occurs under conditions of external stress. In this case human agency is claimed to be central to the theoretical approach, but it is a long way from Giddens and Bourdieu (neither of whom are cited).

In contrast Earle (1997) looks at the issues raised by practice theory for the study of social evolution among chiefdom societies. His study of ideology (see above) takes one of its starting points from Geertz's ideas about the creation and existence of culture through the enactment of public ritual. Using Bourdieu and others, Earle argues that 'cultural phenomena are not rules held in people's heads, but the daily actions of people habituated and instructed as they go about their routine lives' (1997: 148). Taking structuration theory on board, Earle enthuses that 'culture exists as a constantly moving objective world, experienced as it is created by its members' (1997: 149). At the same time, his approach to ideology is still developed from the perspective of the ruling élite, and practice theory and structuration do not direct his analysis of particular archaeological sequences.

Clark and Blake (1994: 17) construct an influential model of the emergence of institutionalized inequality, based on 'self-interested competition among political actors vying for prestige or social esteem'. Following Giddens, they assume that social systems consist of 'regularized practices', which are not endowed with rationality or the ability to adapt. Social actors possess knowledge of the system and the constraints on it (e.g. past practices). The ambitious actors 'vying for prestige or social esteem' are males (itself a gendered bias – see Gero 2000) and known as 'aggrandizers', and their ability to promote themselves depends to a large extent on favourable environmental conditions and the long-term, unintended consequences of the cumulative actions. For Clark and Blake this approach shows social systems, through these individuals, acting on, rather than reacting to, ecological variables. They open up consideration of long-term change, which does not figure in the work of either Giddens or Bourdieu, in their proposal that the transition to institutionalized inequality requires the introduction of new social practices before structural change. Such practices have to be maintained for a sufficient (but unspecified) length of time so that they become 'habitual'. This raises questions as to the continuous or discontinuous nature of change within the structuration model, and the degree to which the recursive relationship between practice and structure is equally balanced. Criticism has also been made of such 'individualist' models, since 'the action of any one individual can have no historical consequence unless others participate in the moments of interaction' (Pauketat 2000: 117). According to this view, we should focus on the social practices of the many rather than the few.

This does, of course, raise the question as to how far in general practice theory, which has been developed within the context of synchronic studies, can be applied unchanged to the study of long-term change, using the particular kinds of data available to archaeology. Structuration theory has been criticized within the social sciences, and that critique, both positive and negative, has extended into archaeology (e.g. Last 1995; Meskell 1999).

There have also been attempts to build intellectual bridges between practice theory as a whole and both evolutionary and historical materialist approaches to the past. Shennan (1989, 1991) noted the criticism that structuration theory undervalues the constraints exercised by social structure upon social action, and that it fails to account for the development of social institutions. But his main point was that the theory fails to account for cultural transmission, the persistence of human societies through space and time. For this, Shennan sought to establish a rapprochement between structuration theory and neo-Darwinian evolutionary theory, arguing that they are complementary rather than antagonistic approaches to social change.

Earle (1991a) also pursued the same aim, focusing on individual choice and the transmission and transformation of human behaviour between generations. Choice has been viewed in terms of economic, evolutionary or cultural rationality, and Earle proposed a synthesis between these which took into account the arguments that (a) there is a biological basis to cultural transmission (cf. Shennan) and (b) individual choice is constrained by group association. Other authors have also tried to distinguish between short-term, human agency and strategies, and the long-term evolutionary mechanisms which select for the persistence of particular strategies over generations (e.g. Plog and Braun 1984; Spencer 1997: 230).

Construction of different bridges has been proposed between practice theory and historical materialism, given that the work of Marx provided one of the roots for practice theory. McGuire argued that 'we should seek our explanations for history in the real dialectical interplay of nature, structure, culture and agency in the specific cases we study' (1992: 143–4), but that this should be done at the level of the group rather than the individual (1992: 134), given the Marxist maxim that 'humans make history as social beings'. There is no room for methodological individualism (which focuses on the actions of individuals as the determinant of social change) in classical Marxism, although it has resurfaced recently in what has become known as analytical Marxism. However, Callinicos has provided an excellent critique of the primacy of individual action in this school of thought and a reaffirmation of the classical Marxist position: 'historical materialism specifies the structural capacities possessed by agents by virtue of their position in productive relations i.e. their class position' and 'it claims that these capacities, and also the class interests which agents share, have primacy in explaining their actual behaviour' (1987: 94).

Conclusions

Views of society and social change have clearly taken several forms during the last four decades. Neo-evolutionism, with its focus on social structure, institutions, statuses and roles, attempted to bring order to the ethnographic record of non-capitalist societies. Proponents defined and redefined types of society, which were placed in an evolutionary sequence (with due allowance for debate over the originality of tribal societies). Processual archaeologists used these types to structure their study of past social systems. At the same time, the use of societal typologies was subjected to rigorous criticism, from both processual and non-processual camps. Within North American archaeology in the 1970s, the focus on ecology and adaptation in neo-evolutionary thinking gave way (although it did not disappear) to one on administration, as a theory of social evolution (especially towards state society) based on information processing and decision-making hierarchies was developed. *Homo economicus* had been replaced by *Homo bureauraticus*!

By the mid-1980s, and in spite of continued criticism, the societal types of neo-evolutionism were still embedded in archaeology. But now talk of chiefdoms, hierarchies, inequalities and social complexity was viewed in terms of power and political strategies, conflict, control and exploitation. Politics was no longer subsumed under administration. Within this tradition, opinion was divided as to the kinds of political strategies used by leaders and élites, as well as the material conditions of their existence, the processes by which complexity evolved, and the utility of neo-evolutionary concepts. Opinion was also divided as to the role of ideological, as opposed to material, factors in social evolution. This reflected the permeation of historical materialist thinking, mainly in the form of neo-Marxism, into Anglo-American archaeology. Some explored regional and even world systems of social reproduction, and the existence was recognized of both evolutionary and devolutionary cycles of social change. Debate ensued as to the role of non-economic factors in social change, as well as the existence (or not) of classes in precapitalist societies, and the degree to which essential concepts of historical materialism could be operationalized in the archaeological record.

Opposed to both neo-evolutionist and historical materialist approaches to society and social change, practice theory also 'hit' archaeology in the mid-1980s. Proponents focused on individual agency, rather than groups, classes and institutions, and advocated a non-deterministic relationship between agency and social structure. Continuity and change were no longer opposed to each other.

This history of different approaches to society and social change is important both in itself and as an example of the complexity of disciplinary change. Rather than a simple, linear sequence of approaches we see ongoing traditions of thought. Debate occurred within and between these traditions. While they appeared initially to be mutually exclusive (as probably intended by their proponents as part of the process of self-definition), ideas and concepts were adopted in spite of the tradition boundaries. Paradigms were seen to be permeable rather than incommensurable. This permeation occurred when what may be regarded each time as the 'mainstream' came under attack from new approaches. Whether the result of internal variation, productive tensions, or the desire to explore new approaches as the productivity of existing approaches succumbs to the law of diminishing returns, the boundaries between traditions have been crossed by intellectual bridges. The agents of such engineering projects are individual archaeologists. The bridges they build may provide theoretical links (e.g. structuration and neo-Darwinism) and practical ones (e.g. operationalizing concepts such as property and exploitation in the archaeological record, and using common units of analysis, such as the household) between different traditions of thought. For some archaeologists (those in the mainstream?) this process is to be expected, as we look to develop the intellectual tools to study the past. There is no monopoly on wisdom. For others, this may amount to a process of homogenization, with the loss of distinct theoretical identities.

These ideas and scenarios need to be explored in greater detail within archaeology, to move us away from simplistic ideas of paradigm replacement. For now I want to move on from looking at approaches to the study of society and social change to scrutiny of key concepts such as 'egalitarian', 'inequality', 'hierarchy' and 'complexity'. In the next chapter I look at their definition, especially as dichotomies, and their use in the study of contemporary and past societies.

4

MATTERS OF TERMINOLOGY
Back to basics

In Chapter 1, I argued that the world in which we live is both complex and full of inequalities. Trends towards such complexity (which subsume inequalities of wealth, gender, etc.) have been the focus of interest among scholars since the eighteenth century, before the social sciences came into existence. Evolutionary sequences of society and culture have been proposed since then, whether based on living or past societies. Since the 1960s archaeologists have wrestled with concepts of society and social evolution (although some prefer the, to them, less loaded word 'change'), as we have seen in Chapter 3. Disagreements in Anglo-American archaeology are clearly visible in definitions of society, in the motors of social change, in the form such change takes and in the scales of analysis which are required to study that change. At the same time, there are various terms that are used widely in the literature, and which have been mentioned in Chapter 3, but which have yet to be defined. In this chapter I will focus on the definition of such terms, and on their use in the study of both contemporary and past societies. I hope this will enable the reader to negotiate his/her way through a potential terminological minefield and to understand the obsession with the dichotomous thinking that pervades social thought. According to this, societies are either egalitarian or not, hierarchical or not, and simple or complex. I will begin with concepts of equality and inequality, egalitarian and stratified, hierarchical and heterarchical, before considering the concept of complexity.

Egalitarian relations and egalitarian societies?

If our world is complex and unequal, then it is no surprise to find speculation that the societies of our earliest ancestors were 'simple' and egalitarian. In other words, there was some 'original state of man', a baseline from which social evolution sprang. Whether this 'original state' was to be envied and admired or regarded as inferior to later stages of evolution became a matter of opinion. For some scholars, our earliest ancestors were 'noble savages', endowed with dignity in their simple state, while for others their hunter-gatherer descendants represented an 'original affluent society' (to quote Sahlins 1972), well off in the basic necessities of life, even if they lived on the margins of modern states and lacked their technologies.

This belief in the dichotomy between equality and egalitarian societies on the one side, and inequality and complex societies on the other, has a long ancestry in the social sciences. It was emphasized in an influential study of African political systems by Fortes and Evans-Pritchard (1940). The authors defined three types of political organization among indigenous African societies. While hunter-gatherer groups, with their ties of kinship, were defined as one of these types, it was the opposition between the other two types, those of states and stateless societies, which has proved so influential. As Flanagan (1989: 245–6) has pointed out, stateless societies were defined by negative traits: they lacked the centralized authority and institutionalized hereditary inequality of state societies. Where positive traits were stressed, they focused on the segmentary lineages and situational leadership of African stateless societies. The key point is that the terms equality and egalitarian were not defined in themselves, but as the opposites of inequality and stratification. Analysis began with a dichotomy, and worked back from states to stateless societies.

But what do we mean by egalitarian, or equality? We could mean equality of opportunity, by which all members of society are born with the same opportunities to earn social position and wealth during the course of their lives. This, of course, is the ideological basis of North American society, in which the farm boy can rise to be president or earn a vast fortune, and all are equal before God and the law. Such a triumph for democracy may be due to unequal abilities, whether these are intelligence, hard work and effort, entrepreneurial flair or sheer deviousness and dishonesty. Not for nothing have two modern presidents of the United States of America been nicknamed 'Tricky Dicky' and 'Slick Willy'!

But individual abilities do not tell the whole story and must be placed in their social context. Although North America, along with other Western democracies, adheres to this equality of opportunity, and aspiring leaders advocate wider access to the benefits of education and health, it is clear that this definition of equality is an ideal that fails to find support in practice. We are a long way from equality of opportunity for immigrants and ethnic minorities, for the homeless (what has become known as the 'underclass'), for women, and so on. The degree of equality in the conditions of life counts for more than any ideology of equality of opportunity. Democracy and universal suffrage allows regular opportunities to exercise one's vote, but this does not necessarily result in any change in the conditions of life. The right to vote may also be prevented or impeded, as was seen in the case of ethnic minorities in Florida during the last US presidential election.

In ethnographic contexts equality of opportunity and outcome may or may not coincide. While the !Kung Bushmen and New Guinea highlanders share equality of opportunity, this does not apply to outcome: the equality of outcome seen among the !Kung is less visible in the New Guinea highlands, where political and economic inequality may be achieved during individual lifetimes (Flanagan 1988: 166). It is important here to specify how equality or inequality are measured: Western scholars tend to use economic criteria, but social scientists have reminded us of other criteria valued in ethnographic contexts such as differential knowledge, access to the supernatural or the exotic, and different skills and abilities.

These issues show that distinctions need to be made between egalitarian social relations and practices, egalitarian societies (see Chapter 3) and egalitarian ideologies (i.e. egalitarianism). Flanagan (1989: 248) located inequalities and hierarchies of inequalities between individuals in the realm of everyday, interpersonal relations, or social organization, in contrast to stratification (the division of society into ranked, institutionalized categories of people such as classes and castes), which he argues is part of social structure. According to this argument, individual social systems can have elements of hierarchy and equality, depending on the criteria used and the daily practices of social life. 'There are no egalitarian societies', but 'there are egalitarian contexts, or scenes, or situations' (Flanagan 1989: 261).

What we may classify as non-egalitarian, or hierarchical, social systems may show egalitarian social relations, while so-called egalitarian societies exhibit different kinds of inequalities. There are degrees of equality and hierarchy. Even capitalist societies include egalitarian relations. These may be expressed and practised at different levels of society. They may often occur at local levels such as industrial or workers' co-operatives and communes of various kinds (e.g. Greenwood 1988 on the Basque region of Spain). Egalitarian relations may be practised on the margins of state societies, in both the spatial and the social sense of the word. Salzman (1999) argues that there are differences in the degrees of equality and inequality in the social relations of pastoralist tribes, depending on the extent to which they are integrated into state societies. Such relations do not, of course, change the dominant, economic relations that structure capitalist society. As Donner (1988: 158) wrote, 'subsystems that are based upon egalitarian relationships may be valued by people who simultaneously participate in larger social systems that are based upon hierarchical and stratified social interactions.' Perhaps the best examples of this are the kibbutz communes of Israel, which are based upon the communal mode of production (Keene 1991). Some 3 per cent of the population of Israel live on kibbutzim, but they produce around 50 per cent of the country's agricultural produce, as well as 75 per cent of its industrial output. This is by no means a marginal activity. And yet, while being fully integrated into the capitalist world system, egalitarian social relations are practised within kibbutzim.

We return to the classification of societies (as we may count the kibbutzim for purposes of analysis) as either equal or unequal. In these cases there is clearly variation in degrees of egalitarian relations and practices in daily life, in spite of integration into, and subordination to, dominant, unequal economic relations. This variation and the problems posed by dichotomous thinking have been raised in other ethnographic and archaeological contexts. Plog (1995) notes the coexistence of egalitarian and hierarchical dimensions in the ethnographic records of Pueblo societies in the American Southwest. An egalitarian ideology stressed social integration through sodalities, while hierarchical relations were witnessed in differential control of scarce resources (especially prime agricultural land) and knowledge of ritual. Tensions and conflicts were just as much a part of Pueblo life as was integration.

McGuire and Saitta also argue that the ethnographic and archaeological records of Pueblo societies show them as being 'complex, communal societies' (1996: 201) which 'embodied both consensual and hierarchical social relations' (1996: 198). While the means of production were held in common, and surplus was collectively appropriated, individual Pueblo groups did not necessarily have equal access to property and resources, the labour of some groups was appropriated by others, and there were inequalities (including the exercise of power *to* and *over*) within and between groups. Rather than continue the search for unequivocal traits that allow us to classify Pueblo societies as either egalitarian or hierarchical, we should recognize the complexity of real-life situations in which equal and unequal relations and practices are present. Each may also become dominant social relations in turn, as can be seen in the oscillations between predominantly egalitarian and hierarchical society among the Kachin (Friedman 1975), and in parts of sub-Saharan Africa (Keech McIntosh 1999a). The ethnographic record of the Americas has also been used to support the argument that short-term political unification of autonomous villages under the leadership of chieftains can occur in contexts such as increasing levels of warfare (Redmond 1998). The emergence of such leaders by no means implies that their position will become permanent and hereditary, nor that it will impose on all aspects of daily life.

In some contexts, as we have seen in Chapter 3, relations and practices of inequality are concealed behind an ideology of egalitarianism (defined in the *Oxford English Dictionary* as 'that which *asserts* equality'). For example, Mars (1988) showed how the emergence of élites in some Israeli kibbutzim since their creation in 1948 has been concealed by the predominant ideology of egalitarianism. Gerlach and Gerlach (1988) argued that the assertion of egalitarianism among the Digo tribe of Kenya was a means of concealing and coping with their history of hierarchical and stratified society (including the practice of slavery) under colonial rule.

Where they exist, egalitarian social relations do not define some idyllic state of innocence and happiness that requires no effort. As Rayner (1988) argued, there is no dichotomy between the rules and constraints of stratification on the one hand, and a kind of unconstrained, rule-less freedom of egalitarian relations on the other hand.

> Egalitarian relationships are not simply non-hierarchical, but are achieved and maintained by the social and symbolic manipulation of often complex rule systems governing decision-making. Hence egalitarian systems of social organisation place costly demands upon their members for participation and vigilance.
>
> (Flanagan and Rayner 1988: 2–3)

According to Rayner (1988: 21) the most frequent combination of such rules is between 'homogenizing' rules (e.g. communal ownership, rules of poverty), which promote strict equality, and 'equal-opportunity' rules (e.g. allowing uneven accumulation of personal property, but not inherited wealth), which promote equity.

Ideologies of generosity, reciprocity and sharing among small-scale, non-capitalist societies counter tendencies to the individual accumulation that might accentuate inequalities. Richard Lee (1982) has documented the variety of levelling devices used in everyday social relations among the !Kung Bushmen: these include joking, teasing, accusations of stinginess, praise for generosity, playing down the size of kills or the value of gifts, all within the context of social practices carried out in the open and not concealed from public view.

Circulating information to all members of a group, or an organization, so that decision-making can take place by consensus, is also costly in terms of time, resources and money. Great energy goes into the prevention of internal schisms by such circulation and communal decision-making, as Rayner (1988) shows in a study of the International Marxist Group in the 1970s. The costs of decision-making in relation to information communication have already been discussed in Chapter 3, with special regard to the emergence of social hierarchies when what are called critical thresholds of information processing are reached. That such an emergence of hierarchies is not an automatic consequence of scalar stress (as proposed by Johnson 1982) is supported by Keene's observation that such stress has not removed communal ownership of production and appropriation of surplus from kibbutzim (1991: 384).

It is important, then, to make distinctions between egalitarian relations, societies and ideologies, and to recognize that all societies may exhibit tensions between egalitarian and hierarchical relations. This is particularly important for our understanding of what Fortes and Evans-Pritchard (see above) called 'stateless' societies, which have always included a wide variety of social forms in which such tensions were present and acted out daily. Once this observation is accepted, the task of archaeological analysis becomes both more challenging and more realistic.

Inequalities and hierarchies

Inequalities are now recognized in all societies, from hunters and gatherers to states. They take different forms and are expressed in different ways. In spite of ideologies of egalitarianism among hunters and gatherers, there are inequalities in practices as basic as the sharing of food. This is often regarded as a means to ensure the prevention of inequalities in access to nutrition, and as a means of pooling risk during periods of shortage. However, Speth (1990) showed how differences in access to nutrition can result from the sharing out of different parts of animal carcasses: the best hunters may have preferential access to the parts of animals with the best fat values at kill sites, while the same parts of their carcasses may vary in nutritional value according to seasonal variation in fat depletion. Taboos may prevent both children and women from access to proper nutrition during critical periods of their life cycles. Women may be kept undernourished as part of male strategies to maintain gender inequality. Such nutritional differences are also noted between different groups of hunter-gatherers: there are no common levels of stature, body weight, mortality, etc. There is even evidence among the N.Aché of Paraguay that supports the hypothesis that hunting ability leads to greater reproductive success (Kaplan and Hill 1985).

In such societies, along with small-scale agriculturalists, which have been broadly classified as egalitarian, band or tribal societies (see Chapter 3), inequalities centre on personal attributes, as well as age and sex, as males control the labour of females, or elders are superior to juniors. Among the !Kung there appear to be equal roles for men and women (e.g. the women participate in decision-making and have a predominant role in production), but the position of women in other hunter and gatherer societies varies (Lee 1990).

Godelier's (1982) study of the Baruya of highland New Guinea serves as a good example of inequalities and social hierarchies in agricultural societies. Godelier began by listing the personal attributes, or 'talents', which distinguish, and are used by, 'big men': these include magical powers, oratory, strength and courage displayed in warfare and ability and energy expended in agricultural production. Then he examined inequalities of gender. Males control the means of both production and destruction: women take no part in the ownership of land, tools for forest clearance, and weapons, nor in the manufacture of salt (for exchange), the pursuit of trading expeditions, and the possession and use of sacred objects. As Godelier said, 'Baruya women are thus subordinate to men materially, politically and symbolically' (1982: 11). Symbolic differences are also marked in the initiation ceremonies for males and females: male initiation may take up to ten years, whereas ceremonies for females only last a few weeks, and the latter include both instruction in, and representation of, female submission to men. Thus 'the role of male and female initiations is to produce, and at the same time legitimate, the general domination of men, of all men, whatever may be their personal attributes, over women, all women, whoever they are' (1982: 15).

Other social hierarchies are also present among the Baruya. Selected males prepare and direct the initiation ceremonies. The males of particular lineages inherit the knowledge required by tribal tradition for these ceremonies. Inequalities are also evident in the ability to become warriors, shamen or cassowary hunters: in the case of warriors and hunters, the inequalities are between males and females, who are not allowed to participate, while women can be shamen, but of lesser status than male shamen (Godelier 1982: 23). Lastly, for both males and females, seniors enjoy superiority over juniors: for example the initiates are superior to non-initiates, and those in the later stages of initiation enjoy the respect of those beginning their initiation. At the same time, it should be noted that a boy who has been initiated then becomes senior to all of his elder sisters. The big men, great men and great women who receive the greatest attention in accounts of inequalities in highland New Guinea societies are the tip of the iceberg when it comes to assessing the full range of their social hierarchies.

In another highland New Guinea society, that of the Duna (Modjeska 1982), elder brothers possess secret knowledge and carry out rituals which are accepted as necessary for the reproduction of the fertility of a lineage's land, its wild and domesticated animals (especially its pigs) and its people. The magical powers associated with this knowledge and ritual practice, along with the myths through which these powers are affirmed, are the ultimate sources of the superiority of elder over younger brothers. Juniors are dependent on elder brothers for the reproduction of life, and give them their labour when required. While the latter are responsible for gardening and family life, the elder brothers engage in hunting. Such superiority of age and kinship is frequently cited in African ethnographies, in which, for example, the superiority of elders over juniors is based on the control of bridewealth in return for labour.

Inequalities and gender relations have been studied for other areas of Melanesia (e.g. Strathern 1987). For example, in Kwaio society there are inequalities between males and females in the control of resources such as pigs and valuables, in magical knowledge, in access to public ceremonies, in the control over weapons, and so forth (Keesing 1987). Elsewhere debate has taken place on the extent to which gender hierarchies and lower status for women occur, or occurred, in all societies. In particular the degree to which women's status changed with the emergence of the state (taking up a tradition of thought initiated by Engels) has been the focus of recent differences of opinion (Silverblatt 1988). Current thinking is against excessive generalization. Leacock (1983) cited examples of stratified West African societies in which women hold positions of public authority. Nelson (1998) argues against any universal subordination of women to men in state societies: she notes the examples of ruling women in a variety of early state societies, from the European Celts to early Sumer, Japan and Korea. The Silla state of the first to seventh centuries AD in Korea is notable, among other things, for the fact that the largest and most distinguished of the royal tombs was constructed for a woman. Gender inequality as a whole appears to have been absent.

Social inequalities, then, can occur in all societies and are negotiated and contested within the context of everyday interpersonal relations and practices. They are also resisted, as we have seen in Chapter 3, although this capacity varies according to, among other things, the effectiveness of physical and ideological coercion. Inequalities take different forms, and the presence of one form (e.g. economic inequality) need not necessarily imply the presence of another (e.g. political inequality). This reminds us of Hastorf's 'decoupling' concept, which was mentioned in Chapter 3. Whatever their form, such inequalities occur, somewhat confusingly, within what are usually described as egalitarian societies.

More than anything else, this distinction of egalitarian as opposed to stratified society highlights the ways in which inequalities are organized (Berreman 1981). In so-called egalitarian societies inequalities are unranked, status is based upon criteria such as age, gender and personal characteristics, and reciprocity and generosity are valued more highly than selfish accumulation of wealth and resources. In stratified societies inequalities are institutionalized: they occur 'as a result of rules that act effectively to bar part of the population from social, economic, or political resources' (Jones 1981: 151). Such rules divide society into non-kin-based classes, which can be further divided into the exploiters and the exploited. Persuasion has now given way to coercion. Such stratified societies can still include egalitarian social relations and practices, albeit under the control of the dominant economic relations. One of the challenges for archaeology is to trace changes in the forms of social inequality, and the extent to which these forms coexisted in the same societies, while at the same time analysing major transformations in social structure.

Hierarchy and heterarchy

The integration of hierarchy into the structure of society, as proposed for stratified as opposed to egalitarian societies, was central to the study of early states by Henry Wright and Greg Johnson, which was discussed in Chapter 3. They argued that the problems posed by greater information communication and regulation in larger-scale societies required the emergence of centralized and specialized administrators and decision-makers. 'Decision-making hierarchies essentially allow the co-ordination of a large number of activities and/or integration of a larger number of organizational units than would be possible in the absence of such hierarchies' (Johnson 1978: 87). Societies were divided vertically into different administrative levels, with higher levels integrating, co-ordinating and regulating the activities of lower levels, and horizontally into different administrators responsible for different activities. These hierarchies of decision-makers were now integrated into the structure of society, rather than simply pursuing interpersonal relationships. For Wright and Johnson, these decision-making hierarchies were most clearly identified in the archaeological record in hierarchies of settlement area sizes, which served as a proxy measure of population size. All political and economic activities were centralized within such hierarchies.

Johnson (1982) also made a terminological distinction between the hierarchies present in these stratified societies and those that existed in the interpersonal relations of non-stratified societies. Simultaneous hierarchies

> are hierarchies of the familiar sort in which system integration is achieved through the exercise of control and regulatory functions by a relatively small proportion of the population. Such functions may be exercised simultaneously at a number of hierarchically structured levels of control. As such, the entire control hierarchy 'exists' at any given time.
>
> (Johnson 1982: 396)

In contrast, the decision-makers in sequential hierarchies are not specialized, and different leaders emerge in different contexts (e.g. resolving disputes, leading warfare, organizing exchange, etc.). Consensus may be negotiated initially within nuclear families, then extended families, the village, and so on. The development from sequential to simultaneous hierarchies was a central focus of

Johnson's research, and has subsequently been pursued by other scholars (e.g. Paynter 1989: 382; Aldenderfer 1993; Spencer 1993).

But need all stratified societies be centrally organized, such that a single, regional, decision-making and settlement hierarchy co-ordinates and integrates all aspects of political and economic activity? This is the question raised by a different concept, that of heterarchy, which was introduced into archaeology by Carole Crumley (1979), who queried the automatic correlation of social and spatial hierarchies. Her definition of heterarchy was 'the relation of elements to one another when they are unranked . . . when they possess the potential for being ranked in a number of different ways' (1979: 144). Crumley used the example of an automobile company which

> may be seen as hierarchically organized in terms of corporate decision-making, and heterarchically organized in terms of the production of an automobile: into the final product goes the expertise of administrative, research and design, assembly and sales departments. If the unit of study is the automobile, all aspects are equally important. If the study has as its focus departmental efficiency or an interdepartmental softball tournament, however, the departments might be variously ranked.
>
> (1979: 144)

According to this perspective, aspects of hierarchy and heterarchy may be present in the same society, while political centralization need not be as pervasive as is implied in the decision-making model outlined above. Multiple, parallel hierarchies can exist within the same society: for example, there were lay, Church and craft hierarchies within early medieval Ireland (Wailes 1995). Among the lowland Maya there were hierarchical settlement and ceremonial centres (e.g. Tikal, Palenque, etc.), but economic and craft production were not automatically subject to central control: whereas politically and ritually valuable items were probably under central control, community specialization near to the key resources accounted for mass-produced pottery and lithics (Potter and King 1995). A stratified political system coexisted with a horizontally structured economic system.

Levy (1995) argues for the existence of chiefdom society in Bronze Age Denmark, most conspicuously visible in the hierarchical burial treatment. In contrast, there is only what Levy describes as a 'limited and flat' settlement hierarchy. She argues that the basis of the chiefs' power was not one of economic control: for example, the evidence for metalworking on almost all Later Bronze Age settlements argues against the existence of attached specialists. There was no centralized control of the main subsistence and productive resources. The basis of chiefly power, according to Levy, was in the control of ritual and esoteric knowledge.

Similar issues are raised for early states in South-east Asia by White (1995), who argues that control over commodity production and distribution was not the main basis of the political power of regional élites. Craft specialization and long-distance exchange were decentralized. Metallurgy was based on household production, and there was community specialization in the types of metal artefacts produced. In the absence of centralized control, ritual activities may have served to solve occasional inter-community conflict. There was even evidence for decentralized rice production and irrigation systems. As White points out, such heterarchical structures occurred in state societies in which there are examples of non-hierarchical factors such as age and 'virtue' being used to decide on succession to office. White argues that hierarchical and heterarchical relations belong on a continuum within complex societies, and that an awareness of heterarchy allows us to bring into our analysis of specific cases the possibility of flexibility in social status, gender relations, political relationships and rules for individual behaviour, as well as decentralized economies and multiple ideologies (1995: figure 9.2).

This perspective on hierarchy and heterarchy, coupled with the earlier discussion of equality and inequality, allows us to pursue more subtle analyses of social systems than those based on societal typologies. It also has implications for our conception of the term complexity, to which I now turn.

A complex issue?

Price (1995: 140) is of the opinion that 'there seem to be as many definitions of complexity as there are archaeologists interested in the subject.' While there are clearly divisions as to the degree of complexity shown by particular societies (e.g. whether they should be regarded as chiefdoms or states), there is some unanimity among Anglo-American archaeologists as to how complexity is defined and measured. Price's preference for the dictionary definition – 'things complex have more parts and more connections between parts' (1995: 140)– has much in common with how complexity has been studied during the last three decades. It is also in accord with the wider usage of the term 'complex' within archaeology: we refer to simple/complex house and settlement plans, architecture, pottery designs and forms, technologies, rituals, artistic motifs on rock art, and so forth.

Flannery (1972) initiated this tradition of thought. For him state societies were complex systems (in line with his cultural ecology approach, see Chapter 3), and complexity was measured in terms of two variables. *Segregation* was defined as the degree of differentiation and specialization within an individual system ('more parts'), while *centralization* referred to the degree to which the internal parts of a system were linked to each other ('connections') and to different levels of social control. These variables became the basis of subsequent analyses of decision-making hierarchies in early state societies (see Chapter 3). Later authors used Flannery's definition as the basis for the distinction between horizontal and vertical dimensions of complexity: the former focused on the individual parts of a system and the degree to which they were functionally specialized, while the latter was concerned with ranked differences between the individual parts. Perhaps the clearest example of this distinction is seen in Blanton *et al.*'s (1981) study of the development of the early state in Mesoamerica.

McGuire (1983) followed this line of thinking in arguing that complexity must be divided into its component variables before being subject to archaeological analysis. He distinguished two major variables, namely heterogeneity ('the distribution of populations between social groups') and inequality ('differential access to material and social resources within a society'). Inequality is further divided into absolute, proportional and relative forms (McGuire 1983: 102), and the difference between the two variables is expressed as follows: 'whereas heterogeneity indicates how many individuals have comparable access to resources, inequality measures how much difference there is between comparable levels of access' (McGuire 1983: 102). The key point of McGuire's argument is that these two variables are not positively correlated, so that an increase in heterogeneity accompanies an equivalent increase in inequality. He uses the example of Predynastic and Dynastic Egypt to propose that the construction of the pyramids marked the development of a relatively high degree of inequality, but a lower degree of heterogeneity.

The argument that complexity must be broken down into its constituent variables, so that different forms of complex society can be distinguished, and different degrees of complexity can be measured, is widely held in Anglo-American archaeology. Recently, for example, Nelson (1995) has listed a number of characteristics of complexity, including large populations, horizontal and vertical social differentiation, hereditary ranking, and élite appropriation of production, which need not all be present in all examples of complex society. He focuses attention on two variables, scale and hierarchy, and argues that these need not be positively correlated with each other: for example, the pueblos of Chaco Canyon, in the American South-west, show larger scale, in terms of population and spatial size, while the monumental centre at La Quemada, in northern Mexico, shows evidence of a more hierarchical structure. For Nelson these differences are those of different types of chiefdoms (collaborative vs coercive).

In all of these studies a distinction is made between the 'surface' traits (e.g. hereditary ranking) and the 'deep' variables (e.g. differentiation, integration) which archaeologists use to identify more complex societies in the past. Some authors (e.g. Minnegal and Dwyer 1998) have criticized the focus on these traits and variables at the expense of a clear statement as to what complexity actually *is*. For Flannery, as we have seen, the focus was on early states as examples of complex systems. This followed the divide between state and stateless societies initiated by Fortes and Evans Pritchard (see above, page 72). Archaeologists and anthropologists have raised two major problems with this dichotomy during the last three decades. The first problem concerns the status of hunters and gatherers as the 'simple' baseline from which all human societies evolved. The second problem focuses attention directly on the state–stateless divide and the definition of the state.

Hunters and gatherers: the 'simple' baseline?

Lee and Devore (1968: 11) set our image of hunter and gatherer societies in the much-cited observation that '(1) they live in small groups and (2) they move around a lot.' This emphasis on the small-scale and mobile aspects of hunters and gatherers was emphasized within the neo-evolutionist concept of band societies (see Chapter 3). Although exceptions such as the North-west coast Indians were recognized, the sub-Saharan African and Australian hegemony of hunter-gatherer studies in the 1960s only allowed neo-evolutionists to speculate that band societies may not have been universal in the Palaeolithic.

Anthropological research in the 1970s posed problems for this model of 'simple' hunters and gatherers. The extent to which hunters and gatherers practised a traditional lifestyle, fossilized and isolated from more 'complex' societies, was subjected to radical criticism. Their coexistence with agriculturalists and pastoralists (often in close proximity and marked by exchange relations) was shown through historical and ethnohistorical analyses (e.g. Headland and Reid 1989). Even the Kalahari San Bushmen, the archetypal isolated, mobile, small-scale hunters and gatherers, have a history of herding and planting activities (Schrire 1984). As we have seen already, inequalities in such basic aspects of life as food sharing were also documented among the 'simplest' hunters and gatherers.

The biggest challenge to the African/Australian model of hunters and gatherers came from ethnographic and ethnohistoric research along the Pacific coast of North America. The north-west coast groups such as the Haida, Tlingit and Tsimshian have long been characterized as having hereditary social ranking, sedentary villages and dense populations, part-time craft specialization, intensive warfare, ownership of productive resources (whether individual or private), wealth differences and even slavery (Maschner 1991; Lightfoot 1993). The presence of such characteristics of complex societies among non-agricultural groups made the north-west coast Indians very much an anomaly. However, the publication of ethnographies of Californian Indians in the 1970s showed that a wider pattern of behaviour could be seen along the length of the Pacific coast. Evidence was cited of intensified subsistence strategies (including management of nuts and seeds), sedentary villages and dense populations, craft specialization, long-distance exchange (including prestige goods), regional alliances, hereditary chiefs and (more rarely) social classes (for references, see Lightfoot 1993).

These temperate hunters and gatherers were very different from those in sub-Saharan Africa and Australia. They exhibited characteristics normally associated with tribal rather than band societies, and provided a challenge for neo-evolutionary typologies (see Chapter 3). The implications for archaeology were clear: more 'complex' hunters and gatherers may not have been such an anomaly in the past, especially in the kinds of temperate environments in which hunting and gathering was more widely practised before the advent of agriculture. The case studies published in Price and Brown (1985) highlighted these kinds of societies, in which complexity was expressed in terms of their increased scale, size and organization. Demographic, environmental and social causes were sought for the emergence of such societies. In the majority of cases these societies were dated to the Holocene and included famous examples from the American Mid-west (Late Archaic and Early Woodland), southern Scandinavia (Ertebølle), the Near East (Natufian) and Japan (Jomon). Bender (1989) looked for the roots of social inequalities (especially in the access to ritual knowledge) in the Upper Palaeolithic, while Soffer (1985) inferred the existence of 'nascent' hierarchies and some specialized production before 18,000 BP and intensified procurement and storage, limited residential mobility, increased population aggregation and hierarchical social and economic relations after that date.

Of course it could be (and was) objected that the American Pacific ethnographic record, which stimulated the growth of archaeological research on 'complex' hunters and gatherers in other parts of the world, was the outcome of European contact: 'complex' hunters and gatherers were a modern creation. The answer to this challenge lay in archaeological research in the Pacific region itself. Lightfoot (1993: 177–85) summarizes the evidence for changes in variables such as subsistence intensification, long-distance exchange, population aggregation, social ranking and warfare in different regions of the Pacific coast of North America. For the north-west coast, for example, there are claims for the existence of social ranking by 500 BC (Maschner 1991). Along the length of the Pacific coast, the time lag between the earliest hunters and gatherers and those that are called 'complex' varies from c.5000 to c.9500 years. What is more, the different aspects of complexity listed above do not develop together within this time span (Lightfoot 1993: 182).

Arnold has placed her research on the archaeological sequence in southern coastal California within the broader context of the whole coastal region. She defines complexity in terms of 'chiefdom like organisation', which she argues had three basic characteristics: hereditary inequality, hierarchical organization (including some multi-community political authority) and the ability of elites to manipulate domestic labour (Arnold 1992, 1993, 1995, 1996a, 1996b). Arnold centres her attention on the third of these characteristics: 'the separation of household labor or products from head-of-household management – where individuals outside family units begin to manipulate these resources – represents a significant restructuring process' (1992: 62). This control of labour was used to mobilize surpluses that were then invested in social strategies of competition through such means as feasting and exchange. Comparative analysis shows that variation existed in such factors as the extent of elite authority, the means by which labour was appropriated, wealth disparities and societal scale (Arnold 1996b: 79).

The archaeological record of the Pacific coast challenges neo-evolutionist thought (hunter-gatherer chiefdoms?), while at the same time maintaining it and using one of its basic concepts. However, before we get carried away with the complexity of American Pacific coast hunters and gatherers, it is worth noting that their spatial scales and degree of hierarchization do not approach those visible in the archaeological and ethnographic records of the agricultural societies in the American South-west, South-east and Mid-west. Regional political units here were organized on a larger scale, with settlement hierarchies and public monuments. The larger population densities of the Pacific coast at the time of European contact did not translate into the kinds of polities seen in these regions. As Lightfoot argues (1993: 183–5), the labour control and surplus mobilization strategies used by Pacific hunter-gatherer élites were unable indefinitely to support the kind of social intensification which was open to agriculturally based economies. The Pacific 'complex' societies 'represent the upper range of socio-political development supported by hunter-gatherer economies' (Lightfoot 1993: 185).

These ethnographic and archaeological examples show us that the description of hunter-gatherer societies as 'simple' fails to do justice to empirical variation. In the archaeological cases it is now recognized that arguments for complexity proposed in the 1970s were overstated: recent analyses of Natufian mortuary practices, for example, reject the inference of hereditary social inequalities and chiefdom-like society (Byrd and Monahan 1995) and focus on the use of communal rituals to promote social integration (Kuijt 1996). While we now hear reference to more 'complex' hunters and gatherers, their forms and structures are light years away from those of state societies. Indeed the dichotomy between states and stateless societies, as proposed by Fortes and Evans Pritchard, emphasized the scale of such differences, defining stateless societies, as we have seen, by the characteristics of state societies that they *lacked*. This implies a clear grasp of what states actually *are*, and an assumption that the emergence of the state was the major structural change in cultural evolution. Thus the state should be different from all other forms of society.

States and the Great Divide

There is no one definition of the state on which all scholars agree (Claessen and Skalnik 1978: 3), whether they are historians, anthropologists, sociologists (Abrams 1988: 59) or archaeologists. This observation should not surprise us, given the different theoretical perspectives that scholars bring to bear on the different kinds of data they study. But problems of definition do not exist only between disciplines. Within archaeology there have been major differences of opinion as to whether particular societies were, or were not, states. If such disagreements stem from a desire to fit a given society into one or other of a series of evolutionary stages, as part of a typological exercise, then they can become what Kohl (1984: 128) has called 'tiresome disquisitions', which emphasize the description of societies and the simplification of reality. But the definitions and concepts we use determine our ability to undertake comparative research: if societies A and B are defined as states, then we can compare and contrast their forms and structures, learning more about such societies in the process. The concepts we use initiate, rather than conclude, analysis.

Let us look at three examples of disagreement between archaeologists as to the existence of state societies. The first concerns the monumental centre of Cahokia (Figure 4.1), where more than a hundred earthen mounds are known within an area of 10sq km of the floodplain of the Mississippi River, just outside the city of St Louis (Milner 1998). During the eleventh century AD there was rapid population nucleation at this site, with the most recent calculations proposing that a maximum of some 10,000 people lived here during the next two centuries (Pauketat and Lopinot 1997). Other calculations of the population have reached as low as 500 and as high as 50,000 people. It is these calculations, along with the population nucleation, the construction of the impressive monumental architecture (the central focus of Monks Mound, seen in Figure 4.2, with its surrounding palisade and plazas, each of which was surrounded by smaller mounds), the settlement hierarchy and layout, the evidence for social hierarchy, centralized economic control and regional trade which have led some scholars to argue that Cahokia was the 'urban center of a theocratic state' (see Emerson 1997 for a discussion and critique of this proposal). Critics of this view disparage it somewhat as the 'little Teotihuacan-on-the-Mississippi' model (Pauketat and Emerson 1997: 3).

In spite of the characteristics listed above, as well as the symbol-

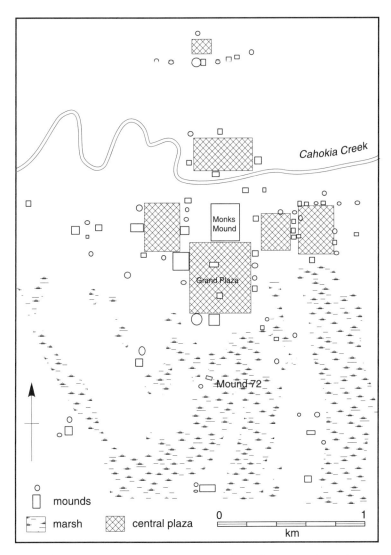

Figure 4.1 The central mounds and plazas of Cahokia in the eleventh century AD (adapted from Pauketat 1998: figure 3).

izing of coercive force in the central burials (and the far from symbolic evidence for violent deaths and dismembering in Mound 72), the use of such force to direct population nucleation at Cahokia, and evidence for the appropriation of labour in both monument

Figure 4.2 Monks Mound, Cahokia. (Photo by the author.)

construction and craft production (Pauketat and Emerson 1997: 47), most scholars now argue that Cahokia was a complex/paramount chiefdom. For example, Emerson (1997) uses Wright's definition of a complex chiefdom (see Chapter 3) to propose that Cahokia evolved from a simple to a 'sacral paramount chiefdom, perhaps on the verge of becoming a state' (1997: 251). The inference of 'specialized ritual and political functionaries', which Emerson interprets as 'the institutionalization of non-kin forms of leadership and *power over*', leads him to make the following suggestion: 'at its height, Cahokia may have had some characteristics of an incipient state that died "aborning"'(1997: 251; cf. Hall 1991: 33 on 'a city-state in process of formation' and Kehoe 1998: 171 on Cahokia as a 'secondary state of Early Post-Classic Mesoamerica'). Even proponents of the complex chiefdom model for Cahokia accept that, in social evolutionary terms, it was only just 'this side' of a state.

The influence of Wright's complex chiefdom model, and of Wright and Johnson's information-theory approach to early states (see Chapter 3), is also evident in another debate over the existence, or not, of state society. In this case it concerns the Huari polity of the Middle Horizon period (AD 550–950) in the central Andes. Isbell and Schreiber (1978: 372) began by stating what they called 'agreed' criteria for state definition.

First, the state exercises a monopoly upon the right to use force in the execution of decisions and in the maintenance of order. Second, the state defends a territory against encroachment upon its sovereignty. Third, a state administers public affairs within its territory through a hierarchy of officials. Additional special interests may also appear, such as private property, control of foreign trade or formalization of law. Such criteria are often difficult to identify from the archaeological record.

The last sentence is critical. As we saw in Chapter 3, Wright and Johnson's model of decision-making hierarchies in early states finds its main archaeological application in the analysis of site size hierarchies. These are based on data from excavations and surface survey, and are analysed for the Ayacucho valley, providing the main support for the inference of statehood (Figure 4.3).

The attribution of statehood to pre-Hispanic societies more widely in the Andean region has also been the subject of disagreement. For example, was Nasca society on the south coast of Peru in the first seven centuries AD a state or a complex chiefdom? Carmichael (1995) uses mortuary analysis, the absence of full-time craft specialization and commitment to monumental architecture, and the evidence of settlement patterns to argue that the best description of Nasca society would be that of a simple chiefdom. This recognizes the 'tremendous range of social formations' (1995: 181) which can be included under the title of chiefdom. But just when these chiefdoms, of whatever level of complexity, gave way to states in the Andes depends on how one defines the state. The studies contained in Haas *et al.*'s (1987) edited volume used different criteria (e.g. site hierarchies, labour control, monument size) to place the appearance of the state anywhere between *c.*2500 BC and AD 500 (Bawden 1989).

Third, there is the example of the Olmec culture of the Gulf coast of Mexico *c.*1150–300 BC. For some, the Olmec, with their ceremonial centres, public monuments, colossal carved stone heads, mobilization of public labour, and evidence for craftsmen, were Mesoamerica's first state society, its 'mother culture' (see sources cited in Grove 1997). Clark cites the existence of social stratification, an upper class of kings, nobility and priests, as well as craftsmen and traders, the upward mobility of tribute and labour to legitimize élites by the construction of public monuments, to propose the existence of a 'kingdom', which could be either a complex chiefdom or a state in the ethnographic record (1997: 215). Elsewhere he

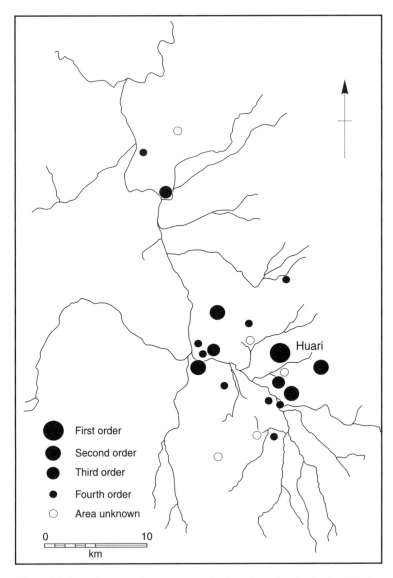

First order

Second order

Third order

Fourth order

Area unknown

Huari

0   10

km

Figure 4.3 Four-level settlement hierarchy based on site size in the Middle
Horizon period in the Ayacucho valley, Peru (adapted from
Isbell and Schreiber 1978: figure 3).

suggests that future research will produce evidence of more than one state within the Olmec heartland (Clark 1993: 167). However, Flannery and Marcus (2000) argue strongly that the Olmec are to be classified within the range of chiefdoms known from ethnographic and archaeological records: 'they built mounds and plazas like Tongan chiefdoms, carved jades and wooden statues like the Maori, erected colossal heads like Easter Island, and concentrated thousands of farmers, warriors and artisans in sprawling settlements as the chiefs of Cahokia did' (2000: 6). The Olmec do not compare, in terms of complexity, with the urban and primate political centres of the Monte Alban and Teotihuacan states. Instead of being the 'mother culture', they argue, the Olmec were just one of the regional chiefdoms of Mesoamerica prior to the emergence of the state.

These examples, as well as the history of neo-evolutionary studies (see Chapter 3), could suggest that the categories chiefdom and state have become so inclusive as to be 'catch-all' social types. Marcus and Feinman (1999: 5) acknowledge the heterogeneity of societies classified as chiefdoms and states, but how much of this heterogeneity is necessary before new types need to be created? Rather like the term 'postprocessual archaeology' (see Chapter 2), it has been argued that there is more variation between what are called state societies than exists between states and other types of human societies (McGuire 1983: 115; cf. Keech McIntosh 1999a: 2, on the variation in societies defined as states by Fortes and Evans Pritchard). And if the criteria for defining states keep changing, then it is no surprise that archaeologists differ about the distribution of such societies in the past. For some the focus is on the emergence of legitimized force and bureaucracy (e.g. Service 1962, 1975), and there is a sharp divide from chiefdoms. For others the development of stratification marks the beginning of state formation, even though that may not happen for some time (e.g. Fried 1967: 185; cf. Wright's view that class formation preceded state formation in Mesoamerica and Mesopotamia, 1984: 69; Claessen and Skalnik 1978: 20). A further source of difference lies in the view that what some call complex chiefdoms should in fact be regarded as archaic states, with social stratification and economic exploitation, but lacking the bureaucratic structure of 'full' states (Kristiansen 1991: 18). These examples also highlight divisions over the extent to which state formation is a result of continuous evolution or a major structural change: as further examples of the latter, Gledhill (1988: 10) refers to a 'rather substantial jump' from complex chiefdom to state, and Kohl (1987: 29) uses the concept of punctuated equilibrium in relation to state formation. For the majority of scholars, early state formation, however defined and however rapidly it occurred, was a rarity in social evolution.

This exclusive club, which resists the addition of further members (e.g. Cahokia and the Olmec), has its membership defined mainly in two ways. First, there is the presence of decision-making hierarchies (see Chapter 3), through which political and economic activities are centralized and specialized. These are expressed in regional settlement hierarchies. More than three levels in such hierarchies are required before a state can be recognized (most recently, see Marcus and Feinman 1999: 6–7). However, it has been argued that decision-making hierarchies are not always expressed in settlement hierarchies (e.g. Cordy 1981; Brumfiel 1995), and that centralization of economic activities is not necessarily associated with political hierarchies: rather than a regional hierarchy, there can be multiple heterarchies (see above). Stein (1998: 26) has argued recently that the concept of centralization has been unduly stressed in the definition of the state, and that the extent of such centralization is the outcome of conflict between the interests and power of ruling élites and the resistance of other social groups. As Stein writes, 'the resulting view of society is a "fuzzy model", grounded in culturally unique configurations of conflict and contingency, rather than the clean lines of monolithic hierarchy that we might see on a corporate table of organization' (1998: 27).

Second, the use of decision-making hierarchies, with the measurement of regional settlement hierarchies, has been developed in the study of the so-called 'primary' or 'pristine' states of Mesopotamia and Mesoamerica. These have long been called the world's first 'civilizations' in Anglo-American archaeology, and the comparative, processual approach to their study as state societies was initiated in Flannery's classic paper (1972). Given their physically impressive monuments, labour mobilization and large-scale population aggregation, it is no surprise that social evolution seems to be based on the view from the top of the plazas and pyramids of Monte Alban and Teotihuacan or the ziggurat of Ur. This is, literally, a 'top down' view of past societies! When it comes to such characteristics as centralization, stratification, specialization, public works, and so on (all in Flannery's 1972 definition of a state), these sites (as well as those of the Inka Empire and China) are without comparison. If they characterize early states, then it is no surprise that the Olmec and Cahokia are viewed as chiefdoms. When it comes to criteria of size and scale, they just do not cut the mustard; neither does Mycenaean Greek society (described by Renfrew 1972: 369 as 'something more than chiefdoms, something less than states'), nor the Harappan civilization of the Indus valley (Possehl 1999).

It is interesting to observe the ways in which regional ethnographic or archaeological records have set the agenda for comparative research on social change. The ethnography of sub-Saharan Africa and Australia gave momentum to the study of band societies until the publication of the North American Pacific coast record of complex hunters and gatherers in the 1970s (see above, p. 85). State societies have been viewed from the perspective of the biggest and most impressive. For chiefdoms and the development of social stratification, there has been what Keech McIntosh calls an 'Oceanic hegemony' (1999a: 4), with political and social systems being viewed in the light of the ethnographic records of Polynesia and Melanesia. This has raised doubts as to the extent to which concepts like chiefdom and state are applicable to African societies.

The distinctive nature of the African ethnographic and archaeological records has been stressed recently (Keech McIntosh 1999b). Of particular interest is the evidence for less economic stratification in agricultural societies (given abundant land and the practice of shifting agriculture), the absence of correlation between population densities and political centralization (Goody 1977), the absence of centralized organization and vertical control hierarchies in favour of heterarchies in some regions, and the presence of only some of the characteristics that are normally used to define more complex societies. For example, the city of Jenné-jeno, in the inland Niger delta (Mali), shows rapid population growth and settlement nucleation, but no evidence for subsistence intensification, impressive public monuments, marked social ranking or stratification (Keech McIntosh 1999c). As with hunter-gatherer studies, comparative research has to take into account such regional variation and not subsume it in over-generalized models.

Alternative states?

Clearly differences of opinion exist as to the definition of, and the transition to, statehood, as well as its material recognition. Most scholars in the Anglo-American world agree that early states were a rarity, usually associated with what are called the world's earliest 'civilizations'. Cherry went as far as to describe the state as 'a particular, highly successful, form of organizational adaptation' (1978: 413). And yet, the state also brings with it success for the few, and oppression, exploitation and coercion for the many. There is a

downside to states! To focus on 'organizational adaptation' is to neglect these relations of inequality. States do not behave adaptively to
solve problems; they create problems for population numbers, health,
the environment, stability of political units, and so forth. Such problems are recognized within the tradition of historical materialism
discussed in Chapter 3, along with the need to focus social analysis on
class, conflict, contradiction, physical and ideological coercion and
exploitation. We have seen already the effect that historical materialism had on Anglo-American archaeology in the 1980s. Now it is
time to examine the approaches to the study of the state, both within
and outside Anglo-American archaeology, which this theoretical
tradition has stimulated in recent years. As was stated in Chapter 3,
there is a diversity of approaches within this tradition. A book
would be needed to cover them all in sufficient detail. What follows
is selective, but offers a challenge to mainstream thought.

Let us begin with the concept of class.

> Class implies a relationship of permanently or consistently
> unequal control over the goods, resources and labor that
> ensure the continuity of the social group. In class relations,
> there is always a power relationship: at least one group is
> permanently removed from direct production and extracts
> goods and services from other groups in the society.
>
> (Gailey and Patterson 1987: 7)

Class-based societies are different from kinship-based societies in the
exploitation of this power relationship, which is exercised through
coercion. This exploitation is not only that of the producing classes
as a whole, but, it is often argued, increasingly that of the productive and reproductive capacity of women (e.g. Gailey 1987), although
this is by no means universal (see above, p. 79).

For historical materialists class relations are the basis of state societies, and, following Engels (1972, originally published in 1884)
and Lenin (1969, originally published in 1917), the state is
developed to preserve class society: state formation is 'the emergence
of institutions that mediate between the dependent but dominant
class(es) and the producing class(es), while orchestrating the extrac-
tion of goods and labor used to support the continuation of class
relations' (Gailey 1987: ix). The institutions of the state serve to
guarantee the interests of the dominant class: as Lull and Risch put
it, 'the class which is economically dominant also becomes the class
which is politically dominant' (1995: 99). Social coercion, whether

physical or ideological, is the basis of the institutionalized and legit-imized power of the state. They follow Gramsci's view that the state is hegemony protected by coercion. State formation follows the emergence of class relations, although by what length of time is a matter for debate. In this respect there is agreement with the neo-evolutionist tradition (e.g. Wright 1984: 69). The critical question here is how long a class system, and particularly the interests of the dominant class, the non-producers and exploiters, could survive without the institutions of the state.

The main interest that the state is intended to guarantee is that of the private property of the dominant class. Private property is, fol-lowing Marx, 'the most direct expression of the unequal appropri-ation of human labour and its resulting product, and therefore the cause of the existence of workers and non-workers, or put another way, the cause of the development of a class society' (Lull and Risch 1995: 100). It is argued that property relations are best studied in the archaeological record through analysis of differential production and the generation of surplus (Lull and Risch 1995: 100). In this context surplus is not defined as simply production in excess of need, but as when such excess is appropriated by others than those who have produced it. Surplus is the product of a relationship of exploit-ation. Property itself may take the form of natural resources such as land (as in the case of feudalism), human labour (e.g. slavery), the means of production (as in capitalism), or the products themselves (for a theory of production and products, see Castro *et al.* 1998a).

The association of class and state societies is not without its prob-lems. Neo-Marxist anthropologists such as Rey and Terray have argued that relations of dominance and exploitation (e.g. by age and gender), namely class relations, exist in all societies. Saitta has defined class in terms of how surplus labour is produced and distrib-uted in society, rather than using property, wealth or power rela-tions (1988, 1992: 889). As a result he argues that 'all societies are class societies, in that every society requires the production and dis-tribution of surplus labour' (1992: 889). At the same time Saitta admits that not all societies are what he calls class-divided, that is with relations of exploitation between producers and appropriators of surplus labour, and thus leaves intact the major structural bound-ary of class and pre-class societies. Bloch (1985: 83–4) cited some nineteenth-century African states as examples of what he calls class-less states, although, as he said, the neo-Marxist argument for class relations not being restricted to state societies reduces the impact of these ethnographic 'spoilers'. On the same pages, Bloch also cited the example of the Tuareg of North Africa as one of a stateless society with classes.

In spite of these definitional differences and debates over the ethnographic record, it is clear that the historical materialist perspective on states directs our attention to concepts that are not widely discussed in the Anglo-American world. A clear distinction is also made between the structural relations by which the state is defined and the material form it may take in individual cases.

> a state structure does not consist of the visible forms of power, pomp and circumstance (e.g. palaces, writing and exotic wealth items), but the systems of exploitation, extortion and physical and ideological coercion which in each case can take distinct forms, given the possibilities of social development which are dialectically related to the needs of the dominant class.
>
> (Lull and Risch 1995: 108)

This distinction between structural relations and material form marks a distinction that is not usually made within the Anglo-American tradition; for example, Flannery (1999) focuses on the recognition of a state in the archaeological record (settlement hierarchies, monumental palaces, temples, priests' residences, royal tombs, etc.) without defining what exactly a state *is*. As we shall see in Chapters 5 and 7, the distinction between structure and form leads to claims for the existence of state societies in prehistoric Europe which would be strongly disputed by those looking for the usual neo-evolutionary criteria.

The historical materialist perspective focuses not only on the structure of the state, but also on the structural change(s) which took place between kin- and class-based societies. Rather than quantitative changes in the degree of specialization, centralization and the number of levels in an administrative hierarchy, emphasis is placed on qualitative differences in the emergence of classes, changes in property relations (e.g. communal/private), the allocation and exploitation of labour and so on (e.g. Gailey 1987; Kristiansen 1991). In this sense we are dealing with a structural evolution.

For example, the Chilean archaeologist Bate (1998: 83–94) distinguishes what he calls initial class societies in the following way: they are divided into exploiting and exploited classes (with the former removed from physical production and appropriating the surplus of the latter), have distinct property forms and relations in different societies, and have institutions of ideological and physical coercion (cf. Bate 1984; Lumbreras 1994). The initial states that supported these class relations were based on upward tribute in return for downward services, and were inherently unstable, as the costs of maintaining the state led to increased tribute demands and conflict (e.g. through expansion of the state) and collapse, before the emergence of more 'military' states. Like Lull and Risch, Bate attempts to reformulate classic Marxist thought in developing his model of class and state. In the Anglo-American world, Gailey and Patterson (1988) share his focus on tribute from producers to non-producers as a distinctive factor in early states: civil production for the state is superimposed on subsistence production for the local communities. These tribute-based states vary in strength according to the level of resistance from these primary producers. Where such resistance increases, the state relies increasingly on appropriating a labour force of captives or slaves, whereas in stronger tribute-based states, it is the products of labour which are appropriated.

Not only does the historical materialist approach define the state differently, using different concepts as well as a notion of structural discontinuity, but it also departs from the 'top down' view of early states mentioned earlier in this chapter. Although it uses concepts such as the state, as opposed to, for example, tribal societies, and can have the same difficulties in dealing with periods of structural change (e.g. Kristiansen 1991 on stratified societies as 'an archaic form of state organisation'), it challenges us to look at our familiar categories of thought and practice in a new light.

Conclusions

The main aim of this chapter has been to introduce the reader to the usage of a range of concepts by archaeologists in social analysis. I emphasize the word 'introduce', as I do not claim the coverage to have been comprehensive. The archaeological literature is full of words like egalitarian, inequality, hierarchy and complexity, and it is important that we understand how they are being used, and the theories that lie behind them.

Many of the examples in this chapter illustrate the need to be wary of dichotomous thinking in social analysis. There are inequalities in egalitarian societies, which exhibit tensions between egalitarian and inegalitarian social relations. Hierarchical and heterarchical relations can exist within the same society. Societies cannot be classified into either 'simple' or 'complex'. And yet we need to use concepts in order to structure thought and analysis. For many in the Anglo-American world, these concepts are neo-evolutionary and derived from cross-cultural comparison of the ethnographic record. In other areas, such as the Mediterranean and Latin America, the concepts of historical materialism lead us to different representations of the past: for example, what might be classified as a complex chiefdom in one tradition may be viewed as a structurally different state in the other. This may seem like a trivial, semantic argument, but it has very real implications for the kind of history we construct, our ability to compare historical sequences between different regions of the world, and our understanding of the ways in which structural change is given material expression. It is important for contemporary archaeology that we go outside our own, regional traditions of thought and see how others view the past. How far are the different representations of the past mutually exclusive?

In the following two chapters, I want to look at a case study in what has been called 'emerging complexity' in south-east Spain, to see how concepts are used, and what kind of past is constructed; and then to consider examples of social analysis and the use (consistent or not) of concepts such as complexity in other parts of Iberia and the Mediterranean basin. What do these studies tell us about social change in this region and the way it is being studied?

5

A CLASS ACT

Representing the prehistoric past of south-east Spain

In Chapter 2, I drew attention to the theory and practice of archaeology outside the Anglo-American world. The greatest space was devoted to the critical, challenging materialism that is being developed within the Spanish-speaking world. This focuses on the material conditions of life as the basis of society and social change, and uses the analysis of production and relations of production in the study of the archaeological record. Concepts such as exploitation and property play more central roles in this work, and lead to different representations of social change in the past.

In this chapter I present a case study of such representations, using the sequence of social change seen in the archaeological record of south-east Spain c.5000/4500 to 1550 cal. BC. This gives me the opportunity to examine the relationship of theory and practice with regard to an area that has been widely cited in publications on the emergence of social complexity in prehistoric Europe. How have different models been evaluated against the empirical record? How far have research projects been structured to contribute to this evaluation? What evidence is there for structural changes in these prehistoric societies? How far do the representations of these societies agree with, or differ from, those based on models of social complexity used in the Anglo-American world? And how does this record of theory and practice, as well as the representations it produces, help me to evaluate my own earlier work on this topic?

I begin with an introduction to south-east Spain and to the history of research in the area, with a central focus on the relationship between theory and practice. Then I define, and highlight problems in, the current chronological and spatial scales of analysis. This provides the context for an outline of the evidence for production and social change in successive periods from Neolithic agricultural colonization to the end of the Early Bronze Age. The representations of change in palaeoecology, production and social inequality are then drawn together as a challenge to existing models of change and to those current in Anglo-American archaeology.

Theory and practice

South-east Spain is broadly defined in terms of the modern provinces of Almería, Granada and Murcia, with a 'core' area in lowland Almería, and a more 'peripheral' area extending north into Murcia and west into the uplands of eastern Granada (Figures 5.1–5.2 show the region and the main sites mentioned in this chapter). The core area is now the driest in Europe and exemplifies processes of both short- and long-term desertification (Figure 5.3). In a previous publication (Chapman 1990) I have given a more detailed account of the contemporary environment, the archaeological record and its study.

What interests me here is the historical relationship between theory and practice. To assess this relationship, I have divided the history of archaeological research in south-east Spain into three periods: 1880–1975, 1976–84 and 1985 to the present.

1880–1975

The year 1880 is taken as a starting point, as it marks the beginning of systematic archaeological fieldwork by Louis and Henri Siret. While their excavations were to cover a range of sites from the Middle Palaeolithic to the Classical period, and from lowland Almería to southern Murcia and eastern Granada, it was those belonging to later prehistory that attracted the greatest attention. In a major publication (Siret and Siret 1887) and subsequent syntheses (e.g. Siret 1913), the later prehistoric sites and materials were divided into a succession of cultural assemblages that were argued to represent ethnic groups known from literary sources. The materials found in mainly megalithic tombs and a few, poorly defined, settlements of the Neolithic were identified with the Iberians. The more complex communal tombs and enclosed settlements (e.g. Los Millares) of the Copper Age/Eneolithic were equated with the Phoenicians. Succeeding them were the Celts, who constructed hilltop Bronze Age settlements (e.g. El Argar, Fuente Álamo, Gatas) with intramural, individual burial, intensified metallurgical production and the use of metal and other items to mark out social distinctions among the dead.

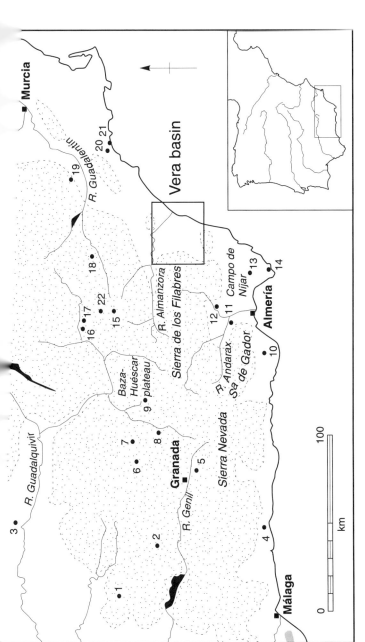

Figure 5.1 Map of south-east Spain showing the main sites mentioned in this chapter, apart from those in the Vera basin (see Figure 5.2). Land over 500m altitude stippled. 1 Cuerva de Los Murciélagos, Zuheros. 2 Las Peñas de los Gitanos, Montefrío. 3 Peñalosa. 4 Cuerva de Nerja. 5 Cerro de la Encina, Monachil. 6 Carigüela de Piñar. 7 Cerro de Los Castellones, Laborcillas. 8 Cuesta del Negro, Purullena. 9 Las Angosturas. 10 Ciavieja, El Éjido. 11 Los Millares. 12 Terrera Ventura, Tabernas. 13 Tarajal/El Barranquete. 14 Borronar, Cabo de Gata. 15 El Malagón. 16 Cerro del Real. 17 Cerro de la Virgen. -8 Cerro de las Canteras. 19 La Bastida de Totana. 20 Ifre. 21 Cueva de Los Toyos. 22 La Venta.

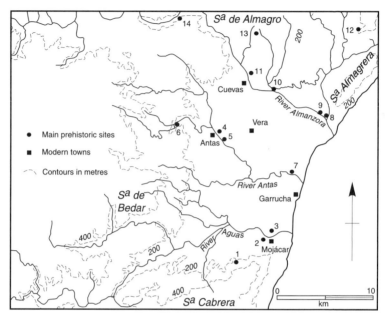

Figure 5.2 Map of the Vera basin, south-east Spain, showing the main sites
mentioned in this chapter. Contours mark land above 200m and
400m altitude. 1 Gatas. 2 Las Pilas. 3 Cuartillas. 4 El Argar. 5 El
Gárcel. 6 Lugarico Viejo. 7 Cabecicos Negros. 8 Almizaraque.
9 Cerro Virtud. 10 Zájara. 11 Campos. 12 El Oficio. 13 Fuente
Álamo. 14 Santa Bárbara.

The archaeological sequence of south-east Spain and its interpretation in terms of culture, ethnicity and diffusion was in keeping
with the theory and practice of late nineteenth- and early twentieth-
century archaeology in Europe. It also set the agenda for fieldwork
and interpretation until the end of the 1960s (e.g. Chapman 1990:
24–30). Fieldwork was sporadic and unevenly published. The re-
excavation of Los Millares in the mid-1950s (Almagro and Arribas
1963) recovered new data on the plan of the settlement and its
defences, as well as the layout and contents of the adjacent cemetery
of megalithic tombs, and the first two carbon-14 dates for south-east
Spain; but the culture historical framework of interpretation was
unchanged. During the 1960s and early 1970s, excavations on the
periphery of the south-east recovered, for the first time, stratified
data on Neolithic (the caves of Nerja, Carigüela de Piñar, Los
Murciélagos and the settlement at Las Peñas de los Gitanos, Montefrío), Copper Age (Cerro de la Virgen) and Bronze Age (Cerro de la

Figure 5.3 The eroded landscape of the middle and lower Aguas valley in the Vera basin, looking east from the foothills of the Sierra Cabrera towards the Mediterranean. (Photo by the author.)

Virgen, Cerro del Real, Cerro de la Encina at Monachil and Cuesta del Negro at Purullena) occupations, as well as more samples for carbon-14 dating. The main focus was on the greater continuity seen in the material assemblages from these sites. With the exception of the Copper Age settlements of Almizaraque, Terrera Ventura and Tarajal/El Barranquete, no comparable stratified excavations took place in the lowland core area of Almería.

The fieldwork of the 1960s and early 1970s began to raise questions about the extent of cultural and population discontinuity in later prehistory. The growing number of radiocarbon dates raised challenges for existing absolute chronologies. Local debate was minimal, but south-east Spain was included within broader critiques of diffusionism, based on radiocarbon dating, in later prehistoric Europe (e.g. Renfrew 1973b). These critiques followed an earlier attack on diffusionism and the supposed cultural links between south-east Spain and the eastern Mediterranean (Renfrew 1967). An even broader critique of culture historical approaches and diffusionism was taking place in Anglo-American archaeology at this time (e.g. Binford and Binford 1968), but the basic sources were not yet translated into Spanish.

1976–84

The proposal of alternative models to culture history and diffusionism in south-east Spain came in the second period, from 1976 to 1984. These models have been discussed in detail elsewhere (e.g. Chapman *et al.* 1987: 95–106; Chapman 1990: 141–9, 211–19) and will only be summarized here. In all cases the focus was on local processes of social and economic change, although none of the models covered the entire sequence from agricultural colonization to stratified Bronze Age societies.

Three models were based on the argument that the climate of south-east Spain from the fourth to the second millennia BC was as arid as it is today. I proposed that water control was required by local populations for successful adaptation to this environment and for the intensification of production required by population aggregation around the best water sources. This aggregation posed problems for access to land and water, as well as for social control and inheritance, leading to the emergence of higher-order settlements such as Los Millares during the Copper Age. Larger numbers of cohabiting people also favoured the development of craft specialization, which in the case of copper metallurgy provided desirable wealth and status items (Chapman 1978, 1982). The focus throughout was based on systems theory and adaptation.

Mathers (1984a, 1984b) adopted a similar theoretical perspective and was concerned with the risks posed for cereal agriculture in arid, lowland Almería, even if some form of water control were practised. Agricultural production had to be stabilized to ensure adequate yields, and this required local leadership and the development and maintenance of extensive networks of kinship and alliance. Such networks provided the means by which crop shortages and failures could be offset by food obtained through exchange. In essence this was the social storage model of Halstead and O'Shea (1982).

A different perspective was adopted by Gilman (1976, 1981), who rejected the role of adaptation in social change and focused on the means by which hereditary leadership emerges and supports the interests of the few rather than the many. As in the previous two models, water control was regarded as essential for successful agricultural production in south-east Spain and, along with polyculture, acted to tie people to particular areas of land and capital investment (e.g. terraces, ditches, olives and vines) and, by extension, to each other. Such areas of capital investment also required defence. The egalitarian society of early agriculturalists would have been strained by the limits on group fission and the increased potential for social conflict. The changes seen in the archaeological record from the Copper to Bronze Ages, with increased social inequalities, reflected the outcome of contradictions between the forces of production and the social relations of production. Historical materialism was the avowed basis of this model.

The remaining two models depended on the reconstruction of more humid climates and less denuded landscapes during later pre-history in south-east Spain. The model of Lull (1983, 1984) was concerned with the earlier part of the Bronze Age (the Argaric), when increased metal production acted against local self-sufficiency and led to complementary production within the south-east (i.e. between metal-producing and non-metal-producing areas). The division of labour required for this production, and for the transport of raw materials and goods, implied the development of a social hierarchy, removed from direct production. Early Argaric chiefdoms evolved into a class society. At the same time population growth led to intensified agricultural production in the lowlands, as in the Vera basin. The combination of intensified metallurgical and agricultural production led to widespread deforestation, land exhaustion and the collapse of the Argaric system. Lull's emphasis on systems of pro-duction and reproduction was also based on historical materialism. Ramos (1981, although it was actually published after Lull's model) focused only on the Copper Age and argued that population growth stimulated both settlement expansion and intensified agricultural production (including irrigation), as well as the social competition that led to the emergence of 'Big Men' by the later Copper Age and chiefdoms by the Bronze Age. Ramos also claimed his intellectual ancestry in historical materialism.

The first point to note about all these models is that they made substantial use of archaeological materials that had been collected, since the time of the Siret brothers, with other questions in mind. Thus Lull assembled and re-analysed data on Argaric sites and materials and I examined Copper Age tombs and grave goods. We both produced interpretations of social process to replace those of cultural history and diffusionism. Both of us were led to question existing chronologies based on typologies of artefacts and tombs. At the same time new data were collected with different questions in mind. Thus Lull carried out a morphometric analysis of pottery and metal artefacts to determine the extent of standardized production during the Argaric; I studied site locations in relation to the poten-tial for irrigation; while Mathers undertook systematic survey in the

Guadalentín valley in southern Murcia to determine changes in settlement patterns from the Copper to Bronze Ages.

Taken together, and whatever their theoretical differences (essentially functionalist/adaptationist vs shades of historical materialist), the models highlighted the need for the collection of controlled data on local palaeoenvironments, climatic change, the availability of water and the nature of past subsistence strategies, the degree of agricultural intensification, the amount and timing of population growth, and so forth. It was also clear that existing chronologies were, at best, open to question and, at worst, totally inadequate.

All the models also focused on the regional scale, at the level of 'cultures' (e.g. Millaran, Argaric), and periods such as the Copper Age or the Argaric Bronze Age, even though it was already clear that each of these spanned hundreds of years. Discussion of changes in subsistence potential and intensification did make a distinction between the coastal lowlands and the interior uplands, but further differences in scale (e.g. regarding demographic change) were not much in evidence. Data on such variations of scale were pretty scanty at that time and were not of importance within predominantly culture-based models of the past.

The excavations that were undertaken during the period from 1976 to 1984 existed in a parallel universe to the models and were of two main types. In the interior uplands of Granada, excavations continued to establish relative and absolute chronologies on stratified sites, as, for example, on the Copper Age settlements of El Malagón, Las Angosturas and Cerro de los Castellones (Laborcillas). The same aims were shared with fieldwork projects in the coastal lowlands, but here the emphasis was on the re-excavation of sites that had been the original subject of study by the Siret brothers during the last two decades of the nineteenth century. Excavations (in some cases long term) began at Los Millares, Campos, Almizaraque and Cabezo de la Cueva del Plomo (Copper Age) and Fuente Álamo (Bronze Age) and some interim results were published (e.g. Arribas *et al.* 1979, 1981; Schubart and Arteaga 1978, 1980). These were combined with the published and unpublished records and materials of the Sirets (and any subsequent excavators) to reinterpret occupational sequences and to develop knowledge of site plans. For example, the post-Argaric, Later Bronze Age occupation suggested at Fuente Álamo by a handful of sherds published by the Sirets (Siret and Siret 1887) was confirmed by the stratigraphic excavations.

1985–present

During the period from 1985 to the present some additions to, and expansions of, the models appeared. Mathers (1994) published data on settlement patterns from his survey in the Guadalentín valley, as well as from existing sources on the Vera basin and the Andarax valley. Lull proposed the possibility of an Argaric state society, in the Marxist sense of the term, on the basis of analyses of Argaric intramural burials (Lull and Estévez 1986). Gilman argued that intensive study, using site catchment analyses, of the location of later prehistoric settlements in relation to agricultural and irrigable potential strengthened his argument that capital intensive technologies were practised (Gilman and Thornes 1985). He also turned to historical and ethnographic analogies to buttress his model (e.g. 1987a, 1995), and contrasted the sequence of the south-east with other areas of Iberia (using Earle's concept of 'wealth' vs 'staple' finance – Gilman 1987b) and the Aegean (1991). In a book on the south-east, I presented the maximum evidence for water control in south-east Spain, as well as trying to give a balanced treatment of all the models (Chapman 1990). Others attempted to develop arguments about the responses of later prehistoric communities to the need to live and reproduce in 'risky' environments (Hernando 1987, 1997). The models were now widely cited in the Spanish literature (e.g. Martínez Navarrete 1989) and occasionally subjected to detailed critique (e.g. Micó 1991).

Fieldwork projects were marked by substantial continuity of excavations and of research teams. The excavations of Los Millares have continued, with interim publications of their results (e.g. Arribas *et al.* 1985; Molina 1989; Molina and Arribas 1993), while the first monograph of the excavations at Fuente Álamo in 1977–91 has just appeared (Schubart *et al.* 2001). Following on from the Campos excavations further Copper Age sites (e.g. Zájara, Santa Bárbara, Cabecicos Negros, and Las Pilas) were located and sampled in the Vera basin (for details and synthesis, see Cámalich and Martín Socas 1999) and important rescue excavations took place at the stratified (mainly Final Neolithic–Copper Age) settlement of Ciavieja (El Éjido, see Carrilero and Suárez 1989–90). For the Bronze Age a small-scale excavation took place at Lugarico Viejo (Ruiz Gálvez *et al.* 1987) while geophysical survey and small-scale excavation were carried out at El Argar (Schubart 1993). On the periphery of the south-east a major programme of excavations was carried out on the Bronze Age settlement of Peñalosa (Contreras 2000 and other references contained therein).

Extensive and intensive survey projects developed out of these projects, in the Almanzora valley and in the Vera basin (e.g. Cámalich *et al.* 1987, 1990; Delibes *et al.* 1996). Collaboration between excavation and survey teams resulted in an European Union-funded programme of archaeo-ecological survey, called Archaeomedes, in 1992–4 (Castro *et al.* 1994). Further field survey and more intensive study of palaeo-environments took place in the south of the Vera basin in the Aguas project, also funded by the EU in 1994–6 (Castro *et al.* 1998b). Given the intensity of this survey, it is argued that the further discovery of major prehistoric settlements is improbable in the Vera basin (Delibes *et al.* 1996: 163). Field surveys have been carried out throughout the south-east, in the uplands as well as the lowlands, usually arising out of excavation projects on major sites such as Los Millares (e.g. Cara and Rodríguez 1986). Survey intensity, methods and publication details have varied, making difficult the evaluation of site distributions in terms of changing settlement patterns and population densities.

This fieldwork has clearly produced a massive amount of new data on different periods of the later prehistoric occupation of south-east Spain, as we shall see later. The publication record of this fieldwork is uneven and makes definitive evaluation difficult. Interim reports and interpretive publications outnumber definitive monographs, while specialist reports (e.g. on animal bones and plant remains) are the subject of PhD theses, or published in instalments, relating to excavation campaigns, or in scattered articles without detailed contextual archaeological evidence. However, it is clear that none of these projects was initiated with the explicit aim of testing the strengths and weaknesses of the different models outlined above. Occasionally they refer to one or two aspects of the models, as they relate to data recovered from the projects, but there is no sense in which the models have guided or structured the practice of field archaeology in the region. There has been no explicitly theoretical context in which practice has been designed and pursued.

The one exception to this generalization is the Gatas project, which was set up in 1985 with the specific aim of testing the different models, although it did recognize, from the very beginning, that the kind of regional project that this required, with common methodologies, was impossible in the existing scientific and political context (Chapman *et al.* 1987: i). As elsewhere in Andalucía, fieldwork projects have been mainly site-based, with individual methodologies. The disjunction between theory and practice has been matched by that between individual examples of practice. If the Gatas project was to contribute to any testing of the models, then it would have to begin from the evidence (with all its strengths and weaknesses) of a single site. It is fair to point out that there was no discussion of the methodological procedures by which the models might be tested, or one preferred to the others, apart from the recognition that we were dealing with speculative 'prototype' models (Chapman *et al.* 1987: 221) based on inadequately contextualized data.

The Gatas project was designed to be both dynamic and flexible, with three phases of fieldwork: initial synthesis of current archaeo-ecological data in the south-east and physical survey of Gatas and its immediate environment at the present day (Figure 5.4); sondage excavations to test the preservation and nature of deposits at Gatas and sample its archaeo-ecological sequence; and finally extensive, area excavations (Figure 5.5). The results of each phase were integrated into the planning of the following phase. The fieldwork for phase 1 took place in 1985 (Chapman *et al.* 1987), followed by the phase 2 sondages in 1986–7 (Castro *et al.* 1999a) and the area excavations in 1987, 1989, 1991 and 1995 (Castro *et al.* 1991, 1993, in press; Buikstra *et al.* 1995). The controlled data on successive occupations of the site, their absolute chronology, the evidence for productive activities (e.g. Risch 1995 on lithics), stratified human burials and environmental change have been augmented by, and

Figure 5.4 The hill of Gatas (centre) in the foothills of the Sierra Cabrera, viewed from the modern farm to the north of the site. (Photo by the author.)

Figure 5.5 Vertical view of an area excavation of an Argaric house with internal burials at Gatas. A cist burial is visible to the right of centre at the bottom of the photograph. (Photo by Vicente Lull.)

placed in the context of, other excavation and survey projects within the Vera basin and further afield, including the Archaeomedes and Aguas projects (e.g. Castro *et al.* 1993/94, 1998b, 1999a, 1999b, 2000). As we shall see later, all of these data have contributed to our evaluation of the models outlined above.

At the same time, internal debate has led to the development of theoretical perspectives by individual and collective members of the project since 1985 (e.g. Lull 1988; Castro *et al.* 1996a; Castro *et al.* 1998a). Some of these have already been discussed in Chapter 2. Note that here, rather than theory just 'determining' practice, as in some kind of linear sequence, both are transformed in a dialectical relationship. The internal dynamic of research projects, with con- flicting views on theory and practice, is often overlooked in studies of the creation of knowledge, perhaps because of the hierarchical, rather than democratic, structure of research teams.

This history of the theory and practice of later prehistoric archae- ology in south-east Spain is not intended to be exhaustive, but illustrative of the points I have made. It is now time to move on to archaeological evidence as it stands at present. I begin with the organization of this evidence in time and space.

Space, time and scale

The organization of archaeological data in time and space has important implications for the scale of research. Finer-grained chronologies permit analysis of shorter-term activities and practices, while spatial differences in sites and materials help us to articulate local and regional systems of production and reproduction. During the first two periods of research in south-east Spain, the sites and materials were organized by the Three-Age system, with subdivisions by relative position (Early-middle-late) or letters of the alphabet (A–B), and by archaeological cultures. This approach to space and time was based on the assumptions that regional cultures reflected the existence of past 'peoples', in the Childean sense, and that prehistory was marked by long periods of stability and short periods of change. Change in material culture was a marker of all change in past societies.

The excavations of the last three decades, together with programmes of radiocarbon dating, are now the bases of finer-grained chronologies, although not necessarily for all periods of later prehistory or for all areas of south-east Spain. Many scholars retain the use of the term 'culture', while some prefer to use the term 'group' and reject the notions of 'peoples', with their common traditions, ideas, subsistence practices, and so on (González Marcén *et al.* 1992: 24–5).

Castro *et al.* (1996b) present and discuss the absolute dates for the Copper and Bronze Ages of south-east Spain within their Iberian context. This is the fundamental source for the organization of the archaeological data of these broad periods in space and time. In what follows, I draw on this source, as well as sources relevant to individual periods. The reader is directed to these sources for more detailed information. My purpose here is to present the general sequence of archaeological materials in time and space for the Neolithic, Copper Age, and Argaric Bronze Age. The Postargaric periods are mentioned more briefly, and will be referred to in this chapter as and when they are relevant to its themes.

What are the implications of the periodization for the scale of research in the region? The focus is mainly on the lowlands of south-east Spain, as the sequence here has been the object of explanation for the models mentioned above. Within this area, the Vera basin has seen the most intense research for the entire sequence of occupation in later prehistory. The more detailed discussion that follows in this chapter will centre on the Vera basin but will also include mention of other parts of south-east Spain where relevant.

Secure evidence for the changes associated with the Neolithic (e.g. pottery production, plant and animal domestication) in Iberia appears at *c.*5500 cal. BC, from Valencia and Cataluña in the east, through the intermontane basins and sierras of western Granada to central and southern Portugal (e.g. Zilhão 2000). Stratified deposits of this Early Neolithic period are lacking in south-east Spain, apart from on its western fringes. Open-air settlements and cave sites containing what have been called Middle and Late Neolithic materials have been recognized and studied since the 1880s (Chapman 1990: 59–69). In lowland Almería these materials are poorly contextualized and lack significant numbers of reliable absolute dates (Román Díaz and Martínez Padilla 1998). Fernández-Miranda et al. (1993) focus on the ephemeral traces of small sites such as Cuartillas and date them, by analogy to materials in Granada (cf. Cámalich and Martín Socas 1999), to the fourth millennium BC. Circular, stone-built communal tombs have also been assigned to the Neolithic, but lack absolute dates.

However, a collective burial in a pit (which in turn cuts through an earlier occupation level) at the site of Cerro Virtud, in the north of the Vera basin, has now been dated consistently to c.4900–4620 cal. BC (Montero and Ruiz Taboada 1996; Montero et al. 1999). This now extends the chronology of Neolithic activity in the Vera basin by a millennium, stretching out the known record from a few hundred to some fifteen hundred years.

The archaeological record of the Copper Age is more clearly defined than the Neolithic. Both sondage and area excavations on stratified settlements have yielded a greater number of radiocarbon dates. Open and enclosed settlements, along with collective dry-stone tombs with passages and corbelled vaults, are known from both lowland Almería and the uplands of eastern Granada (Chapman 1990: 69–84). Excavations of stratified deposits have allowed inferences to be made about sub-phases of the Copper Age, most notably at Los Millares (Arribas et al. 1985), but these have yet to be supported by definitive publication. Micó has questioned the extent to which a unified culture or horizon can be recognized on settlements in the south-east during this period, pointing out that the only settlement that has all of the defining characteristics of the Millaran culture is the type site itself (Micó 1991). In the absence of more detailed studies (e.g. pottery morphometry), it is difficult to lump together all the known sites within the same regional unit of analysis.

Using the radiocarbon dates, Castro et al. (1996b) distinguish three broad periods, c.3000–2800/2700 cal. BC (although possibly beginning in the late fourth millennium cal. BC), c.2800/2700–2500 cal. BC and c.2500–2250 cal. BC. The last of these periods contains Beaker materials. The overall timescale of the Copper Age is at least eight hundred years, and possibly a millennium.

The sites and materials of the Argaric group (equivalent to Early Bronze Age groups elsewhere in Europe) show marked changes from the preceding Copper Age. Hilltop, naturally defended settlements appear all over the south-east; intra-mural, individual burial replaces the collective disposal of the dead in megalithic tombs; metallurgy increases in frequency, diversity and composition; and both metal and ceramic artefacts become subject to clearly defined norms in their production (Lull 1983). Argaric materials are found all over the south-east, extending west to Granada and Málaga, north-west to Jaén and north to Murcia, covering an area of nearly 50,000sq km and showing the same homogeneity.

Programmes of radiocarbon dating on the Argaric have been undertaken on individual sites and as part of a regional programme on the dating of tombs and grave goods. Castro *et al.* (1993–4) cite 116 dates for the Argaric, with the majority from Almería and from two sites, Gatas and Fuente Álamo. The dating of the beginning of the Argaric is still controversial. Although the earliest dates go back to *c.*2500 cal. BC, they are few in number and Castro *et al.* (1996b: 121) begin the Argaric at *c.*2250 cal. BC. This agrees with the earliest dating of Gatas. In fact the latest Copper Age dates in the Vera basin, from sites at Almizaraque and Las Pilas, overlap with the earliest dates for the Argaric in the same area, at Fuente Álamo and Gatas, posing an interesting question as to the nature of cultural change at this time. The end of the Argaric is dated to *c.*1550 cal. BC. The current dates from Gatas and other sites suggest that there are three Argaric phases, 2250–2000 cal. BC, 2000–1750 cal. BC (the phase marked initially by the expansion of the Argaric inland from the lowlands of Almería and Murcia to the uplands of Granada and the upper Guadalquivir valley), and 1750–1550 cal. BC.

This phasing of the Argaric, based upon stratigraphies and radio-carbon dating, removes the need for a division into periods A and B, based on typologies and associations of tombs and grave goods. For example, there is substantial chronological overlap between types of tomb containers, such as artificial caves and stone cists on the one hand (previously included in Argar A) and pottery urns (included in Argar B) (Castro *et al.* 1993–4). These are now seen as the material reflection of contemporary, rather than successive, social practices within Argaric society in south-east Spain. In other words, we can begin to separate chronological from social variation in the disposal of the dead. Schubart *et al.* (2001) argue that the stratigraphy of Fuente Álamo supports the division of the Argaric into periods A1–2 and B1–2. However, it should be noted that the radiocarbon dates from this site are widely dispersed within the first three occupa-tion 'horizons', as well as overlapping between all of the Argaric horizons, and 36 out of 40 dates are from both individual and pooled charcoal samples in domestic contexts. Direct dating of skeletal materials from the intra-site tombs at Fuente Álamo is needed to test the absolute chronology of the settlement.

The Postargaric period has been divided into various groups and phases (see Castro *et al.* 1996b: 168–70), and is broadly dated *c.*1550–900 cal. BC. The first part of this time period, *c.*1550–1350 cal. BC, shows marked continuity in settlement layout and occupation, as well as pottery traditions (although lacking large urns and cups) from the Argaric, but now lacks intra-mural burial and the concentrations of metal objects associated with them. Conspicuous consumption of such items now occurs on the fringes of the south-east in gold and silver hoards. More marked changes in settlement layout and material culture appear *c.*1350–900 cal. BC, alongside the appearance of extra-mural cemeteries of urned cremations.

For most authors, the sequence from Neolithic to Copper and Argaric Bronze Age societies in south-east Spain is one of increasing complexity. It should also be clear that it is one of increasingly finer-grained chronologies. If we include more detailed analyses of cultural materials, we would also expect to be able to focus more attention on changing productive activities. When we compare these through time, we are not comparing like with like, as far as detail and chronological resolution are concerned. The detail of the long-term record of human activities and social practices in the Vera basin (e.g. Castro *et al.* 2000) also exerts a spatial bias on our knowledge of south-east Spain as a whole. Taking these problems of scale into account, the next three sections will focus on production, inequality and social change from the fifth to the mid-second millennia cal. BC.

Production, inequality and social change: the Neolithic

A common feature of the models proposed to explain the changes seen in the sequence from Neolithic to Bronze Age societies in south-east Spain is their focus on matters of production. For example, was it domestic or specialized, self-sufficient or comple-mentary, risky or not? As we have seen in Chapter 2, production also lies at the heart of a materialist analysis of social change. The discussion of alternative views of state societies in Chapter 4 looks at the development of economic into political domination and the emergence of exploitation and property in terms of the appropriation of social production. What is the evidence for production and social inequality in south-east Spain? How does it change through time? Is there evidence for exploitation and property?

Rather than present a full-scale materialist analysis (see Castro *et al.* 1998a), I will focus on the production of food and material culture, and the social changes seen through time. Dichotomies such as simple/complex or egalitarian/unequal societies will be avoided, for the reasons stated in Chapter 4. Inequalities appear to be present in all societies, as well as tensions between egalitarian and hierarchical relations in everyday social practices. Such tensions may, of course, be difficult to see, given the resolution of the data at our disposal.

Knowledge of Neolithic societies in south-east Spain is still poor. The low density of sites and, by inference, population (at best in the low hundreds, see Castro *et al.* 2000) shown in the Vera basin is even more marked when the absolute chronology is taken into account (see above, p. 114). Small sites were located either in the lower parts of river valleys, close to the sea, where there was potential for both dry and wet farming, or over 5km inland in the foothills of the mountains, where access to dry farmland was combined with the exploitation of the sierras (Castro *et al.* 1994: 94–6). Sites occurred only up to 150m in altitude and were less than 1ha in size. Excavations at Cuartillas (Fernández-Miranda *et al.* 1993) in the lower Aguas valley revealed a single-phase occupation of mainly perishable structures (of no clear form) and pits. Similarly, ephemeral circular structures on artificial terraces and storage pits were excavated at Almizaraque (e.g. Delibes *et al.* 1996), where they were dated to the late fourth and early third millennia cal. BC. At Cerro Virtud, small-scale excavations on a site heavily disturbed by modern mining exposed two phases of Neolithic occupation; the first phase contained pits excavated in the rock and a later hearth, both pre-dating the collective burials of *c.*4900–4620 cal. BC; the second phase post-dated these burials (Ruiz Taboada and Montero 1999a: 208–10).

Outside the Vera basin, the main clusters of Neolithic sites are found in the upper Almanzora valley, the Andarax valley and the coastal region to the west of Almería, and in eastern Granada (see Román Díaz and Martínez Padilla 1998: figure 1). The known site density amounts to about 1 site per 165sq km. If we exclude the communal, stone-built cists and 'round graves', then the density of caves and open-air sites is even lower. Coupled with their ephemeral nature and small size, this density has supported the inference of non-sedentary populations (e.g. Molina 1983; Fernández-Miranda *et al.* 1993; Castro *et al.* 1994). Such mobility is not incompatible with production based on domesticated plants and animals, as has been pointed out by Román Díaz and Martínez Padilla (1998). Direct evidence of this production is rare. Systematic sampling of Neolithic deposits through flotation is rare right across Andalucía: even the systematically collected evidence for cultivation of wheat, barley and legumes from fifth-millennium cal. BC occupation of the Cueva de Los Murciélagos (Zuheros, Córdoba) was based on small samples of plant remains from non-habitation contexts (Peña-Chocarro 1999). In the Vera basin, bones of domesticated sheep/goat, cattle and pig, as well as red deer and rabbit, were found at Cuartillas (Castaños, in Fernández-Miranda *et al.* 1993: 82–3), while grinding stones and storage vessels were found at Cuartillas and Cerro Virtud, and storage pits are known especially outside structures at Almizaraque (e.g. Delibes *et al.* 1996). Storage pits in Neolithic levels are also known to pre-date Copper Age occupations elsewhere in the lowlands, as at Terrera Ventura (Gusi and Olaria 1991) and Ciavieja (Carrilero and Suárez 1989–90). The locations of sites in the Vera basin mentioned above, coupled with the results of pollen and charcoal analyses (see below), also support the potential for animal grazing and cereal cultivation.

The materials found in these Neolithic sites are mainly clay, stone, flint, bone and shell. Absolute, and even relative, dating is poor for all categories of sites; there are few studies of production, and insufficiently large-scale excavations to provide contextual data on the processes and social contexts of production. Studies of stone tool production in Granada (Carrión and Gómez 1983) and Valencia (Orozco-Köhler 2000), to the west and north of our main study area, show the predominance of local (within 10km) rock used for polished stone axes in the Early and Middle Neolithic. Sources of sillimanite and schist, used respectively for axe and bracelet production in Valencia, are located up to 350km away in south-east Spain. The exchange relations that linked these regions were probably small in scale: the percentages of analysed Valencian stone axes made from south-eastern rocks in the Neolithic (Harrison and Orozco-Köhler 2001: 118) work out at an average supply rate of one every two hundred years. Within the Vera basin, the site of Cabecicos Negros shows little typological diversity in its lithic tools and little evidence of the use of such tools for cereal cultivation, while the flint used to make blade tools is argued to have come from the Vélez region of upland Almería, some 50km to the north (Cámalich and Martín Socas 1999: 244). This observation could also support the inference of mobility among Neolithic populations in this region.

A recent study of bone artefacts suggests that the earlier examples were few in number and poor in quality, requiring little technological skill or investment of effort, while later examples increased in frequency (especially in funerary contexts), numbers of types and investment of labour (Maicas Ramos 1999). Exploitation of local clay and temper sources is proposed for pottery production at Cuartillas (Fernández-Miranda et al. 1993: 64), as in Granada (Navarrete et al. 1991). The evidence for metal production, both from the fifth millennium BC site of Cerro Virtud (Ruiz Taboada and Montero Ruiz 1999b) and from the later third millennium phase 1 occupation at Almizaraque (Delibes et al. 1996: 157) is confined to 'vase-ovens' with slag adhesions and fragments of partially reduced ore. The earlier evidence from Cerro Virtud is particularly difficult to interpret in terms of the organization of production. Even if we accept the hypothesis that 'knowledge of metallurgy at Neolithic Cerro Virtud cannot have been an isolated phenomenon' (Ruiz Taboada and Montero Ruiz 1999b: 902), more controlled data are needed to evaluate any suggestion of either domestic or specialized production.

The best evidence for on-site Neolithic productive activities comes from two sites. The Cueva de los Toyos in southern Murcia (Siret and Siret 1887: 17–20) yielded a three-handled globular pot containing sea shells at different stages of working in the production of small beads. More recent evidence of the production of stone and shell ornaments comes from the settlement of Cabecicos Negros, near the mouth of the river Antas in the Vera basin (Goñi Quinteiro et al. 1999). In addition to the evidence for different stages of production of objects such as shell beads and stone 'bracelets' and the lithic technology that was used for this production, there is contrasting evidence for the labour investment required for the making of the shell beads as opposed to the more time-consuming bracelets. The authors conclude that the scale of production of shell and stone ornaments at Cabecicos Negros exceeded normal domestic requirements; such a surplus was used for purposes of exchange among semi-nomadic populations. While this is a plausible hypothesis, and these kinds of objects are known from other Neolithic sites in the Vera basin, there is no calculation as to what 'normal domestic requirements' would have been and no published contextual information on the productive activities.

This limited evidence of daily social practices in Neolithic settlements, especially in the south-eastern lowlands, supports the inference of small-scale, mobile communities; these lived off domesticated and wild animals and plants; engaged in domestic production and perhaps even production beyond domestic need, particularly of artefacts used to mark out social distinctions based on age, gender, or group affiliation; and exchanged raw materials and/or finished products during the course of annual cycles of movement (cf. Sánchez Romero 2000 for a model of mobility between open-air sites and caves in Granada during the Early and Middle Neolithic). Evidence for the disposal of the dead is also difficult to interpret in this context. Communal burials are found in caves (mostly on the peripheries of the south-east), stone cists (mostly in the southern lowlands) and circular stone tombs, or 'round graves' (Leisner and Leisner 1943). Cists are *c*.1–2sq m and 'round graves' are 3–9sq m in size, and both may contain one to ten individuals. Examples of larger 'round graves' with up to eighty individuals are attributed to the Copper Age on typological grounds. The patchy nature of the data and the lack of absolute dates for the tombs make difficult a more detailed interpretation than that of the disposal of family or kinship groups within these tombs.

The burial pit at Cerro Virtud was of similar size (11sq m) and contained a minimum number of eleven individuals, all but one being adults (Montero *et al.* 1999). The oldest male, over 50 years of age, was clearly differentiated from the remaining burials by the presence of five pots, one of which was the largest vessel found in the pit. Was this the senior member of the kinship group, the first one interred after the construction of the burial pit? As in other areas of western Europe, such collective burials could have provided the focus for mobile communities, a material embodiment of social identity. Any inequalities do not seem to have been based on lasting control of productive activities.

Production, inequality and social change: the Copper Age

There is a marked increase in the number of known sites for the Copper Age throughout south-east Spain, as well as in numbers of radiocarbon dates and both stratigraphic and area excavations. In the Vera basin, survey in the lower Almanzora valley shows that the six sites dated to the Neolithic increased to sixteen in the Copper Age (Delibes *et al.* 1996: 165). In only three cases (including Cerro Virtud and Almizaraque) did occupation continue on the same site, and settlement aggregated as well as expanding into new areas. In the lower Aguas valley, in the south of the basin, discontinuity of site occupation through local relocation and aggregation has also been proposed (Fernández-Miranda *et al.* 1993: 81). In addition to settlement evidence, artefact typologies have been used to argue for continued mortuary rituals in some communal 'round graves' from the Neolithic to the Copper Age. When we move to the Vera basin as a whole, 90 per cent of the Copper Age sites are newly founded at this time (Castro *et al*. 1994).

Data on site areas have been used to propose an overall population of *c*.1300–1600 in the Vera basin at this time (Figure 5.6), about one person per sq km, more or less evenly divided between the north and south (Castro *et al*. 1998b: 71). Differences in site areas also suggest that population was not evenly divided between settlements. Within the lower Almanzora valley, the largest sites are Almizaraque (0.5ha) and Zájara (0.3ha), but seven other sites are less than 0.1ha in size (Delibes *et al*. 1996: 165). The largest settlement in the whole basin is at Las Pilas (at least 5ha), in the lower Aguas valley. This pattern of a small number of sites over 1ha in size, and a much larger number under 1ha, is broadly repeated over the entire lowlands and uplands of south-east Spain (e.g. Chapman 1990: 152). The depth of deposits, together with the radiocarbon dates, from larger sites such as Almizaraque and Las Pilas, support the inference of occupancy of such sites over longer periods of time, although such

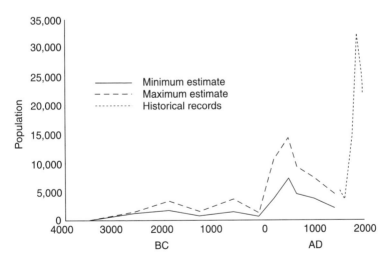

Figure 5.6 Population change in the Vera basin from *c*.4000 BC to the present day. The maximum and minimum estimates are based on site surface areas. Estimates based on historical records are added from the sixteenth century AD (adapted from Castro *et al*. 1998b: figure 17).

occupancy may not necessarily have been continuous (e.g. Almizaraque – Delibes *et al.* 1996).

Whereas Neolithic sites were mostly ephemeral in nature, labour investment in domestic structures (now circular with stone foundations and timber superstructures), enclosing stone walls (e.g. Los Millares, Las Pilas, Campos, El Malagón, Cerro de la Virgen) and accompanying communal tombs increased markedly in the Copper Age (for details, see Chapman 1990: 69–83). This investment varied within regions (Román Díaz and Martínez Padilla 1998).

This evidence from site types, sizes and numbers, as well as their degree of labour investment, has led to the hypothesis that there was a distinction between a small number of larger, longer-lived and more densely populated settlements and a larger number of smaller, short-lived and thinly populated settlements (Castro *et al.* 1998a). A degree of mobility was still visible among these smaller settlements.

As in the Neolithic, analysis of site locations suggests the potential for cereal production and animal grazing (e.g. Gilman and Thornes 1985; Castro *et al.* 1994). For the Vera basin, it was again noted that there were two main groups of sites: those suitable for dry farming in the main basin and close to the sea and other sources of water; and those inland sites in the foothills of the sierras, which had access to cultivable land and to the resources of the mountains (Castro *et al.* 1994: 102). This distinction between lowland, riverine sites and those at the junction of the valleys/basins and the foothills of the sierras is repeated in the Guadalentín valley in southern Murcia (Mathers 1984a).

Direct evidence for subsistence activities is of variable quality and states of publication. The presence of domesticated species of wheat, barley and legumes was recorded by the Siret brothers (e.g. from Almizaraque, see Martínez Santa Olalla 1946; Téllez and Ciferri 1954) and has been confirmed by modern excavations (e.g. Delibes *et al.* 1986). The same species, along with a range of wild plants, have been recovered from Las Pilas (Rovira 2000) and Campos in the Vera basin, as well as at Los Millares, El Malagón and Cerro de la Virgen (Buxó 1997). There are publications of fauna from Terrera Ventura (Driesch and Morales 1977), Los Millares (Peters and Driesch 1990) in the lowlands and Cerro de la Virgen (Driesch 1972) in the uplands. Together they show the dominance of bovids and ovicaprids, followed by pigs, as well as the exploitation of horses and red deer. Species were used for both primary and secondary products (e.g. Chapman 1990: 136).

Where and how was this food production carried out? The

locations of both Neolithic and Copper Age sites in the lowlands suggest the potential for both dry and wet farming. The extent to which these were practised depends upon the scale of production, the water and nutritional requirements of different species of plants and animals, and any constraints on cultivation and grazing posed by local climate. The current evidence for environmental change will be presented later in this chapter. As for the succeeding Bronze Age I argue that (1) dry farming would have been a sustainable strategy for cereal cultivation; (2) the fallow regime would have depended on the intensity of production, soil types and annual rainfall; (3) livestock could have been maintained by grazing on stubble and on valley bottom and river mouth pastures and stabled within settlements, as at Campos (Cámalich and Martín Socas 1999: 322); (4) soils with greater humidity and higher water tables, along with more continuous flowing water and the potential for natural irrigation, would have existed in the valley bottoms; and (5) the water requirements of legumes would have led to their cultivation in these naturally humid soils (see Castro *et al.* 1999b). Such production does not appear to have been capital intensive, nor as 'risky' as some have argued. There is also no evidence to suggest that there was unequal access to production between Copper Age communities.

Within settlements, evidence of production takes the form of the basic instruments of production (e.g. grinding stones, stone axes and adzes, flint artefacts), as well as storage in pits and pots. Pits have been found in most Neolithic and Copper Age settlements, although it is the ones with the narrower mouths, such as over 300 examples found at El Gárcel (Gossé 1941), that have been most often identified as used for purposes of storage. Román Díaz (1999) summarizes the storage data from sites in the lowlands of south-east Spain. Evidence varies for the numbers of pits found, their contents (e.g. carbonized cereals at El Gárcel, refuse), and their locations (inside/outside structures). The presence of impermeable linings has suggested that some pits were used for water storage, but they could just as easily have been used for grain storage, as is shown by pit 1 at Campos, which contained an assemblage of threshed cereals, of which 98 per cent were seeds of barley (Cámalich and Martín Socas 1999: 296). Areas devoted to pits outside any domestic structures (e.g. Almizaraque) have led some authors to propose that these were for communal access for the community as a whole (e.g. Chapman 1990: 157). Allowing for the reliability of data from old, limited or unpublished excavations, it should be pointed out that pits also occur within structures, storage vessels are found within structures, and pits dug into bedrock go out of use after the later Neolithic and early Copper Age occupations of these sites (e.g. Almizaraque, Ciavieja). The proposal (Román Díaz 1999: 204) that storage vessels contained grain for consumption, while sealed storage pits kept grain for sowing or special purposes (feasting?) would apply only to the earliest phases of occupation on such sites.

Micó (1990) has suggested that the change in internal/external storage from the later Neolithic through the Copper Age was one from community or lineage group to individual household control. Open access for all gave way to inter-household differences based on hidden stores and possible increasing inequalities in access to productive activities and consumption. Given the variation in evidence for storage between sites, such a model may only apply to certain areas and sites. What would, then, be of interest would be differences in storage capacity between houses, as well as evidence for greater access to instruments of production such as grinding stones. The only evidence for this to date is from Fort 1 at Los Millares, where the quantity of grinding stones and storage vessels exceeds those necessary for the food production of its inhabitants (Molina *et al.* 1986).

What is known about the sources and production of implements of various kinds, whether used as the means of production or not? Taking lithic materials as a whole, Risch (1995) calculates that an average of only 10–20 per cent were of non-local origin; these include rocks for grinding stones, building materials, axes and adzes, as well as flint (see below). For grinding stones the figures can be much lower on individual sites: at Almizaraque and Los Millares, for example, only 5–6 per cent were on non-local andesite. A potential source for this rock type, along with evidence claimed for all stages of the production process, has been found at Borronar (Cabo de Gata, Carrión *et al.* 1993: 304) although Risch (1995: 129) was unable to locate these quarries and found the only blocks of a suitable size for grinding stones in local riverbeds. Along with other volcanic rocks, andesite was used for small amounts of lithics at sites like Los Millares and Terrera Ventura, that is within a distance of *c.*40–55km from the source. However, the majority of rocks used on Copper Age sites were selected from secondary sources in local riverbeds and little effort was put into producing a standardized product (Risch 1995). A predominance of local sources of hard rock is also noted in Murcia (Barrera Morate *et al.* 1987), Valencia (Orozco-Köhler 2000) and Granada (Carrión and Gómez 1983), although materials or finished products could still move over distances of 100–200km. In all areas lithic production and the use of 'exotic' lithologies increased in the Late Neolithic/Copper Age, that is, the fourth and third millennia cal. BC. South-eastern rock types such as sillimanites and amphibolites provided 41 per cent of the analysed Copper Age stone axes in Valencia (Harrison and Orozco-Köhler 2001: 118), roughly one axe every six years.

Flint sources were more unevenly distributed in south-east Spain. The inhabitants of Campos and Zájara, in the northern Vera basin, used secondary flint nodules from the bed of the Almanzora river for flake production, and non-local flints for the production of prismatic blades, while opal was introduced from an unknown source to produce large denticulates at Las Pilas, in the south of the same basin (Cámalich and Martín Socas 1999: 244–5.). The best data on flint sources come from the survey and excavations at La Venta, some 20km to the north of the settlement of El Malagón (Ramos 1998). Twenty mines, each with a diameter of *c*.4m and a depth of 2m–3m, have been found within an area of 1ha. There was no evidence of permanent occupation, but flintworking did take place on site. La Venta was the principal source of flint for El Malagón, and smaller quantities came from locally available superficial nodules.

More localized sources have been proposed for copper ores, based principally on two arguments. First, copper ores were so widely available in Almería that it has been calculated that 66 per cent of a sample of sixty-eight Copper Age settlements and tombs were located within *c*.3.5km–10km and 8 per cent were within 3.5km of such sources (Suárez *et al.* 1986: 205). Allowing for variation between sites, copper ores would have been available within one to two hours' walk. Second, the copper sources of the Vera basin have been surveyed and sampled for trace element analysis, leading Montero (1993, 1994) to propose that individual settlements exploited their nearest sources throughout their occupation. Such exploitation was small scale, with no evidence for mining.

Few studies have been published on pottery sources during the Copper Age. The most extensive analyses now come from Campos: mineralogical study supports the use of multiple clay sources, including local sources for coarse wares used for storage and other sources used for a range of forms, possibly from at least 50km away in the Andarax valley, the Sierra de las Estancias or the Baza-Huéscar plateau (Cámalich and Martín Socas 1999: 174–221). Schüle (1980: 55) cited coarse sherds from Cerro de la Virgen which have micaceous inclusions that must have come from a distance of 20–30km. Of other raw materials used in the third millennium BC, ivory and ostrich-eggshell were from North African sources; the nearest source of jet was in the Sierra Morena in southern Spain; the nearest amber source was in Murcia; and although a source of callais has been cited at Adra, to the west of Almería, this is now known to be chlorite, leaving the nearest potential sources in south-west, north-east or north-west Spain (Harrison and Orozco-Köhler 2001: 112–14).

The best evidence of productive activity on Copper Age settlements relates to flint and metal artefacts. Evidence of flint 'workshops' has been found at a number of sites, including Almizaraque (Siret 1948), Campos (Siret and Siret 1887), Cerro de las Canteras (de Motos 1918), and Fort 1 at Los Millares (Ramos 1998) (Figure 5.8), and flint production is also known from other sites. The principal products were flakes, blades, arrowheads and sickle teeth. Ramos (1998) proposes a model of surplus production of arrowheads, with the pressure-flaking requiring greater skill and possibly specialized production, in contrast to domestic production of the other artefacts. However, the evidence from their consumption, especially in tombs, does not imply that flint products were not widely available within Copper Age communities.

Evidence of copper working has also been found within settlements. At Los Millares (Figure 5.7) metalworking took place in two of the bastions in the outer defensive wall, in a rectangular structure inside the third wall and in one of the bastions of the outer wall of Fort 1 (Figure 5.8) (Arribas et al. 1979, 1981, 1985). All these were peripheral areas, suitable because metallurgy presented (a) a potential fire hazard and (b) the danger of arsenic poisoning. In contrast, at Almizaraque, where evidence of copper working was present in all phases of the Copper Age occupation, it is claimed that there were no spatial, and hence social, restrictions on production (e.g. Delibes et al. 1986, 1989). According to this 'Almizaraque model', copper working was small scale, based on local sources, non-specialized, with no major division of labour and no complementary production between sites and regions (Montero 1993). The majority of copper objects were instruments of production: axes, knives/daggers, saws, chisels and awls (the latter constituting just over 50 per cent of the known copper artefacts) (Table 5.1). An awl was associated with the production of pressure-flaked flint arrowheads in Fort 1 at Los Millares (Ramos 1998) and saws were probably used in making ivory objects (Pascual-Benito 1995: 27). Castro et al. (1998a) propose that the attraction of copper artefacts lay not in any supposed advantages over stone or bone, but in their ability to be recycled; although the production cycle was longer and labour investment greater, less time

126

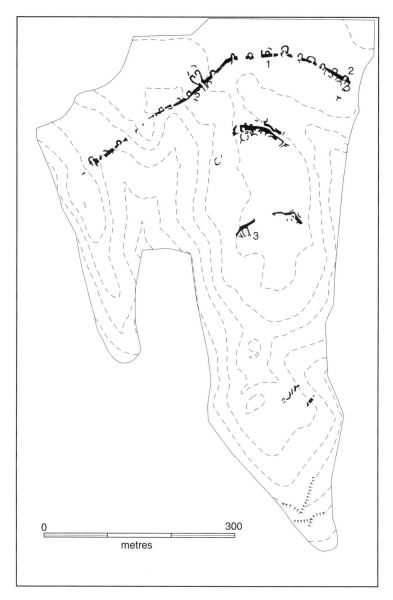

Figure 5.7 Location of metalworking evidence (1–3) at Los Millares (adapted from Arribas *et al*. 1985: figure 2).

Figure 5.8 Location of metalworking and lithic production areas in Fort 1, Los Millares (adapted from Arribas *et al.* 1985: figure 9). External ditches stippled.

and energy were devoted to obtaining the raw materials. This is an important point, since, when added to the other evidence of implements, it suggests that any changes in production overall during the Copper Age were not based on improvements in the means of production.

While it can be argued that there was neither major capital investment in production (see below for discussion of the irrigation hypothesis), nor major changes in the means of production, the case

Table 5.1 Frequencies of Copper Age and Argaric metalwork in south-east Spain

	Copper Age		Argaric	
	Number	%	Number	%
Awls	300	50.7	408	14.0
Chisels	35	5.9	27	0.9
Saws	16	2.7	6	0.2
Axes	59	10.0	139	4.8
Daggers	51	8.6	588	20.2
Points	44	7.4	77	2.6
Swords	–	–	10	0.3
Halberds	–	–	40	1.4
Bracelets	10	1.7	279	9.6
Rings	31	5.2	1,080	37.1
Beads	7	1.2	175	6.0
Diadems	–	–	8	0.3
Various	12	2.0	67	2.3
Undetermined	27	4.6	10	0.3
Total	592	100.0	2,914	100.0

Source: Data from Montero 1994: 213

for greater inequalities in access to production is more debatable. A growing population was divided into, at best, a two-level settlement hierarchy (Chapman 1990; for a proposal of a three-level hierarchy, see Martín Socas *et al.* 1992–3), as settlement expanded and aggregated. But larger settlements, at least in the Vera basin, did not have access to correspondingly larger amounts of cultivable soils. Fort 1 at Los Millares is the best evidence so far for concentration of the means of production above the amount necessary to cater for domestic consumption, but this has still to be understood within the context of the larger complex of Los Millares and its surrounding forts and settlements before any relations of tribute or exploitation could be proposed.

Mainly local sources and domestic production have been proposed for hard rock and metals, while some stone lithologies and flint, some pottery and various exotica support the inference of inter-regional exchange relations. Specialized surplus production is proposed only for flint arrowheads. Although production areas have been identified within settlements, some may be determined by the needs or dangers of the craft being practised (as in the case of copper metallurgy), and the extent to which they were carried out within distinct households (which may comprise more than one structure) is not clear. For example, food production, flint arrowhead production and metallurgy were all carried out within Fort 1 at Los Millares (Figure 5.8).

There is also evidence for increasing social tensions. Site locations were dictated not only by cultivable potential, but also by the need for visual control of territory, as at Las Pilas (Martín Socas *et al.* 1992–3). In addition to greater labour investment in food production (to support the growing population, as well as increasing inequalities in access to food production, see above), and in the production of flint and metal implements, surplus labour was invested in the construction of fortifications and larger and more elaborate communal tombs (for initial calculations, see Monks 1997). Castro *et al.* (1998a) suggest that social tensions and physical conflict intensified in the later Copper Age, as shown by the record of fortification construction at sites such as Los Millares, Campos and El Malagón, and destruction or burning levels at sites such as Campos, El Malagón and Cerro de la Virgen.

Taking all these inferences together, there is some evidence for hierarchical relations and inequalities within Copper Age societies in south-east Spain. But both equal and unequal social relations appear to co-exist. The settlement evidence has also been used to infer the existence of some differences in consumption: for example, Ramos uses the concentration of flint products in the large structure G at El Malagón to infer the existence of a chief (1998: 33). Such village chieftains owed their position to manipulation of production and exchange relations in a tribal political economy and developed out of Neolithic 'Big Men' (see Ramos 1999).

The funerary evidence also changes at this time. Communal stone tombs with entrance passages, side-chambers and false corbelling over the main chamber are constructed. Whereas the ephemeral nature of Neolithic settlements made their contemporary tombs the focal expression of community identity, this role was largely taken over by the fortified settlements of the Copper Age. The association between such settlements and groups or cemeteries of communal tombs is taken as a defining feature of this period, but the cemeteries associated with sites such as Los Millares and El Barranquete are the exception (Micó 1991). Within such cemeteries, differences in the labour expended in the construction of tombs and in the consumption of grave goods have led to inferences of social differences within these communities. Chapman (1990: 178–95) proposed that differences in access to prestige goods distinguished the tombs of higher-ranked kinship or descent groups, which were able to locate their dead closer to the settlement at Los Millares. The critical question is whether such groups controlled the production of these goods; the fact that they occurred in other tombs besides those in which they were concentrated may suggest otherwise, but this emphasizes the need for better data from settlement contexts.

Micó (1993) has extended the study of funerary monuments by undertaking a principal components analysis of tombs of both Los Millares and El Barranquete. His main observation is that the size of the tombs is correlated not only with the number of interred individuals, but also with the wealth of objects deposited. From this he infers that the larger kinship groups (lineages?), because of the size of their labour force, were able to build the larger tombs and accumulate, through more extensive exchange networks, the greatest amounts of wealth items for consumption in their tombs. An association has also been observed between the size of settlements and the presence (Delibes *et al*. 1996: 166) or numbers (Castro *et al*. 1998a: 53) of collective tombs in the Vera basin. The size of the community, as well as individual lineages, appears to have been of critical importance in the ability to invest surplus labour in both conspicuous consumption in funerary contexts and the production of food and desirable social objects. The eight hundred or more years of the Copper Age in south-east Spain saw increased tensions within and between communities, and between egalitarian and hierarchical social relations. These tensions were given material form (and not hidden, as argued by both Mathers 1984a and Gilman and Thornes 1985) and based firmly on productive relations. The society that was being reproduced was one of increasing inequalities, but apart possibly from gender relations (Castro *et al*. 1998a: 70) these had yet to amount to exploitation.

Production, inequality and social change: the Argaric

From *c*.2250–1550cal. BC the distinctive settlements, burials, material culture and society of the Argaric Bronze Age occupied an area of nearly 50,000sq m, stretching from the 'heartland' of the Vera basin north to southern Murcia and Alicante, west to Granada and north-west to Jaén (Lull 1983). Within the coastal lowlands of Almería and southern Murcia, there were marked disjunctions of settlement location and architecture. In the Vera basin, for example, the major Copper Age settlements of the plains (e.g. Almizaraque,

Campos, Zájara, Las Pilas) were all abandoned. Although small Argaric sites have been found in the valley bottoms, it is the larger settlements in the peripheral foothills (e.g. Gatas, Fuente Álamo, Lugarico Viejo, El Oficio), with their artificial terraces on which rectilinear structures were built (Figure 5.9), that became the focus of Bronze Age society. Many of these sites were intervisible (in contrast to settlements in southern Murcia, see Risch and Ruiz 1994: 80–1), as well as having extensive views of the sites in the valley bottoms. Although there were fewer sites, more were in the 1–4ha range in this period than in the Copper Age, suggesting a process of population nucleation (Castro *et al.* 1994). Where the foothill sites had been occupied during the Copper Age (e.g. Gatas, Fuente Álamo), they were now so extensively remodelled that all traces of previous structures and settlement layout were removed. Calculations of population size in the Vera basin suggest that there was an increase from the 1,300–1,600 range in the Copper Age to *c.*1,700–3,400 people in the Argaric (Castro *et al.* 1994) (Figure 5.6). These calculations are based not only on surface areas, but also on the cereal

Figure 5.9 Argaric settlement at El Oficio, showing the plan of the settlement excavated by the Siret brothers (above), as well as sections through and more detailed plans of domestic structures and burials (below) (Siret and Siret 1887: plate 18).

production inferred from the frequency of grinding stones present at sites such as Gatas (Risch 1995). The population increase marks what Castro *et al.* (1998a) call intensification in basic production.

As in the preceding periods, studies of site locations show the potential for dry and wet farming within walking distances of settlements (Gilman and Thornes 1985; Castro *et al.* 1994; Risch and Ruiz 1994). However, the larger settlements in the Vera basin were not supported by greater amounts of cultivable land; in fact there is an inverse relationship between site size and available productivity (Figure 5.10), suggesting unequal access to, and participation in, primary food production. I will return to the significance of this observation a little later.

More direct evidence of food production comes from animal bones and plant remains, as well as the instruments of production found within settlements. The principal (published) collections of animal bones are from Gatas and Fuente Álamo (Table 5.2) in the lowlands, and Cerro de la Virgen, Cerro de la Encina and Cuesta del Negro in the uplands (see discussion and sources in Chapman 1990: 116–18, 131–8; Castro *et al.* 1999a: 186–93). Publication of plant remains is restricted to Fuente Álamo (Stika 1988, 2001), Gatas (Clapham *et al.* 1999) and El Argar (Stika and Jurich 1998). Comparison of faunal reports suggests the exploitation of primary and secondary products, with a shared emphasis on ovicaprids and bovids in the early Argaric and a division between upland (increased emphasis on horses and bovids) and lowland (increasing emphasis on ovicaprids and suids at the expense of bovids) sites (Castro *et al.* 1999a: 191).

The sequence at Gatas (supported by the data from Fuente Álamo) provides the basis for a model of agricultural production in the

Table 5.2 Animal bone weights (% of total) at Gatas and Fuente Álamo

	Gatas			*Fuente Álamo*	
	2	3	4	I + II	III + IV
Cattle	52.3	23.5	12.6	46.3	46.2
Sheep/goat	40.6	33.0	46.9	38.6	33.0
Pig	1.8	6.8	24.5	9.9	8.9
Horse	1.7	–	6.8	0.7	2.1
Others	3.6	36.7	9.2	4.5	9.8

Sources: Data from Castro *et al.* 1999a and Schubart *et al.* 2001

Note: The absence of coherent absolute dating for the occupation phases at Fuente Álamo makes it difficult to compare their animal bone weights with specific phases at Gatas

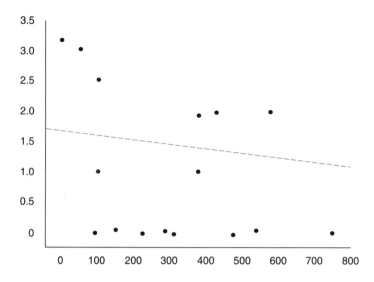

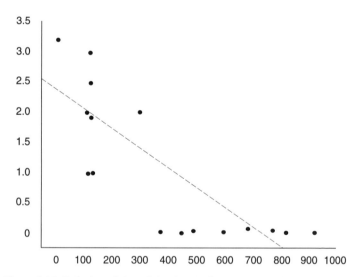

Figure 5.10 Relation of size of site (vertical axis) to areas (horizontal axis) in hectares of dry (above) and wet (below) farming within 2km of Argaric sites in the Vera basin (adapted from Lull and Risch 1995: figure 4).

lowlands (see Castro *et al.* 1999b, with all relevant references). Throughout the three phases of the Argaric occupation, and whatever the sample size, cereals dominate over leguminous species in the plant remains, and barley dominates wheat among the cereals. The frequencies (per volume of excavated deposit) of cereals and legumes, together with those of grinding stones and other macrolithic tools (Figure 5.11) are used as indicators of an increase in agricultural production from Gatas phases 2 (*c.*2250–1950 cal. BC) to 3 (*c.*1950–1700 cal. BC) and 4 (*c.*1700–1550 cal. BC). By phase 4, barley monoculture was being practised. The increase of agricultural production during the Argaric is even more marked at Fuente Álamo (Stika 1988).

Barley is the main crop cultivated today in the Vera basin and was also the dominant cereal in historic periods. This is because of its greater adaptability to arid and semi-arid conditions, its early maturity and greater resistance to parasites. It is grown extensively under a regime of dry farming with varying periods of fallow. Legumes have greater water requirements than barley: peas and vetch are sensitive to lack of water during growth, while the quality of beans declines under annual rainfall regimes of less than 400–500mm. Another cultivated species, flax, is also sensitive to water conditions (especially near the surface) and temperatures. While barley could have been grown under extensive, dry-farming conditions (a proposal supported by the observation of smaller seeds at Fuente Álamo and El Argar – Hopf 1991; Stika 1988), with one to two years fallow, the legumes and flax required cultivation under conditions of water enhancement, near river courses and/or in areas with higher water tables or seasonal inundation. This model is supported by what is known of habitats of weeds of cultivation found at Gatas, by soil micromorphology at the southern foot of the hill (Courty and Fedoroff 1999) and by the sheer dominance of cereals over legumes, which argues against a model of cereal–legume rotation. Castro *et al.* (1994) also note that the only Argaric settlements with higher frequencies of legumes are located in the low-lying areas with humid soils of southern Murcia.

Finally there is an independent source of evidence that supports this model for Argaric agricultural production. Carbon isotope discrimination analyses on seeds are a measure of their water status during growth. Analyses of Copper and Bronze Age seeds from both lowland and upland sites in south-east Spain show no support for the cultivation of wheat and barley under conditions of natural or artificial water enhancement, while the slightly higher delta carbon

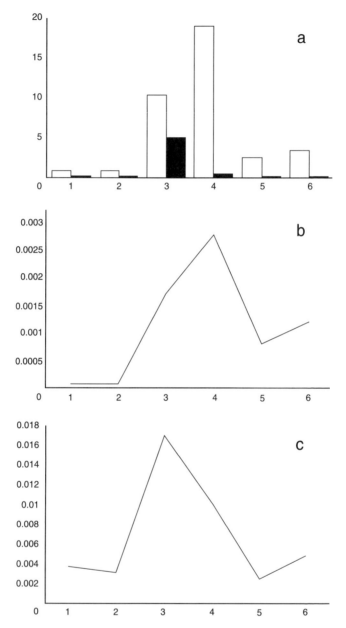

Figure 5.11 Agricultural production at Gatas during occupation phases
1–6: frequency of (a) cereals (white) and legumes (black), (b)
grinding stones and (c) lithics, per volume of excavated deposit
(vertical axis) (Castro *et al.* 1999a: figures 168, 178 and 174).

values for beans could support the inference of growth in such conditions (Araus *et al.* 1997a, 1997b).

The practice of barley monoculture, and the increase in agricultural production, would have had major implications for human labour, given the greater time taken to get to and from fields, the costs of cereal processing, the organization of livestock grazing (and manuring) on stubble and the provision of animal traction. The evidence of charcoals and pollen from Gatas also suggests greater clearance of woodland at this time. The cultivation of legumes under conditions of water enhancement also implies increased labour costs for weeding, hoeing and so on, as well as the benefits of an important source of protein. Further protein was gained from animal meat, and it is worth noting that meat consumption increased markedly in Gatas phase 4, at the same time as the practice of barley monoculture.

How was Argaric production organized? According to the evidence of site locations in the Vera basin (see above) there was an inverse relationship between site size (and by inference population) and available land for dry and wet farming. This leads to the hypothesis that there was some unequal access to basic agricultural production from the late third to the mid-second millennia cal. BC. This hypothesis is strengthened by two observations. First, the cereal crop found so far at Gatas is a clean one, suggesting that primary processing took place (a) somewhere else within the settlement, (b) immediately outside the settlement associated with local cultivation, or (c) in the bottom of the Vera basin, associated with the smaller settlements and the larger areas of cultivable land. The fact that sondage and area excavations have taken place across and below the settlement of Gatas makes (a) unlikely. This leaves (b) and (c) as possibilities, while the latter would imply the existence of tribute from smaller to larger settlements.

Second, excavations of the foothill and larger Argaric settlements from the 1880s up to the present day have revealed evidence for (Lull 1983) and inferences of (Schubart and Pingel 1995) the storage of grain, as well as of instruments of production such as grinding stones and flint sickle blades. For example, in Ifre house C there were ten grinding stones piled up next to an oven (Siret and Siret 1887: 89), in Fuente Álamo one occupation floor of 10.5sq m in trench 39 contained twenty-two complete or partially broken grinding stones in various piles, and in area C of Gatas there were separate areas for cereal processing, using grinding stones, and for cereal storage in large vessels. Trench 39 at Fuente Álamo also produced a deposit of nearly fifty sickle teeth, many of which had no signs of use

(Risch 1998: 137). The important point to note is that such concentrations, especially of grinding stones, far exceeded the subsistence needs of the populations in the low hundreds that lived on these sites. Risch (1998: 144) calculates that three hours' grinding per day could have produced flour for more than six times the population of Fuente Álamo during phase 3 of its occupation (c.1900–1780 cal. BC). The grain would have been brought in to hilltop settlements such as Fuente Álamo after primary processing in the valley-bottom settlements for transformation into flour (by the same people?) using the grinding stones that had been concentrated there. Even the harvesting may have been done with the flint sickle teeth produced in the hilltop sites. There is scant evidence for grinding stones from the valley-bottom sites, where they would be expected to be visible on the surface. This is all the more surprising because of the availability of secondary sources for these grinding stones in the riverbeds of the Vera basin closer to areas of greater cultivable potential (Risch 1995, 1998). What we appear to be seeing is a regional, political system in which the instruments of production, and hence the processing of cereals (primarily barley) into food, were under the control of the larger, hilltop settlements in the Vera basin. The same control may also have been exercised over linen production: the flax on which it was based came from low-lying areas along river courses, while textile production in hilltop settlements is indicated by the frequency of loom weights (Castro et al. 1998a). Risch (1998: 148) calls this a 'system of vertical production', in which surplus production is geared to local political and economic factors rather than extensive exchange networks.

What about the production of implements and other social objects during the Argaric? The emphasis on the use of local, secondary, lithic sources that was seen in the Vera basin during the Copper Age was accentuated during the Argaric Bronze Age. For Gatas 60 per cent of the raw materials came from within a distance of 3–5km of the site, with 26 per cent within 1km; only 2 per cent came from more than 10km (Castro et al. 1999a). A similar pattern of use of local sources was seen at Fuente Álamo (Risch 1998) and in the contemporary settlements of southern Murcia (Risch and Ruiz 1994: 81–4). Rocks were selected from riverbeds according to their size, shape and potential for use without extensive working, except for the more standardized main working surfaces, which were prepared by percussion within the hilltop settlements. In addition, experimental studies on the rock types used at Fuente Álamo show that 70 per cent of the grinding stones were of a form of mica schist best suited for cereal processing (Risch 1998: 132–3). These also had the most standardized sizes of all the grinding stones at this site. As has already been mentioned, the frequency of grinding stones increased to a peak in Gatas phases 3–4, coinciding with widespread barley monoculture. The production costs of lithics in general were reduced (note the disappearance of pressure-flaked flint artefacts). Although flint was still used for making sickle teeth, its overall use declined, to be superseded by metal.

In addition to lithics, there was also intensification in the production of metal objects during the Argaric, with nearly five times as many artefacts as in the Copper Age (Table 5.3). However, this increase is the product of both a local and a regional trend: while frequencies increased in Granada and Murcia, 71 per cent of the known objects in south-east Spain come from the Vera basin, and some 72 per cent of these are from El Argar (Montero 1992: 199, 1993: 54). The conspicuous consumption of ornaments and weapons in burials distinguishes this period (the former comprising 53 per cent of the known artefacts, see Table 5.2), although this should not be used as an argument against the importance of metal in productive activities. Tools and weapons together contribute just over 44 per cent of the known metal objects and nearly 75 per cent of the total weight of metal consumed in known Argaric artefacts (Table 5.2 and Montero 1992: table 13). Copper awls, chisels, saws, axes and knives far outnumber the lithic and bone tools that could be used for cutting and perforating tasks. Use wear analysis of flint sickle teeth from Gatas supports the inference that they were important for tasks such as harvesting and threshing (Clemente *et al.* 1999). The cut marks seen on animal bone, shells and hard rock were more likely to have been made by metal tools (Castro *et al.* 1998a).

Table 5.3 Frequencies of Copper Age and Argaric metalwork in south-east Spain

	Copper Age			Argaric		
	Sites	*Objects*	*% of objects*	*Sites*	*Objects*	*% of objects*
Vera basin	22	114	19.2	13	2,080	71.4
Rest of Almería	35	200	33.8	27	112	3.8
Granada	72	220	37.2	66	429	14.7
Murcia	22	58	9.8	31	293	10.1
Total	151	592	100.0	137	2,914	100.0

Source: Data from Montero 1994: 210

For these reasons it can be argued that those who claim a purely symbolic, or 'prestige' value for copper objects (e.g. Gilman 1976; Montero 1999) have underestimated the role of metal in productive activities. Such a 'social-functional' dichotomy overlooks the evidence for the use of metal in productive activities in both the Copper Age (see above) and the Argaric, as well as the likely use of different categories of metal objects. It also fails to take into account the critical question of who controlled the exploitation, production and distribution of metal.

As in the Copper Age, there is no basis for arguing that proximity to copper sources was the major factor determining settlement location, especially in the Vera basin, where ore deposits are widely distributed. Montero (1993) proposes the same model of independent, local source exploitation and domestic production as for the Copper Age (the 'Almizaraque model'). Three major problems exist for this model. First, Montero (1993: 51–2) argues that 'there was no separation or specialisation in activities between settlements', but his data from twenty-one sites scattered throughout the south-east show that only nine of these have evidence for both smelting and casting activities (Table 5.4). Montero's data are qualitative, recording the presence/absence of such activities, and include sites with varying degrees of excavation and publication, as well as multi-period occupations which include evidence for metal production from Postargaric periods (Risch, personal communication).

Second, a pilot programme of lead isotope analyses on artefacts from Gatas and other lowland sites fails to match them to ores from the Vera basin, southern Murcia and south-east Almería (Stos-Gale et al. 1999; Stos-Gale 2000). A possible match is suggested for the Linares area of Jaén, or possibly further afield in the Huelva-Seville region. This finding is counter-intuitive, given the widespread presence of ore deposits in south-east Spain, and suggests an alternative model of exploitation of 'exotic' metal sources through long-distance exchange, perhaps controlled by the dominant classes of society (see below). If small Argaric villages on the plain of the Vera basin only had limited access to locally available rocks for grinding stones (see above), then could not the same also be true of the equally widely available metal sources? If it was, then how did this situation come about? Were local metal sources exploited initially in the Copper Age? A larger-scale programme of sampling of ore deposits, as well as analysis of ores and artefacts from Copper Age sites such as Almizaraque itself, is clearly needed to help resolve this contradiction of lead isotope and trace element analyses. While Montero himself

Table 5.4 Evidence of different stages of metalworking on Argaric settlements

	Smelting	Casting
Barranco Cera		X
Cerro de la Encina	X	X
Cerro de las Viñas	X	X
Cerro del Fuerte		X
Cerro de la Campaña		X
Cuesta del Negro	X	X
El Argar	X	X
El Oficio	X	X
El Picacho		X
El Puntarrón Chico		X
Fuente Álamo	X	X
Gatas	X	X
La Alquería	X	
La Bastida de Totana	X	X
La Finca de Félix	X	
Las Anchuras	X	X
Lugarico Viejo	X	
Pago Al-Rutan	X	
Peñicas Santomera		X
Rincón Almendricos	X	
Terrera del Reloj	X	

Source: Data from Montero 1993: 52

Note: The evidence for smelting includes copper ores, slags and adherences on the vessels in which smelting was carried out, while the evidence for casting comprises crucibles and moulds. In seven cases, the only evidence cited for smelting is the presence of copper ore. If the presence of slags and adherences is regarded as the *necessary* (as opposed to *likely*) evidence for smelting, then the number of sites with evidence for both smelting and casting is reduced in number from nine to five.

(1999: 350) accepts that some of the trace element analyses can be interpreted as showing the existence of metal exchange over longer distances, he clearly regards this as an occasional activity between élites.

Third, it should also be noted that the lead isotope analyses showed that the different sources provided copper for artefacts taken from the same sites (e.g. Gatas, Fuente Álamo and El Argar). This is exactly the opposite of what would be predicted by Montero's model, with its emphasis on individual settlements exploiting the nearest available metal sources. With such widely distributed ores, each settlement had no need of metal from other sources. Montero's acceptance of some degree of metal exchange in the Argaric is matched for the preceding Copper Age (1999: 339), so his position is not incompatible with the lead isotope evidence. However, the small numbers of metal artefacts analysed for each Argaric site makes it impossible to evaluate the degree of exchange that was taking place.

Until the issues of source use and exchange are resolved, it will be difficult to evaluate the arguments for and against the social control of metals in the Argaric. Evidence of restricted areas for metal production within Argaric settlements comes from lowland Almería and Murcia, at sites such as El Oficio, El Argar and La Bastida de Totana: at the last of these, two adjoining rooms provided all the evidence for metalworking in areas of 3,400sq km excavated in the 1940s (Lull 1983: 318–19). These sites support the arguments for non-domestic production, in contrast to Peñalosa, on the north-western margins of the Argaric territory, where evidence of metal production was more widely distributed (Contreras 2000) (see Chapter 6 below). While this can be used to support the Montero model of domestic production, it could also indicate the existence of community specialization, as proposed by Lull (1983).

What are the implications of this production evidence for the changing nature of Argaric society? We have already seen that social tensions and inequalities were visible during the Copper Age, using the investment of surplus labour in fortifications and mortuary rituals as their clearest expression. Destruction and burning levels on fortified sites suggest increased conflict in the later Copper Age. Then at $c.2250$ cal. BC, there is a marked break in the archaeological record of settlements, architecture, material culture and mortuary rituals in the lowlands of south-east Spain, although there is no evidence for population change (Kunter 1990). The processes by which these changes took place are not understood, although active political strategies pursued in a context of social conflict are clearly worth more detailed study. During the next seven hundred years, major changes occurred in production and its organization. There is evidence for an increase in basic production, that is, of population itself, as well as population nucleation. Agricultural production increased, as did the costs of the labour on which it was based. Primary agricultural production in the Vera basin took place in the low-lying areas, while processing into food and its distribution were organized from hilltop settlements, where surplus production is attested. Production costs for implements were further reduced, as can be seen also in the standardization of pottery. All these changes support the inference that social inequalities, coercion and exploitation appeared or increased markedly during the Argaric.

The organization of agricultural production proposed for the Vera basin is one in which human labour was increased to support the appropriation of surplus. Agricultural surpluses may have been produced before, but now they were socially appropriated. There is an increasing disparity between the labour invested in cereal agriculture and the product available to individuals and interest groups. Social inequalities here were based upon differential access to land and to the means of production. The extent of political control increased during the Argaric, culminating in the period *c.*1750–1550 cal. BC, when barley monoculture was imposed across the Vera basin: surplus production was pursued at the expense of labour costs, woodland cover and the need for a balanced diet. The accumulation and distribution of surplus production in the form of flour may have been aided by the use of pottery with a graded series of volumes (Castro *et al.* 1998a: 65).

The standardization of pottery, metals and burials (Lull 1983) right across the territory of the Argaric is seen to be an ideological means by which power was legitimated and accepted in everyday life (Risch and Ruiz 1994: 86). Homogeneity is stressed at the expense of difference. So, for example, the decreasing use of decoration on pottery reduces its capacity as a vehicle for the expression of local group identity. This does not mean that local groups were not attempting to express such identities (the variation in pottery types, locally produced, suggests that difference was being materialized in this way), but that their ability to do so was limited by widely shared constraints on action.

Within this widely shared network of cultural homogeneity and political control, Argaric communities exploited essentially local resources for everyday production. Only a small amount of lithics (e.g. flint, andesite) were obtained from more than a day's walking distance. The extent of exchange of metals is debated (see above), but there is agreement that any such exchange was in the context of élite, or dominant class, activity (as was the obtaining of ivory, Harrison and Gilman 1977).

Metric analysis on Argaric populations in the south-eastern lowlands (Buikstra and Hoshower unpublished) has shown that males were five times more heterogeneous than females and, by inference, more mobile in residence after marriage. A lack of homogeneity among males and greater homogeneity among females has also been noted for the burial population excavated at Fuente Álamo (Kunter 2001). If matrilocality were practised in the Argaric, then some important conclusions may follow. Cross-cultural studies show that matrilocal societies have 'significantly' larger dwellings than patrilocal societies, in order to accommodate families of related women and their 'imported' husbands (see Peregrine 2001: 38). This may be one factor in the change in domestic architecture from the Copper Age to the Argaric in south-east Spain. Ethnographic examples of matrilocality also show that it allows the absence of males engaged in such activities as raiding and trading, while females form the basic economic units in the settlement (Peregrine 2001: 38). Although this is hypothetical at present, it could imply clear divisions of labour in different areas of production, in addition to the contribution of women in 'basic production', which, as we have seen, increased during the Argaric.

Social distinctions have been recognized in Argaric burials since the initial excavations of the Siret brothers in the 1880s. Such distinctions related primarily to individuals interred with a conspicuous number of wealth items, as in the case of the famous grave 9 at Fuente Álamo (Figure 5.12). Lull (1983) examined the associations of grave containers, grave goods and the age and sex of the deceased, along with any evidence for location of intra-mural burial in relation to productive activities such as metalworking. On this basis he proposed the existence of a series of ranked social groups, with evidence for ascribed status in the form of wealthy child burials, that suggested the existence of a chiefdom society. Lull and Estévez (1986) used a principal components analysis to distinguish five levels of Argaric society, the top two of which included grave goods of the highest social value (e.g. halberds, swords, gold, silver diadems). Instead of a chiefdom, they proposed that the top two levels were the dominant class of a state society (cf. Schubart and Arteaga 1986).

Problems for analyses of Argaric mortuary practices are caused by the available samples of burials from both old and more recent excavations, the location of such excavations within settlement areas, and the likelihood that only certain sections of the population were selected for intra-mural burial at any one time (Chapman 1990: 200–1; Castro et al. 1994). The distribution of aged and sexed burials in settlements across the Vera basin also suggests that not all adult males may have been buried in the communities in which they lived (Micó 1993; see also Kunter 2001 on the low numbers of males aged 21–40 years buried at Fuente Álamo).

Making allowance for these problems, systematic programmes of radiocarbon dating on dead individuals (see p. 115) now allow us to begin to separate out social from chronological causes of variation in grave good deposition, age and sex representation, use of different grave containers, and so forth (Castro et al. 1994). For example,

Figure 5.12 Grave goods in tomb 9 at Fuente Álamo, including a sword, two daggers, a silver diadem (top), silver rings (below the diadem) and segmented faience beads (centre, to the left of the sword) (Siret and Siret 1887: plate 68).

although artificial caves have the earliest dates of all Argaric burial containers, they were in use alongside pits, cists and urns during the period *c.*2000–1700 cal. BC. This contradicts earlier schemes based on typology and grave associations alone. Double burials of a female and male, both adults (Figure 5.13), have been dated from four sites in Almería and Murcia: rather than being contemporary and representing married couples, the two individuals were normally interred at least two generations apart (Castro *et al.* 1994; Lull 2000). Rather than being married couples, the double burials reflect relations of kinship within family groups.

Evidence for inequalities is shown in the burial record of the Argaric in differences of wealth and gender. Exclusive associations of metal objects occur with males or females: for example, weapons such as swords, axes and halberds occur only with male burials, while the association of the dagger and awl is restricted to females of Lull and Estévez's (1986) third level of Argaric society. The weapon associations mark out a small number of adult males, compared with the total male population, and are argued to symbolize the coercive powers of this dominant group. Females in this group are marked out by items such as silver diadems (Figure 5.14). Further differences in the symbolism of social position occur through time. Halberds (Figure 5.15) only occur within the period *c.*2000–1800 cal. BC, after which swords are the main symbol of dominant male coercion, while adult males of lesser social position are associated with axes. While these changes are taking place for males, the association of the dagger and awl remains with females of the third level throughout the Argaric. Clearly there are very different 'messages' being conveyed by the associations of these exclusively male (coercive?) and female (productive?) grave goods, while other objects occur with both male and female burials (Castro *et al.* 1994). In contrast to the communal burials of the Copper Age, where social identity was represented by descent, inequalities can now be seen between individuals, as members of different interest groups, in their grave good associations, and between males and females. The inequalities seen in everyday production and the control of women are matched in the burial record and suggest the existence of a class society, if not a state (Lull and Risch 1995; Arteaga 1992).

Evaluating ideas, creating knowledge

This account of some 3,500 years of changing production and inequality is essentially interpretive. I have chosen to highlight

Figure 5.13 Double burial in tomb 37 at Gatas. (Photo by Vicente Lull.)

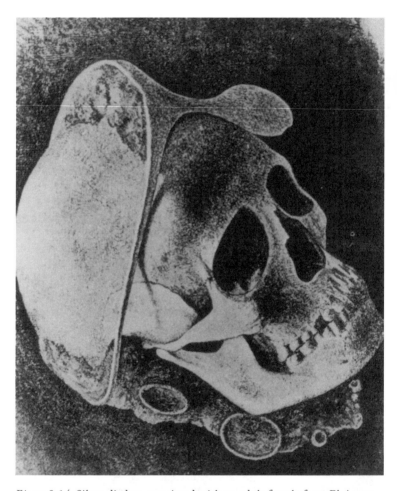

Figure 5.14 Silver diadem associated with an adult female from El Argar
(Siret and Siret 1887: plate 45).

those facts that are relevant to my interest in these two themes. In assembling these facts I have used the reported outcomes of a wide range of archaeological projects undertaken by different archaeologists and other specialists. These projects include small- and large-scale excavations, rescue and systematic fieldwork, surveys, syntheses of existing data, scientific analyses of dating and provenance, and collection of plant and animal remains. An overall account of this record of practice is given earlier in this chapter, as is a summary of

148

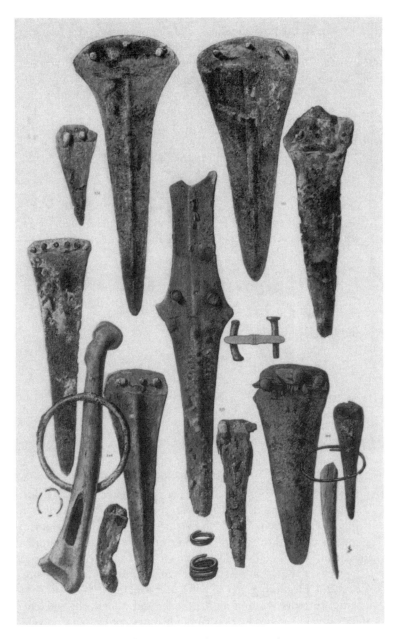

Figure 5.15 Argaric halberds (Siret and Siret 1887: plate 33).

the main models proposed in the period *c.*1976–84 to explain the then known archaeological sequence of Copper and Bronze Age societies in south-east Spain. What are the implications of recent research for these models? Does the current interpretive account, given above, of changing production and inequality have any wider implications? In the remainder of this chapter I will consider these two questions. I make the realist assumption, as discussed in Chapter 2, that there is a 'real' world of experience out there, against which we can evaluate ideas. I freely extract five principles, as follows, from the extensive publications of Alison Wylie (e.g. 1982, 1989, 1992, 2000):

(1) One criterion by which to evaluate our ideas about the past is their internal coherence (e.g. how does the general theory tie in with the operational concepts and methods of analysis? How precise is the idea?).

(2) In addition our ideas must be 'sensitive' to the empirical world, which can challenge and force us to revise our ideas.

(3) Claims to knowledge may be decisively strengthened or weakened when evaluated against a wider range of empirical evidence and different kinds of such evidence.

(4) The archaeological data that we use as evidence are given meaning by 'linking' principles (e.g. an axe mould indicates the presence of metal casting).

(5) At one time there is a body of evidence that is accepted by different practitioners as being the record we are trying to understand, and for which we propose competing ideas.

Earlier in this chapter I pointed out that the models published in 1976–84 were attempts to explain the body of evidence accepted at that time, with its regional scale and period chronology, as well as to collect new, relevant, data. They were proposed as alternatives to existing interpretations based on culture history and diffusionism. The models differed in relation to their theories used (e.g. historical materialism, adaptationism), determinants of change (e.g. dialectical relationships, population pressure, human desires and innate characteristics), the meaning given to particular data (e.g. the palaeoenvironmental interpretation of animal bones and pollen, the inference of intensification of production through water control and polyculture, the degree of social inequality in different periods) and the relationship proposed between the inferences based on the evidence (e.g. between intensification, population change, metallurgy, etc.).

Following the first principle outlined above, we could criticize the internal coherence and theoretical assumptions on which individual models were based. For example, my own model can be criticized as being environmentally determinist and there was an internal contradiction between the small-scale water control needed to adapt to an arid environment and the aggregation of population that was proposed around the best water sources. Ideas such as those of Ramos, based on population pressure arguments, have to explain rather than assume the existence of population growth. However my intention in what follows is to focus on principles 2–4, on the exposure of ideas to evidence. As I argued earlier in this chapter, this exposure to evidence has come about in spite of the rarity of explicit evaluation of ideas through archaeological practice in south-east Spain. Elsewhere I have pointed out inconsistencies between ideas and evidence across the study area (e.g. in population trends, in the relationship between agricultural intensification and increased inequality) that weaken some of the models (Chapman 1990). In what follows I focus on the evidence for the palaeoenvironment, for the nature of agricultural production and specifically the irrigation hypothesis, and for social inequality and especially the existence of the state. In the last case we need to expand our horizons and compare the definition of the state with that commonly adopted in the Anglo-American world.

Palaeoenvironments

The environment of south-east Spain during the last 500 years has been marked by the removal of vegetation cover, increased sedimentation and erosion rates (comparable to the whole of the Holocene in their effects), increased flooding and lowering of water tables. It is one of the key areas of Mediterranean Europe where resources are being devoted to the study of desertification processes (for references, see Castro *et al.* 2000), especially given the need to devise policies of environmental management to cope with global warming. For archaeologists interested in the record of prehistoric societies, the key questions are whether these 'badland' landscapes are a recent phenomenon, whether the area has always been marked by aridity, and to what extent human social, political and economic practices have contributed to landscape formation. How 'risky' for agricultural practices was this region and how necessary for these practices was water control/irrigation?

There has been a marked expansion in the range and quality of evidence on palaeoenvironments in south-east Spain during the last decade (especially compared with the evidence summarized in Chapman 1990). This is the outcome of both excavation and regional survey projects, but the coverage in time and space is still uneven. For this reason I will focus on the Vera basin, as it has the densest coverage for the third and second millennia cal. BC, and make reference to evidence from other regions when available and relevant. Eight lines of palaeoenvironmental evidence are given in Table 5.5, some of which have already been mentioned above. The linking principles (see above) are from the natural and biological sciences. Do these lines of evidence converge on any particular interpretation? Do they strengthen or weaken the models that invoke the need for cultural responses to 'risky' environments?

Let us begin with the evidence for sedimentation and erosion (e.g. Hoffmann 1988; French *et al.* 1998). The record for the Vera basin suggests wetter conditions at the beginning of the Holocene, with increased aridity from *c.*4000 cal. BC. Soils appear to have been of limited formation even before the first agricultural settlement of the basin. Phases of soil erosion are documented in the lower Aguas valley before the Copper Age, when the low population density and higher mobility make an anthropogenic cause unlikely. Two further erosional episodes in the lower Aguas are dated between the late Copper Age and the Roman period, while the erosion of Neogene marls took place further up the Aguas valley before the Roman occupation of Cadimar. The extent to which such episodes are the results of anthropogenic activity is not clear on the basis of geomorphological evidence alone. Much higher sedimentation rates are documented for the last 500 or 600 years, with the formation of two of the four Holocene terraces in the Aguas, and the infill of the lower Almanzora, Antas and Aguas rivers and the deposition of deltaic deposits.

Table 5.5 Lines of palaeoenvironmental evidence for south-east Spain

1 Sedimentation and erosion
2 Pollen analysis
3 Charcoal analysis
4 Habitat requirements of plant species
5 Habitat requirements of animal species
6 Carbon isotope discrimination on plant seeds
7 Oxygen isotope analysis of sea shells
8 Isotopic analysis of secondary carbonates

Although soils may have been of limited development, they had greater vegetation cover than at the present day, as is shown by the pollen and charcoal records (e.g. Rodríguez Ariza and Stevenson 1998). In addition to the *matorral* vegetation, dominated by wild olives and suggesting high temperatures and almost frost-free winters, deciduous species such as ash, willow and elm would have required more humid conditions and higher water tables or greater water flow in riverine areas. The degradation of these species is documented in the lower Almanzora valley by *c.*2300 cal. BC and in the middle Aguas by *c.*1300 cal. BC (Rodríguez Ariza 2000). Exploitation of wood species increased markedly during the Argaric in the Aguas, supporting the argument for large-scale clearance associated with extensive barley monoculture (see above, pp. 133–7). High temperatures and low rainfall are inferred, along with increased salinization in some areas. Outside the Vera basin conditions of aridity, but greater local humidity with greater water flow, are indicated by the presence of similar species, including the deciduous ones in riverine areas (e.g. Los Millares – Rodríguez Ariza and Vernet 1991), while charcoal analyses on the Copper and Bronze Age settlements of the Baza-Huéscar plateau have documented similar evidence for greater local humidity, permanent water courses and vegetation degradation (Rodríguez Ariza and Ruíz Sánchez 1995).

This inference of greater vegetation cover and increased local humidity is supported by the habitat requirements of plant species such as legumes and flax (see above, p. 135 and Castro *et al.* 1999b) and animal species such as pig, red deer, roe deer, as well as the beaver, otter, water turtle and aquatic birds known from Copper and Bronze Age sites in the upland basins of eastern Granada (Lull 1983). But it is the isotopic studies that provide the key, independent measures of climatic change. The carbon isotope discrimination analyses of seeds not only suggest the possibility of bean cultivation under higher water conditions during growth, but seeds from the inland Baza and Guadix basins indicate a wetter climate than today in the third and second millennia BC, along with subsequent decreases in precipitation (Araus *et al.* 1997a, 1997b). The oxygen isotope analyses on sea shells from Gatas (Figure 5.16) show that the mean annual sea water temperature *c.*1900–1600 cal. BC was close to, or even slightly higher than, its present level (Pätzold *et al.* 1998). Seasonal differences in temperature may have been less and winter temperatures milder than today. There is then a decrease in this temperature by 2.5°C in the period *c.*1550–1200/1100 cal. BC and seasonal differences may have decreased even further. The

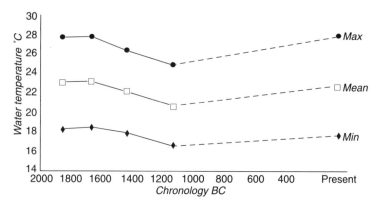

Figure 5.16 Maximum, mean and minimum sea water temperatures for the Almería coast, based on isotopic analysis of *Glycimeris* shells from stratified contexts at Gatas (adapted from Castro *et al.* 1998b: figure 8).

isotopic analyses of secondary carbonates, also from stratified contexts at Gatas, converge with this pattern, showing maximum temperatures and/or aridity at *c*.1600 cal. BC and then a constant decrease until *c*.1000 cal. BC (Dever 1998).

There is a strong degree of convergence between these different lines of evidence. Although soil formations were poorly developed, they had *maquia* and *mattoral* vegetation cover with greater amounts of more continuous flowing water than at the present day. Mean annual temperatures were comparable to the present day, if not slightly higher, at the beginning of the second millennium cal. BC, but then declined. Unfortunately the isotopic data are mainly restricted to the second millennium cal. BC, but there were climatic fluctuations through time, even though the general climate may be described as arid. This is further supported by the (albeit limited) sample of barium/strontium ratios on human remains from Gatas. The decrease in vegetation cover during the Argaric, when temperatures remained broadly the same, was most probably the result of anthropogenic activity.

Agricultural production

The eight lines of palaeoenvironmental evidence converge upon an interpretation of an arid climate coupled with greater local humidity and vegetation cover during the third and second millennia cal. BC.

The impact of human activity, especially cultivation systems, can be seen on this environment during this period of time. The evidence of plant remains and their water requirements matches the palaeoenvironmental evidence in supporting the inference of dry farming based primarily on barley, alongside the cultivation of legumes and flax in small horticultural plots in the Copper and Bronze Ages (see above). The water requirements of the legumes and flax could have been met from riverine areas with more continuously flowing water and/or higher water tables than at the present day. When added to the evidence for barley cultivation under dry farming conditions right up to modern times, even in the arid lowlands, this negates the premise that 'dry farming is not a viable subsistence strategy in the arid lowlands' (Gilman and Thornes 1985: 183). Both Gilman and I argued that simple forms of water control were necessary in order to permit agricultural colonization of the lowlands. But the consistent fifth millennium cal. BC dates for Neolithic occupation at Cerro Virtud in the Vera basin (see above) now remove the evidence for a marked difference in agricultural colonization between the interior uplands and the coastal lowlands. Water control was not the 'key' to coping with an arid and 'risky' environment.

Two other lines of evidence in support of water control are the archaeological structures for conservation and diversion and the locations of archaeological sites (see Chapman 1990: 125–8 for sources). The evidence for water conservation occurs most famously in hilltop Argaric settlements such as El Oficio and Fuente Álamo, as well as in the insecurely dated 'cisterns' at the eastern foot of the Gatas hill (the latter may be of Arab construction and use in the early second millennium AD). Lined pits at the earlier Copper Age sites of Los Millares and Terrera Ventura could have been used for water storage. Ditches filled with waterlain sediments were found at the Copper Age settlements of Cerro de la Virgen (in the interior uplands) and Ciavieja (on the southern coast to the west of Almería). At the latter the two ditches were only used in the earliest, Final Neolithic, occupation phases (Carrilero and Suárez 1989–90), and, if they were used for irrigation, they cannot be argued to have been the basis of a continued and successful adaptation to a risky, arid environment. The cistern at Fuente Álamo is now dated to the very end of the Argaric and the immediate Postargaric period (Schubart *et al.* 2001), so again cannot be used to support the existence of a continuing need for water conservation through the occupation of the site. Even allowing for difficulties of dating and the linking principles by which some structures become evidence for water control, there is little evidence here to suggest that it was central to agricultural production strategies.

The study of the location of later prehistoric settlements in south-east Spain directs our attention to the potential for irrigation within site territories of two hours' walking distance. Settlements such as Los Millares and Gatas have a potential for wet farming, while others such as Fuente Álamo and El Oficio are classified as dry farming locations. The potential for different cultivation systems is one thing, but the extent to which that potential is fulfilled is dependent upon social and political factors. In the cases of Gatas and Fuente Álamo (Figure 5.17), they have different potentials for dry/wet farming, but the archaeological evidence supports the inference of comparable, predominantly dry farming, agricultural regimes at both sites (see above). It could be argued (Castro *et al.* 1999b: 854) that a small area of potentially irrigable land close to Fuente Álamo was sufficient for the cultivation of legumes and flax, while the irrigable potential of Gatas was underexploited in the Argaric. The study of such potential is not without value, especially when compared with what is known of cultivation practices from contextual evidence on each site. But the decisions as to how to exploit that potential are taken within social and political contexts, and not necessarily in the interests of the entire population.

Given this argument, I would now disown completely the model I put forward in 1978. There are also critical, if not terminal, implications for Gilman's model, based heavily as it is on site location potential and the argument that 'irrigation . . . transformed the social relations of production' (1976: 314). The absence of clear evidence for irrigation systems as capital investments removes one basis for his model of contradictions between the forces and relations of production leading to the emergence of social stratification. His other source of capital investment, the cultivation of vines and olives alongside cereals, also lacks irrefutable empirical support. While wild olives (as we have seen above) and wild grapes were part of the vegetational cover of south-east Spain in the Holocene, and examples of stones and grape pips have been recovered from Copper and Bronze Age sites, they are small in number and suggest only incidental consumption. At Gatas there is an increase in evidence for exploitation of both vines and olives only at the end of the Argaric and in the Postargaric, which is after the full development of social stratification. Claims for the cultivation of olives at Los Millares (Rodríguez Ariza and Vernet 1991) depend upon differences in the size of growth rings in wood charcoal samples and observations of

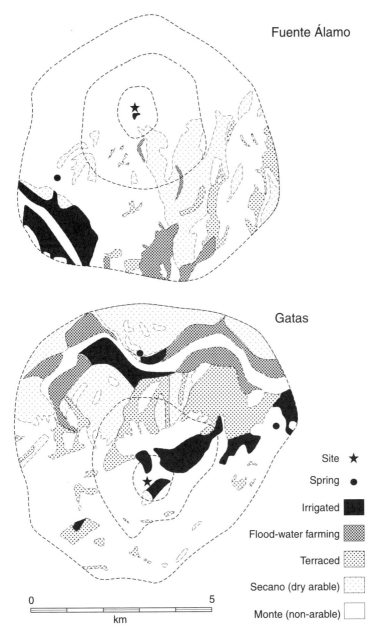

Figure 5.17 Site territories within 12, 30 and 60 minutes' walking distance from the Argaric sites of Fuente Álamo and Gatas (adapted from Gilman and Thornes 1985: figures 5.11 and 5.14).

such differences in modern olive wood from Valencia and Montpel-
lier. Even if cultivation were practised, that still does not tell us the
purpose and scale of cultivation. Terral (1996, 2000) infers some
cultivation in Valencia going back to the Early Neolithic for fuel
and food, with pruning used to support fruit production in the
Bronze Age. But there is no evidence for the production and consumption of either olive oil or wine from any settlement in the time-
span of this study.

Models based on ideas of adaptation through irrigation, or capital
investment technologies, have been decisively weakened by their
encounter with empirical evidence, apart from any other criticisms
of their internal coherence. The 'risky' or 'marginal' nature of the
palaeoenvironment has been over-stressed and assumed undue
importance in creating models of social change. They fail to place
agricultural practices where they belong, within a social and political context. It is to that context that I turn next.

Inequality and the state of the state

Conceptions of society and social change mark one of the clearest
divisions between the approaches of historical materialism and
Anglo-American neo-evolutionism to the study of the past. One of
the interesting aspects of the archaeology of south-east Spain is that
conceptions from both traditions (e.g. 'ranked societies', 'chiefdoms',
'Big Men' and 'the state') have been, and are, used by both foreign
and indigenous archaeologists. How are these conceptions used?
And what are we to make of different uses of the same term, 'the
state'? I will begin by taking an interpretive look at what we have
learnt about Neolithic, Copper Age and Argaric societies, before
confronting different meanings of 'the state'.

The Neolithic societies of south-east Spain appear to have consisted of low density, mobile populations using both ephemeral,
open-air settlements and cave sites. The archaeological record of
these societies is still thin and patchy for the lowlands, given the
period of around fifteen hundred years that they occupied the area.
They used predominantly local resources in everyday life and there is
no conclusive evidence for surplus or specialized production, or the
appropriation of the labour or production of others, or the existence
of groups removed from productive activities. Social distinctions
appear to have been based on age, gender and group affiliation.

Copper Age societies were made up of larger, more sedentary populations who invested greater labour in their domestic

structures, the fortifications that enclosed them and the communal tombs that accompanied them (although this association was not universal). There were no major capital investments in production, nor major changes in the means of production. Through time there is evidence for increased social tensions and physical conflict. The reasons for this are not yet clear. The location of productive activities within settlement spaces provides some evidence for specialization and surplus production (e.g. flint arrowheads, copper metallurgy), but mainly domestic production. Storage may have become more household- than lineage-based, although this would be in contradiction with the treatment of the dead, which now suggests inequalities in access to wealth and exotic items between lineages. Overall there appear to have been relations of equality and inequality, although clear evidence of exploitation is lacking.

This all changes in the Argaric, when there is a major and abrupt disjunction in settlement, burial and material culture, with population nucleation (imposed as part of a political strategy?), an increase in population size (basic production), more extensive dry farming and increasing agricultural production. Once again it was human labour rather than improvements in the means of production that supported this increased production. Unequal access to the products of agricultural labour, as well as the inequalities seen in burials, supports the inference of social classes and the appropriation of surplus production. Women were important both for their basic production and for their labour. Cultural standardization indicates attempts to suppress local identity and exercise coercion both physically and ideologically.

Within the Anglo-American tradition, this sequence might suggest change from Neolithic egalitarian, to Copper Age ranked societies or simple, group-oriented or collaborative chiefdoms, to Argaric stratified societies or complex or coercive chiefdoms. I used the term ranked society when first looking at the Copper Age burials of Los Millares (Chapman 1981), but no longer find this term useful, preferring to focus on the evidence for both equal and unequal social relations seen in domestic and burial contexts. The existence of, and tensions between, such social relations are submerged within societal typologies (see Chapters 3–4). Ramos (1981, 1998) has also used the analogy of 'Big Men' for the leaders of Copper Age communities such as El Malagón. This poses two major problems: first, the highland New Guinea societies that are used as an analogy were in fact the products of colonialism and the collapse of inherited social position, rather than a 'stepping stone' in social evolution (Gosden

1999: 103); second, the 'Big Man''s social position was based on the disposal of wealth, rather than its accumulation and investment in domestic architecture and material culture, thus making him difficult to 'see' in the archaeological record (White 1985).

But it is the use of the term 'state' to refer to Argaric society that is causing the greatest controversy. The historical materialist definition of the state by Lull and Risch (1995) was given in Chapter 4. According to this, state societies are based on class differences, by which surplus is appropriated and society is divided into producers and non-producers; the latter exploit the former. The class that is economically dominant is also politically dominant. Such dominance may be seen in unequal access to labour, natural resources or the means of production. The state consists of institutions designed to guarantee the private property of the non-producing classes and uses both physical and ideological coercion to accomplish this.

As we have seen in Chapter 3, the dominant tradition in Anglo-American archaeology uses information theory to define a state in terms of its centralized and hierarchical levels of decision-making and administration, as well as the specialization of information-processing activities (bureaucracy). Levels of decision-making are measured archaeologically in terms of the number of site levels in a settlement hierarchy: thus early Mesoamerican states had large centres such as Tikal dominating three or more levels of a settlement hierarchy, including the primary producers at the bottom. Given the relationship between site size and population size, it is not surprising that the latter also became an index of the state, especially when looking at the tens and hundreds of thousands of people who were members of early state societies in Mesoamerica and Mesopotamia. Given these criteria, the *at best* two-level hierarchy represented by Argaric settlements (Chapman 1990), with its lack of centralization and the populations of settlements in their low hundreds, along with the lack of palaces, temples, etc., cannot possibly represent a state society. For example, Gilman (1997) admits the existence of a class society in the Argaric, but not of a state.

I have already commented in Chapters 3 and 4 on the way in which early states are members of an exclusive club that is not regarded as open to an increase in size. Cahokia does not seem able to gain admission, opinion is strongly divided over the Olmec, contact-period Hawaiian societies, along with Tonga and Tahiti, lurk on the doorstep, while pre-Columbian Peruvian societies seem to get in at different times according to whether they are thought to have fulfilled different admission criteria! But is this emphasis on specialized bureaucracy (along with legitimized force, a criterion going back to Service), levels of decision-making and centralization, tried and tested on the early 'civilizations', not too restricting? Are the assumptions behind it unproblematic?

The root of the difference between this approach and that of historical materialism lies in the weight given to what Flannery (1972) called exchanges of information rather than just matter and energy. In these terms, concern with exploitation and property focuses very firmly on matter and energy rather than information. Following this criterion, the removal of leaders from subsistence labour, while they may thus enjoy powers of physical and ideological coercion over producers, will get a society admitted to only the 'complex chiefdom' club, but not the states. Until they can process more information, they are out on the doorstep denied admission! And yet, as we have seen in the discussion of heterarchies in Chapter 4, political and economic activities are not always centralized in stratified or state societies, and multiple hierarchies do occur. The absence of centralized organization and vertical control hierarchies in sub-Saharan Africa (see Chapter 4) has raised doubts as to the imposition of social types defined from other regions of the world. Centralization may also have been over-emphasized, depending as it does on the nature of the power relationship between the exploiters and the exploited, between domination and resistance (Stein 1998: 26). And decision-making hierarchies are difficult to identify in contexts where there is dispersed settlement (Brumfiel 1995): the absence of settlement hierarchies does not necessarily imply the absence of decision-making hierarchies (see Chapter 3).

As explained in Chapter 3, the decision-making hierarchies of the Wright-Johnson model emerge in response to the need to process more sources of information and to co-ordinate larger numbers of activities. They solve problems and have adaptive advantages. Critical thresholds are argued to exist in the needs for information processing and these are thought to be related to the scale of the social system. One measure used of this system scale is the size of the population. This in turn allows settlement sizes to be used to define levels in decision-making hierarchies and regional population sizes to be one criterion of the distinction between, for example, simple chiefdoms (low thousands, according to Earle 1991b), complex chiefdoms (tens of thousands, again according to Earle 1991b) and state societies.

But opinion is divided as to the relationship between demographic factors and levels of social complexity (e.g. compare Drennan

1987 and Upham 1987). Feinman (1998) doubts the existence of some universal demographic threshold between chiefdoms and states, citing examples from the archaeological literature of early state populations as low as $c.2,000–3,000$ and as high as the Inka case of 14 million people. He also gives examples of the population overlap between chiefdoms and states and goes on to argue that 'the ways in which ancient states were integrated and interconnected often varied markedly over space, and differences in organisation and integration have profound implications on state size' (1998: 132).

So even within the Anglo-American tradition, there is a recognition of problems with some of the basic assumptions of the definition of state societies in terms of decision-making hierarchies: centralization varies in its extent and strength; not all political and economic activities are carried out under one decision-making hierarchy; such a hierarchy would be difficult to identify from site size data when populations are dispersed; and states occur in a range of sizes. In this context it is interesting to note that the Argaric population in the Vera basin is estimated in the range 1,700–3,400, but that number would at least double with the addition of Argaric settlements in southern Murcia and southern Almería, let alone in the rest of the area in which Argaric materials occur: this area is estimated at nearly 50,000sq m, or over three times the size of Renfrew's (1975) Early State Module.

On the basis of these problems alone, I would argue that we need to reconsider the dominant use of the 'early civilizations' model of the state. There is a case for admitting more of the transitional or disputed examples mentioned in Chapter 4 to the state club. Another way to open up discussion of early states is to consider the perspective of the alternative states of historical materialism. As well as focusing on matter and energy, rather than information (to use Flannery's ecological approach), there is a very different political view of the state, one of exploitation rather than management. Anglo-American archaeologists conceive of the exploitation of plants and animals, but not of human beings! As we saw in Chapter 3, this concept, along with those of class and property, is being addressed by archaeologists whose research ought to serve as a denial of the scepticism of those such as Wenke (1981), who doubt whether such concepts can be 'seen' in our data. Within south-east Spain, the existence of non-producing classes is being addressed by comparison of the treatment of the dead, especially wealth disposal, with evidence of physical activity during life. At the Argaric settlement of Cerro de la Encina, in the Granadan uplands, an inverse correlation has been claimed between wealth and muscular development and degenerative pathologies, although the sample is currently small (Jiménez Brobeil and García Sánchez 1989–90). At the contemporary site of Cuesta del Negro, in the same region, the wealthiest individuals were also marked out by the deposition of finer pottery intended exclusively for such funerary contexts (Contreras *et al.* 1987–8).

Depending on your viewpoint, the state of the early state is either healthy and clearly focused on a limited range of case studies, or challenged by a theoretical perspective that highlights the kinds of inequalities and exploitation that comprise one of the major structural changes in human history. Such changes were not restricted to the 'early civilizations' and did not necessarily receive the same material expression. In both cases, however, they marked out societies with inherent instabilities, as human exploitation was met by resistance and conflict. The dialectical relationship between domination and resistance, along with the potential for, and costs of, the control of increasing production, were key determinants of the length of time that such early states could survive.

Looking forward

This account of a 1,500-year record of change in production, inequality and social change in south-east Spain gives us an example of the relationship between theory and practice, including the evaluation of ideas against an empirical record, as well as a rather different perspective on the most complex of all social types, the state. This perspective deserves wider discussion, in the light of the theoretical assumptions behind it, as well as the concepts it employs to study the archaeological record. For those of us in the Anglo-American world, this challenge to our thinking demands a positive response.

In the next chapter I will try to develop this response by examining a wider range of case studies from the later prehistory of the Mediterranean. Given the space available, this coverage is of necessity selective. What interests me is how archaeologists have used concepts like 'complexity', 'inequality' and 'hierarchy'; how they conceive of societies (including chiefdoms and states); and how they study social change.

6

THE USES AND ABUSES OF COMPLEXITY

Prehistoric societies in the west Mediterranean

In Chapter 1, I argued that the development of more complex and unequal societies has been one of the key topics occupying the thoughts of archaeologists and social scientists since the Enlightenment. In the last four decades, neo-evolutionary thinking has dominated these thoughts in the Anglo-American world, although it has been subjected to criticism from both Marxism and practice theory, as shown in Chapter 3. The use of social typologies guided us through a sequence of more complex societies, while our study of past societies, using dichotomous terms such as equal/unequal, simple/complex or state/non-state, was criticized in Chapter 4. The case study presented in Chapter 5 attempted to avoid such dichotomous thinking and see how a historical materialist approach helps us to represent a sequence of social change in south-east Spain that is widely conceived as one towards increasing complexity. And yet the word 'complexity' was largely omitted from the discussion. I will now examine and criticize its use, not only for this region, but also for other selected areas of Iberia and the west Mediterranean in the same period of time. How is the term defined and used? Is this use clear and consistent? And which theoretical approaches are adopted in the study of society and social change? Throughout the discussion the approach adopted to the study of production and inequalities in south-east Spain will provide the guiding light.

'Complex' societies in Iberia?

The honest scientist, whether natural or social, should always be willing to begin criticism with self-criticism! Over ten years ago I published a book on 'emerging complexity', mainly based on south-east Spain, but also taking into account other regions of the west Mediterranean (Chapman 1990). The approach was strongly influenced by the kinds of decision-making and neo-evolutionary approaches cited in Chapter 3 and conceived of different 'levels' of complexity of regional cultures. The Argaric was the most complex in Iberia, while the contemporary Bronze Age of La Mancha showed 'a cultural complexity more closely comparable to the Argaric culture than any other region of Iberia during the second millennium BC' (1990: 242). In other regions, such as southern Portugal, I referred to only 'some measure of increased complexity' (1990: 237). In all cases I tried to relate such 'levels' of complexity to the colonization of agriculturally marginal or problematic areas.

Looking back, I can understand the criticism of functionalism (the worst insult in the lexicon of the social sciences) that was levelled against such arguments. The definition of complexity followed Blanton *et al.* (1981: 21) as 'the extent to which there is functional differentiation among societal units', dividing such differentiation into 'horizontal' (e.g. specialization of production) and 'vertical' (e.g. ranking, stratification) kinds. Different cultures were then placed somewhere on the ladder of increased complexity, according to a largely unspecified linkage between the horizontal and vertical kinds of differentiation. By merging these two kinds of complexity into one overall measure, important differences in the historical sequences of each region were already being omitted from the interpretation. From rereading the book I get the sense of a classification of west Mediterranean societies into ones which were a little bit more complex, or others which were a little bit less complex, as being the aim of the study, rather than an attempt to analyse changes in production and inequalities, to recognize the existence of social tensions as well as social integration, and to isolate major, structural changes in the organization of prehistoric societies. Given these arguments presented in Chapters 3–4, it is not surprising that the representation of the period *c.*5000/4500–1550 cal. BC in southeast Spain in Chapter 5 is rather different from that given in my previous book. There has also been a fundamental change in the data upon which interpretation is now based.

Other authors have also used the term 'complexity' in Iberia. Mathers (1994: 21) writes of 'a considerable measure of social and economic complexity' in south-east Spain in the third and second millennia BC, although he offers no definition of these terms, while Hernando (1987) compared cultural differences between third millennium cal. BC settlements in the lowland 'arid' and upland 'humid' zones of south-east Spain, thereby relating differences in complexity to differences in environment. For the same period of time, Delibes *et al.* (1995: 46) refer to 'incipient complexity' on the northern Meseta of Spain, an area which was 'not very different, either in socioeconomic complexity or in material culture, from the same period in the "cosmopolitan" areas of the south-east and the Tagus estuary' (1995: 44). Complexity is undefined as a concept, although the text makes it clear that the presence of a settlement hierarchy including fortified settlements, specialist production of metal and flint, and wealth differences in the disposal of the dead all provide evidence of developing stratification and individual leadership, perhaps even an 'élite class' (1995: 52). Kunst (1995) refers to the existence of 'social complexity', also without definition, during the third millennium BC in southern Portugal, but uses similar archaeological criteria to Delibes *et al.* to support such an inference. Forenbaher (1998: 3) notes that the same evidence has supported interpretations of 'full-blown "complex society" complete with hereditary chiefs, political and religious hierarchy, social divisions of labor and elementary forms of private property', or 'hierarchical societies' (chiefdoms), or 'ranked' societies, and he himself refers to a 'relatively high level of socio-economic complexity' by the Late Copper Age of this region. These societies cannot be classified into an evolutionary type. And for northern Portugal at the same time it is stated, without definition again, that 'tendentially hierarchical societies took steps towards a quite significant level of social complexity' (Oliveira Jorge and Jorge 1997: 128).

Díaz-Andreu (1995) points out that complex societies have traditionally been claimed for only south-east Spain and southern Portugal (Portuguese Estremadura) during the Copper Age in the third millennium cal. BC. She proposes to expand the second of these areas to include all the south-west of the Peninsula and add the lower Duero basin in the north of Portugal as a third area. Once again there is no definition of 'complex societies'. Díaz-Andreu argues that there were increases in social inequality elsewhere in the Peninsula (1995: 27), but these were clearly not of a sufficient degree to amount to 'complexity'. This would seem to consist of an increase in inequality beyond a certain 'cut-off' point, but this is not specified. Later in the article she refers to 'the lesser degree of social differentiation, i.e. complexity' shown in areas peripheral to those in which such complex societies emerged. There appears to be a contradiction here between the assertion that there are such things as 'complex societies' and the proposal that there are 'degrees' of complexity, whether between societies described as 'complex' (1995: 30: south-east = most complex, south-west = less complex, lower Duero basin

= even less complex, but still complex!) or between them and the other Peninsula societies.

How are these undefined 'complex societies' recognized in the archaeological record? Like the other authors mentioned above, Díaz-Andreu relies heavily on the existence of fortified settlements, differences of size between settlements, differences in the disposal of the dead and the presence of 'prestige' items (1995: 28, 30, 32). But once again there is no clear statement of exactly which criteria enable us to identify 'complex societies', other than an intuitive feel for the largest settlements, biggest defences and richest burials. Elsewhere Díaz-Andreu (1993: 246) cites 'stable urban structures', the materialization of political power seen in the construction of defensive walls, the unequal distribution of 'luxury objects' and specialized production, but these are very much taken for granted rather than discussed in detail. In both papers Díaz-Andreu follows the arguments of Gilman on south-east Spain, stressing its 'risks' for agriculture and the opportunities for leaders to seize power over long-term 'investments' such as irrigation and polyculture, as well as the use of material culture to distinguish more clearly these leaders from other individuals at the transition to the Argaric Bronze Age. In contrast, south-west Iberia had a less unpredictable climate and did not necessitate the long-term agricultural investments that would have provided the basis of élite power. Long-distance maritime trade provides the alternative basis for such power.

These examples suggest that the terms 'complexity' or 'complex societies' in Iberia are so widely understood that their definition, along with their material correlates, is thought to be unnecessary. Their recognition becomes an end in itself, along with a ranking of societies along a scale of increasing complexity. But this typological exercise tells us little about the specific historical contexts of the societies that we study. What kinds of social, economic or political inequalities developed in the different regions? What kinds of tensions were there between equal and unequal social relations at particular times? What were the material, productive bases of such inequalities? And at what time did these inequalities make the structural change from being kinship- to class-based? These are the kinds of questions that are now being asked in south-east Spain, as we have seen in Chapter 5, and it is fair to say that the quality of data on production and the material basis of inequalities in that area is unmatched in many other parts of the Peninsula. But that should be an incentive for research rather than a deterrent.

The material correlates claimed for 'complexity' in Iberia are not without problems. Let us take the example of Copper Age fortified settlements. Thirty years ago these were known almost exclusively from two regions of the Peninsula, south-east Spain and the Tagus estuary in southern Portugal (Figure 6.1). Indeed the names of the two 'cultures' in these regions were derived from fortified sites at Los Millares and Vila Nova de São Pedro. Then more examples were found extending further south into Portugal and as far north as the Duero valley. A recent survey by Oliveira Jorge provided a catalogue of sixty-nine such sites: according to her map, one group is isolated in the south-east, while the rest extend the length of Portugal and western Spain from the Algarve to north of the Duero (1994: figure 1). It is now clear that fortified sites are even more frequent in the south-east, in both the lowlands of Almería and the uplands of

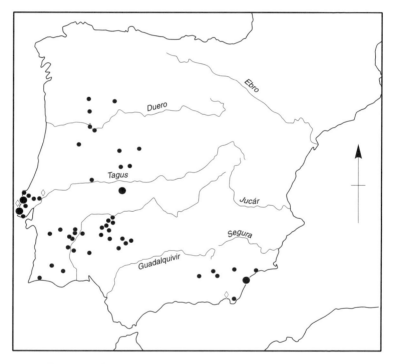

Figure 6.1 Map of Copper Age fortified settlements in Iberia. Larger dots represent concentrations of sites, smaller dots represent individual sites. The open lozenges show the sites known in the mid-1960s (from Savory 1968: figure 44), while the current distribution is drawn from Oliveira Jorge (1994: figure 1). The map excludes monumental enclosures.

eastern Granada, and they extend west into the upper Guadalquivir valley and areas such as the Ronda basin (Pérez Bareas and Cámara 1995; Nocete 2001). There are also examples of 'monumental enclosures' surrounded by a combination of concentric ditches and walls, rather than just dry-stone walls, which are known from the upper and lower Guadalquivir valley, south-west Spain and southern Portugal (Oliveira Jorge 2000: 74–6). Inclusion of these enclosures would raise the number of 'fortified' enclosures to somewhere nearer the 90–100 mark. Not only are they more common than previously thought, but they are not restricted to the areas of so-called 'complex societies'.

The sites included under the heading of 'fortified' also exhibit wide differences in their form, size, degree of monumentality, energy investment, duration of occupation and use. These differences are summarized by Oliveira Jorge for the stone-walled fortified sites, which are nearly all less than 2ha in size, but which embody a wide range of labour investment in their construction. Monks (1997: 19–22) has calculated the construction costs of fourteen sites in Spain and Portugal: ten cost less than 20,000 work days, while one cost twice that amount and three (Los Millares, Cerro de la Virgen and Zambujal) cost over 100,000 work days. The choice of sites for such calculations is heavily restricted by the extent of excavations. The length of their occupation varied from c.200 to 800 years, and the sites with the largest labour investment were in the upper half of this range. The small size of some of the sites suggests something in the order of a fortified farmstead rather than a village or town. Variations are also noted in architectural form, including the number of enclosing walls (Oliveira Jorge 1994: 468–9). It is also worth reminding ourselves that definition of a class of sites according to one characteristic, the presence of fortifications, risks merging together sites that had different functions, productive activities and positions within regional settlement and political hierarchies (see below).

The sites known as monumental enclosures are currently less frequent in number but often conspicuously larger in size. La Pijotilla (Figure 6.2) is located on either side of a tributary of the Guadiana River in an area of high agricultural productivity. It covers an area of c.80ha and is surrounded by a 1km-long ditch, as shown by aerial photography (Hurtado 1997), and seems to have been in use for over 500 years. An inner enclosure appears to contain most of the evidence for domestic structures, while tombs are located in the area between the inner and outer enclosure. It is proposed that the

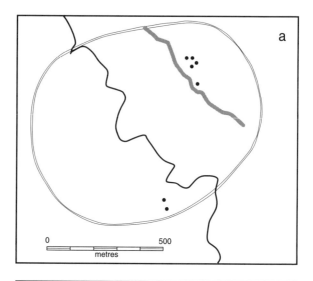

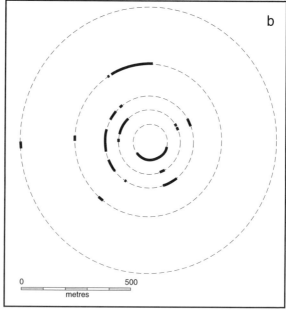

Figure 6.2 Copper Age monumental enclosures at (a) La Pijotilla (double lines show the inner and outer enclosures, black dots show the location of burials) (adapted from Hurtado 1997: figure 6.3) and (b) Marroquíes Bajos (continuous black lines show excavated parts of the enclosures (adapted from Zafra de la Torre *et al.* 1999: figure 3).

enclosure defines an area of cultivated land as well as domestic and ritual areas. At this, and other sites in the region, the high frequency of storage pits, including smaller ones within structures and clusters of larger examples in the open air, has suggested intensified and surplus production, perhaps under the control of particular groups (appropriated?) within the community (Hurtado 1997: 108).

Rescue excavations over the last three decades have revealed the existence of a comparable site at Valencina de la Concepción, just over 5km to the west of Seville in the lower Guadalquivir valley. It would appear that the site complex extends over an area of some 300ha, including a cemetery of megalithic tombs (among which are the famous tombs of Matarrubilla and La Pastora). A more restricted area of settlement (20ha?), mostly covered by the modern dormitory town of Valencina, has yielded evidence of circular domestic structures, wells and storage pits, as well as stretches of V- and U-shaped ditches 4m wide and up to 5m in depth (Ruíz Mata 1983). More recent excavations have confirmed the existence of clusters of storage pits (1.8–2.5m basal diameter by perhaps more than 2m in depth) in the area between the main settlement and the cemetery, and a ditch 7m wide and 4m deep marking the limit of this area. Cruz-Auñón and Arteaga (1995) suggest that this ditch joined up with traces of ditches from earlier excavations to form a large enclosure delimiting the settlement and storage pit areas and extended up to the cemetery. They argue that this supports the inference of one, rather than several, settlement complexes, and that its inhabitants appropriated agricultural production within the lower Guadalquivir valley. The absence of overall plans of the site, or of systematic excavations and extensive series of radiocarbon dates makes evaluation of this interpretation difficult at present.

Oliveira Jorge (2000: 75–6) cites further examples of monumental enclosures in the neighbouring Alentejo region of southern Portugal. The largest, at Perdigões, covers around 16ha, with various concentric ditches and earthworks, may also have walls and includes an area devoted to mortuary practices. It dates to the second half of the third millennium cal. BC. Another site at Monte da Ponte has six multi-phase concentric enclosures comprised of stone and mudbrick walls (one with bastions) and ditches (Kalb and Höck 1997).

But the most impressive of all such enclosures is in the upper Guadalquivir valley at Marroquíes Bajos (Figure 6.2), an area of urban development on the north side of the city of Jaén (Zafra de la Torre et al. 1999). During the period c.2450–2125 cal. BC a settlement complex consisting of at least five concentric enclosures and covering an area of 113ha succeeded earlier, less well-defined and perhaps seasonal, occupation phases. The enclosures consisted of V- and U-shaped ditches 1–1.5m deep and 4–22m wide, and stone and mudbrick walls. The inner enclosure was 100–140m wide and had at least two bastions and an internal palisade. The second enclosure was 280–300m wide and, like the other enclosures, had a ditch of varying dimensions. The third enclosure was 400–420m wide and had the widest stretches of ditch. The fourth enclosure was 660–720m wide and had a 2m-wide and 3m-high mudbrick and stone wall with semicircular bastions on its exterior. This wall was 2km long and incorporated 12,000cu m of mudbrick and stone. In one stretch there was a mudbrick wall on the interior of the ditch as well. This marked the exterior of the settlement area, some 34ha in all. Beyond this a 1,200m-wide enclosure ditch enclosed a further 79ha of cultivable land. In the following occupation phase, c.2125– 1975 cal. BC, this outer ditch may have been abandoned and after that the population appears to have dispersed.

Although dependent upon individual rescue excavations, this is a remarkable picture of rapid population aggregation and labour mobilization during the second half of the third millennium cal. BC. Inferences about productive activities and inequalities are still being developed. Within the main settlement area there are no clear architectural or functional differences between the enclosed areas. There are some examples of larger and better-made domestic structures that are still under study. Domestic complexes are argued to have been self-sufficient in the subsistence and other production needs of everyday life. In the later occupation phase low stone walls delimited these complexes, with streets between them. Some differences in the location of textile production and metallurgy have been identified.

There are three competing interpretations of the concentric ditches at all of these 'monumental enclosures': drainage, defence and agricultural intensification through irrigation. The ditches at sites like Marroquíes Bajos and Valencina de la Concepción appear to be far too large to be simply for drainage purposes, while the association with walls, bastions and palisades argues more for a defensive function. The presence of such features would also argue against, although not necessarily rule out, the irrigation argument. This is where the use of carbon isotope analyses on seeds could be decisive, as in the lowlands of the south-east (see Chapter 5). Cruz-Auñón and Arteaga (1995) and Nocete (2001) place the monumental enclosures within a regional context of 'initial class societies' (see Chapter 4) in the Guadalquivir valley during the third millennium cal. BC. For example, Valencina de la Concepción, La Pijotilla and Ferreira do Alentejo (a large, but not definitely enclosed settlement in southern Portugal) are interpreted as 'primate' centres dominating smaller unfortified and (often peripheral) fortified sites throughout the south-west of the Iberian Peninsula (Nocete 2001: 136–7). This area is viewed as on the periphery of the early state society of the upper Guadalquivir valley. For this region Nocete (1994) proposes a model of a small number of heavily fortified centres (e.g. Albalete, Alcores) located at the centre of a territory of agricultural production, with smaller defensive sites placed for their visual and physical control, especially on the southern and eastern (political) frontier.

Clearly some very provocative interpretations are being proposed for these monumental enclosures and their surrounding lands and settlements in southern Iberia. If we include these enclosures within the category of 'fortified sites', it is clear that one of the key traits used to identify the presence of 'complex' societies in Iberia is more widely distributed than those societies. It is also clear that we are dealing with a heterogeneous category of sites, the function(s) and importance of which need to be studied locally. Rather than pursue fruitless and undefined classifications of regions of Iberia as being 'complex' in some degree, it would be better to focus research on the study of production and inequality, and on the evidence for structural changes in the organization of prehistoric societies.

Following the example of south-east Spain in Chapter 5, we need to focus on evidence for class divisions (producers and non-producers), for the appropriation of surplus and the identification of property. A start has been made on this, but there are significant gaps in evidence and argument. For example, inferences are made of the appropriation of surplus production from a hinterland at Valencina de la Concepción, given the large numbers of storage pits found there (Cruz-Auñón and Arteaga 1995). But how are these pits distributed through time (given that there are examples of pits intercutting each other)? What would they represent in terms of annual cereal production and storage (for consumption or seed)? Did this exceed the needs of the population living at the site(s)? How did the agricultural productivity of contemporary sites in the lower Guadalquivir valley compare with that of the area immediately around Valencina? Was there unequal access to the means of production between domestic complexes? Can we identify producers and non-producers from skeletal evidence? How centralized were other forms of production? Some answers to the questions are already being published (e.g. Nocete 2001: 111–23 on social asymmetries in metal production and consumption, as well as the absence of local agricultural production at Cabezo Juré, and the evidence for the environmental effects of over 500 years of metallurgy along the Río Tinto in the third millennium cal. BC). Until we can document these local relations of production and consumption more reliably in the empirical record, it is premature to construct large-scale models of political systems within the Guadalquivir valley and south-western Iberia.

In some regions a start is being made to research on these questions. For southern and central Portugal, there is still only limited evidence for agricultural production based on large, systematic collections of animal and plant remains (Chapman 1990: 229). For the same region, Copper Age lithic production has been studied by Forenbaher (1998), who argues that craft specialization was limited to large bifacial points, while arrowheads were highly variable and the outcome of dispersed production. Amphibolite was used for the production of most groundstone tools and had advantages of hardness and easier working over other locally available lithologies (Lillios 1993, 1997). Its nearest sources were at a distance of c.150km to the east and south-east and it appears at Copper Age fortified sites in the Tagus estuary region as used and broken tools, as well as tools that were being produced locally. The high concentration of finds in this region argues against a 'down-the-line' model of distribution from the interior to the coast. Lillios proposes a model of two spheres of exchange, reciprocal and competitive, to account for this distribution and the use and deposition contexts of amphibolite tools. This implies that competitive feasting played a major role in the emergence of fortified sites such as Zambujal and Vila Nova de São Pedro. However, there are still huge gaps in our knowledge of all kinds of production at individual sites, as well as of the consumption of this production.

An important Bronze Age settlement with evidence for both production and consumption has been excavated at Peñalosa in the upper Guadalquivir valley. The excavators (Contreras 2000) argue that this evidence supports the inference of a strongly hierarchical, class society. This society was supported by tribute from other, agricultural villages and based on the control of local mineral sources and production. The evidence for metal production is distributed throughout the settlement, as is metal consumption in domestic and funerary contexts, but not all stages in the production process occur in all production areas and there does not appear to have been equal access to products (e.g. silver). The evidence in support of the receipt of agricultural produce from other settlements is not unambiguous: Peña Chocarro (1999: 135) argues that the case for local production is strengthened by soil potential and the presence of chaff remains and weed seeds. The inference of social classes is also problematical, given the poor state of preservation of burial remains and the small size of the available sample (twenty-four individuals from eighteen tombs). From this sample the excavators distinguish three classes, namely the 'nobility', 'warriors/peasants' and 'slaves', with members of the first and third categories being buried in the same areas of the settlement (Contreras 2000; Contreras et al. 1995). However, these social distinctions are not matched by clear distinctions in daily access to production and consumption. In addition to the metal-lurgical evidence, food storage and consumption was practised in nearly all structures. There is no evidence for asymmetries in access to grinding stones, as in the Vera basin (see Chapter 5). The major asymmetry is between the fortified area on the summit, where horse remains (from communal feasting?) were concentrated (cf. the con-temporary settlement of Cerro de la Encina in Granada, Aranda Jiménez 2001), and the rest of the settlement. Given these prob-lems, the available data from Peñalosa are being asked to support a heavy interpretative load.

For the Sierra de Huelva in south-west Spain, a programme of regional survey and excavation has focused on the successive Copper and Bronze Age occupations (García Sanjuán 1999). It is argued that population increase and nucleation occurred between these periods, as well as a major change in the distribution pattern between areas within the region. The choice of more easily defendable site loca-tions, with their potential for greater visual control of territory, was accompanied by investment in defensive walls at sites such as La Papúa and El Trastejón. Arable potential became less important in the choice of settlement location. At El Trastejón the clean wheat grains suggest that processed grain was introduced ready for con-sumption. This evidence, coupled with the poverty of cereal from pollen diagrams, suggests that cereal production could have been of small scale, or that communities were dependent on inter-regional exchange, or that there was some functional specialization between settlements. What is not yet clear is the extent to which relations of inequality structured this movement of agricultural produce, nor the extent to which its consumption was appropriated. Differences of wealth are visible in the burial evidence, but unlike south-east

Spain, these are less marked and the poor conditions of preservation prevent the same kinds of study of osteological materials. It is argued that differences of class do not appear until nearly a millennium later, with 'moderate' rather than 'complex' inequalities. However, the marked differences in the quality of the empirical record of the Sierra de Huelva compared to the south-east need to be taken into account in evaluating this interpretation.

Space does not allow me to go into greater detail, or to expand on the study of production and inequalities, as well as the quality of the empirical record for studying these topics, in other parts of the Iberian Peninsula. Until such studies are pursued in more depth, then comparisons with the sequence of south-east Spain, as presented in Chapter 5, can only be tentative. To compare such regions in terms of rankings or levels of complexity is also a rather meaningless pursuit, leading us away from the kinds of research we ought to be undertaking. How far is this preoccupation with 'complexity' also characteristic of other regions of the west Mediterranean? The next section will answer this question.

'Complexity' in the west Mediterranean?

As in Iberia, the term 'complexity' is widely used and little defined for Mesolithic, Neolithic and Bronze Age societies elsewhere in the west Mediterranean. Skeates (1999: 30) suggests that coastal hunter-gatherers in east-central Italy may have developed 'a degree of social complexity', although generally these societies were 'basically egalitarian'. For the later sixth to the first half of the fifth millennia cal. BC Tusa has recently inferred 'the existence of a fairly complex society' (1996: 54). No formal definition of what a 'fairly' complex society or even a 'complex' society is given, but the inference appears to have two bases. First, there is a widespread distribution of ditched enclosures in southern Italy and Sicily (here with the addition of stone walls), with comparable interpretations to those of sites such as Valencina de la Concepción in southern Spain, including water storage, drainage and defence. A recent example of such a settlement at Stretto-Partanna has evidence of a narrow 13m-deep ditch, one of a series, for which cult or water storage uses are the preferred interpretations. Second, the 'full' adoption of agriculture supposedly enabled surplus production, which, Tusa argues, supported the construction of ditched enclosures and exchange of materials such as obsidian. As in Iberia we are presented with the equation of 'enclosed' or 'fortified' sites with more 'complex' kinds of society.

No distinction appears to be made between the production and appropriation of surplus, between production and consumption, and hence of the existence, or not, of institutionalized social inequalities. The exchange of materials such as obsidian may have required surplus production, but not the appropriation of that surplus, in order to support the creation and maintenance of social relationships.

For the Bronze Age in the Mediterranean as a whole, Mathers and Stoddart (1994) refer to 'greater social complexity' and 'cycles of socio-political complexity', or periods of 'development' alternating with ones of 'decline'. Different regions of the Mediterranean from Iberia to the Levant show between one and five phases of such complexity (1994: 17). Such 'complexity' appears to be related to stratification rather than state formation (which the authors restrict to the east Mediterranean), and even here they argue that stratification is a 'misplaced' term, given that 'the elite did not retain the power to enforce unequal access to resources over long periods of time' (1994: 16). In contrast Mathers and Stoddart prefer the concept of 'fluid and competitive ranking rather than fixed hereditary succession to status' (1994:16). A neo-evolutionary basis to this thinking is visible in the definition of concepts, but even within this terminology there is nothing incompatible between the existence and periodicity of such 'stratification': the physical and ideological means of coercion necessary to support such societies may only have been weakly developed at this time, making them prone to collapse.

For the Bronze Age in central Italy, Barker and Stoddart (1994: 145) suggest some kind of inevitability in social change, with a 'slow momentum towards social complexity at the beginning of the second millennium' and then a rapid change to statehood with the Etruscans. Malone et al. (1994: 188) infer 'a modest degree of complexity' during the same period of time in southern Italy, Sicily and Malta, as if this were some kind of virtue by means of restraint! Again the term is not defined explicitly, although there are references to 'socio-political' and 'socio-economic complexity'. Before c.1300 BC the authors infer limited centralization and a society that was short of the chiefdom level, given the absence, among other things, of any solid evidence for redistribution (although see Cazzella and Moscoloni 1999: 207 for the inference of 'a certain complexity in social structure' on the basis of a 5m-thick stone wall surrounding the Early Bronze Age settlement at Coppa Nevigata in Apulia). Once again there is a strong neo-evolutionary basis to this argument. After c.1300 BC 'élites' are inferred from wealthy grave goods and there is evidence for more settlements (including defended ones), craft specialization, a possible increase in settlement hierarchy, but Malone *et al.* still regard this as 'no remarkably high level of complexity' (1994: 192). By the Late Bronze Age, they state that Sicily was only 'on the brink of quite complex, chiefly societies' (1994: 192). Whatever 'complexity' *is*, it is clearly conceived in relative terms or 'levels', as we have seen in Iberia.

But once again key questions are not being asked: What was the relationship between production and consumption, was surplus production being appropriated by non-producers, and when did classes emerge, for however short a period of time? If classes did not exist, how was production organized and what were the tensions existing in everyday social practices? Although Malone *et al.* state that there is 'no clear evidence of agricultural intensification during the course of the Bronze Age' (1994: 179), the growth of the nucleated, 'semi/proto urban' Middle Bronze Age coastal settlement of Thapsos on Sicily raises questions as to how its population was supported, the extent to which it comprised producers and non-producers and what the nature of the settlement's political relations were with its hinterland and comparable coastal settlements. In turn this is part of a broader series of questions affecting the nature of social change in the central Mediterranean regions of southern Italy, Sicily and Sardinia at the time of Mycenaean trading contacts.

Such questions can only be addressed by focusing research, as we have done in south-east Spain, on the ways in which production and the relations of production are organized in different periods. It is one thing to know that particular species of plants and animals were exploited, but another to infer how production was organized and who had access to, and control over, it. There is also a fundamental difference between inferences of 'intensification of production' and an understanding of its scale and extent (Chapman 1990: 148–9), its mobilization (by whom? for whom?) and its social/political/economic purpose. The failure to make clear this difference accounts for the poverty of systems models that take 'intensification of production' as one variable alongside 'social organization' or 'interaction'. Such variables are usually defined in relation to 'cultures', which in turn are equated with 'societies', and the collection of subsistence production evidence is still structured around these large-scale units in blocks of time.

Even then, the presence of modern, representative samples of animal bones and plant remains is still remarkably patchy in most areas of the west Mediterranean, especially on the islands. This is especially true of the second millennium cal. BC, more or less synonymous with the Bronze Age, and continues into the first millennium cal. BC. In the Balearic Islands, there are still only four published faunal reports from modern excavations: one of these is for the open-air settlement of Son Ferrandell Oleza, the exact dating of which is debated by the excavator (Waldren 2001) and Lull *et al.* (1999) between the late third and early second millennium BC, and three are for sites with stone monuments known as talayots at Son Ferrandell Oleza, Son Fornés and S'Illot (for discussion of all reports, see Chapman and Grant 1997). In Sardinia detailed evidence of subsistence practices associated with Nuragic monuments and settlements of the second and first millennia cal. BC has only recently started to be collected systematically from sites such as Toscono and Urpes on the Marghine plateau (Webster and Michels 1986). This is in contrast to the emphasis that has been placed on the collection of animal bone assemblages from the early phases of human colonization of both Sardinia and Corsica (e.g. Vigne 1988). On the island of Malta, any traces of domestic activity are rare for all periods of occupation from the sixth to the second millennia cal. BC, given the effects of thin soils, soil erosion and landscape remodelling in modern times. Recent fieldwork on Gozo has produced surface traces of settlements, as well as the excavation of two structures where occupation began in the late fourth millennium cal. BC (Malone *et al.* 1988), but the focus of research remains on ritual and the dead in the temples and rock-cut tombs of the Maltese islands, whether in terms of cult activity (e.g. Stoddart *et al.* 1993) or of the creation of identity (Robb 2001).

It is the emphasis on monumental architecture, changes in its form and dimensions through time, and its spatial patterning on Malta, Sardinia, Corsica, Mallorca and Menorca, that has provided the basis for interpretations of Bronze Age society on west Mediterranean islands. In the case of Sardinia, there are also differences of interpretation between foreign and indigenous archaeologists. Webster (1990, 1991a, 1991b, 1996) uses an essentially neo-evolutionary approach to trace the emergence of more complex types of society during the local Bronze Age. This relies on the use of terms such as 'petty chiefdoms' and ethnographic analogies drawn specifically from the African sub-continent, as well as a theoretical framework that makes insular social change an adaptive response to population density and environmental circumscription (1996: 108). The size and form of monumental architecture provides the basis of inferences on the existence of settlement hierarchy, which is taken to be a key indicator of social evolution. Let us follow through Webster's interpretation of the archaeological sequence and then consider the problems it raises.

Webster begins by looking back at social change on Sardinia in the fourth and third millennia cal. BC. During the Late Neolithic there is evidence for increasing settlement numbers and densities, mostly small and unenclosed villages, but with a suggestion of 'regional level ritual integration' (1996: 52) from the site of Monte d'Accodi, with its 10m-high truncated pyramid. Settlement nucleation and enclosure/fortification is seen in the succeeding Copper Age, indicating 'some level of socio-political hierarchisation, probably on a regional level' (1996: 60) and 'societies similar perhaps to those referred to as chiefdoms' (1996: 62). Webster notes that the production evidence does not support earlier interpretations of a stratified society at this time.

Webster divides the period c.2300–500 cal. BC into four cultural phases. Nuragic 1/Proto-Nuragic (c.2300–1800 cal. BC) sees the abandonment of all the enclosed/fortified sites, population dispersion in small settlements which were now moving away from the lowland plains, and the construction of 'proto' or 'corridor' nuraghi (the proposed antecedents of the stone towers, or 'nuraghi' of the following periods). For Webster this suggests 'a reduction in organizational scale and complexity from regional to local levels' (1990: 62): the absence of a settlement hierarchy supports the inference of some kind of 'non-hierarchical' or 'tribal' society 'towards the lower end of the continuum of so-called 'middle-range societies' (1996: 81). Some examples of mortuary practices support the inference of 'Big Men' (1996: 82). Nuragic II (1800–1300 cal. BC) sees the emergence of proper nuraghi. The clusters of these stone towers, along with the absence of any evidence for a settlement hierarchy, suggests the existence of 'more or less autonomous, territorially distinct, sub-regional level socio-political units on the order of localized descent groups or clans' (1996: 99). The following period, Nuragic III (c.1300-900 cal. BC), sees the construction of more complex nuraghi, with multiple towers and, in a smaller number of cases, the kinds of outer walls and towers that have provoked comparison with medieval European castles, as well as a substantial population increase. Webster uses the sizes and forms of nuraghi, as well as the existence of non-tower, open settlements, to infer a two-level hierarchy ('petty/simple' chiefdoms) over large areas of Sardinia, with a three-level hierarchy ('ranked/complex' chiefdoms dominating c.200sq km territories) in the south-west of the island

(Webster 1996: 130–3). Full social stratification, including social classes, emerged in Nuragic IV (c.900–500 cal. BC) in a context of intensified competition and warfare.

Webster's periodization and social interpretation, while well known in the Anglo-American world, are not necessarily accepted in Sardinian archaeology. For example, Perra (1997) divides the Bronze Age into Early, Middle and Late periods, with numbered subdivisions, following the central European model. He argues that nuraghi were initially constructed by 'chieftains', even by 'dominant classes who control production and redistribution of subsistence and luxury goods' (1997: 58). The collective rituals seen in contemporary tombs were an expression of ideological resistance to these dominant classes. Perra also proposes that complex nuraghi were originally more widespread and that their builders consolidated the centralized control over production, with a lower class offering tribute to this élite. This interpretation of more progressive social evolution, from tribal society in the Pre-Nuragic to chiefdoms in the Nuragic, contrasts with Webster's initial devolution and the lack of chiefdoms until the construction of complex nuraghi.

This use of Sardinian nuraghi to make inferences about settlement, and therefore social, hierarchies has been prevalent since the late nineteenth century (Webster 1996: 17). But the supposed evolution from 'simple' to 'complex' nuraghi, along with the division of the Nuragic into four periods, still requires testing by more extensive excavations and by independent dating. We have already seen the advantages of independent dating as a test of Bronze Age periods in south-east Spain (see Chapter 5). Elsewhere carbon-14 dating has been used to show that supposedly sequential megalithic tomb types, in this case the dolmens and passage graves of southern Scandinavia, were actually constructed and used at the same time (Persson and Sjogren 1995). Webster and others (e.g. Tykot 1994) acknowledge the poverty of reliable carbon-14 dating on nuraghi, as well as on other settlements and burials, and we should not assume that sites and materials are as exclusively associated with the four Nuragic periods. For example, Webster notes that burial and tomb types overlap between these periods (1996: 22), while Perra (1997: 54) argues that the most imposing nuraghi were not all constructed during the same period of time. Any such refinement of chronology, as in south-east Spain, will have implications for inferences about Bronze Age society and social change.

The question also arises as to how useful the concepts of tribal and chiefdom societies have been for the social interpretation of Bronze

Age Sardinia. Given all the criticisms of neo-evolutionary theory presented in Chapter 3, to claim tribal or chiefdom status for Nuragic society now seems, at best, to be using a very loose analogy. Decision-making hierarchies are not always expressed in settlement hierarchies and may occur in the context of dispersed settlement patterns (see Chapter 3). Economic centralization does not occur automatically with political centralization (see the examples from South-east Asia and Africa in the discussion of heterarchies in Chapter 4), and the degree of that centralization may vary. The extent of such hierarchies and centralization, as well as that of all inequalities, needs to be studied in each particular context. For these reasons, it seems to me that the use of terms like tribe and chiefdom (both petty/simple and complex) has limited rather than enhanced our understanding of social change in later prehistoric Sardinia.

Confusions also arise. In spite of their different interpretations, both Webster and Perra use concepts like tribe and chiefdom, albeit somewhat inconsistently: for example, Perra includes the class structure in his Nuragic chiefdoms, with centralized control over production and relations of tribute, and yet he does not discuss why this does not make the nuraghi builders members of a stratified society. How early did stratification really appear in Sardinia? While Webster focuses his attention upon the presence or absence of settlement hierarchies, it is surely the evidence of control over production and consumption, of producers and non-producers, and of the appropriation of surplus, which will determine the answer to this question.

Webster (1996) recognizes the poverty of reliable evidence on production and consumption in Nuragic societies and their immediate predecessors. Indeed, one of the main aims of his fieldwork on the Borore plateau has been the collection of precisely this kind of evidence (e.g. Michels and Webster 1987; Webster 1991a), in the context of inferences about the function of nuraghi. He infers tribute of food to élites in Nuragic III (from non-monumental sites? – see Perra 1997) from $c.1300$cal. BC, with larger corralling and storage facilities in complex nuraghi, but there was no evidence for centralized production of metallurgy. In Nuragic IV he refers to household specialists, with examples of metal production on most sites, although production and storage seems to have been greater on the larger, more complex nuraghi. The evidence for centralized production of metal objects is still not clear, but as was mentioned above, this is not incompatible with social stratification. Further work is clearly needed on the relation between all forms of production and consumption to see if the inference of stratification is justified, and at what date.

There are also important observations which are made without comment. For example, in the Nuragic II period, he notes (1996: 95) the find of 28 grinding stones and 122 pestles in the Nuraghe Trobas, but does not discuss the possible implications for the organization of agricultural production (see Chapter 5 on the Argaric settlements of south-east Spain). In the succeeding Nuragic III period he fails to find evidence for control over the means of production, but notes that the 'size and presumably socio-political ranking of individual settlements cannot be so clearly related to the agricultural quality of their immediate catchment area when measured in hectares' (1996: 150). The possibility that this could support the inference of large-scale tribute of agricultural produce is not discussed. This is an interesting observation, in the light of what has already been proposed for the organization of production in the Argaric Bronze Age of south-east Spain. Also of interest is Webster's point (1996: 83) that there is no clear evidence for plough-based agriculture until the Nuragic III period, which is long after the use of such capital investment could have played a major role in the development of major social inequalities on Sardinia. We have already seen in Chapter 5 how such capital investment models based on irrigation and polyculture lack empirical support in south-east Spain.

In addition to monuments and burials, evidence for cult activity and the representations of rock art have been used in recent studies of later prehistoric societies in the central Mediterranean, only this time emphasizing gender, ideology and human agency. Both Robb (e.g. 1999, 2001) and Skeates (1999) have rightly emphasized the different kinds and bases of inequalities that exist in non-stratified societies (see Chapter 4). Both focus on the roles of competitive alliances, exchange, feasting, rituals and access to the ancestors as means by which inequalities emerged in kin-based Neolithic societies in this region. Robb (1994) has traced gender ideologies from the Neolithic to the Iron Age in Italy. His social interpretation for the Middle/Late Neolithic and Copper Ages, broadly speaking the fourth and third millennia cal. BC, focuses on the absence of settlement hierarchies, marked wealth differences in burials, craft specialization, etc., to infer the existence of tribal societies (1999). He turns to Oceania to adopt the analogy of 'Great Men' societies in the Early and Middle Neolithic changing into 'Big Men' societies in the Late Neolithic/Copper Age. It is in the latter societies that we see an

THE USES AND ABUSES OF COMPLEXITY

emphasis on a male gender ideology (e.g. representations of male hunting, weapons deposited with males in burials). This appears to be a strange mixture of standard neo-evolutionism and more post-processual concerns with ideology and agency. While Robb denies the existence of 'a single evolutionary pathway' (1999: 114) and recognizes that Great and Big Men are known ethnographically from the same societies, he attributes them to successive periods of the Italian Neolithic and refers to more stratified societies as the result of 'escape trajectories out of tribes' (1999: 119). The extent to which the New Guinea societal types of Great and Big Men were the outcome of post-colonial processes is not discussed, nor the 'visibility' of such types in the archaeological record (see Chapter 5).

Skeates nails his theoretical colours much more explicitly to the postprocessual mast, especially in his approach to mortuary rituals (1995) and to the symbolic construction of gender differences in Neolithic society (1994). Most recently (2000) he has turned his attention to the ditched enclosures of the Tavoliere in Apulia, arguing against their individual construction as being the outcome of a coherent and intended plan. Instead their depositional fills suggest to Skeates that they were more in a perpetual state of becoming. Further than this, the very acts of excavation and deposition are seen as the products of human agency and integral to the creation, maintenance and transformation of social relations. Such actions are physical as well as symbolic.

The attempts of both Robb and Skeates to tackle matters of gender, ideology and ritual are commendable. They help us to push away at the frontiers of inference on Neolithic and Bronze Age societies in the central Mediterranean. But they are no substitute for a systematic study of production and productive relations in these societies. Without such a study, the ideological representations are hanging in mid-air, and we lack a clear understanding of the material basis of inequalities, whether institutionalized or not. This must now be seen as a major challenge for this, and other, areas of the west Mediterranean.

For example, Skeates (1995, 1999) uses the remains of mortuary rituals as one of the bases of his reconstruction of social relations in the Neolithic of east–central Italy. He follows the argument that such rituals idealize, rather than reflect, social relations. The poverty of palaeoenvironmental and palaeoeconomic evidence from this region means that other ways of 'seeing' those relations, especially as they are based in productive practices, are currently beyond the archaeologist. We have no way of comparing idealized and actual social relations. The existence of ideologies at this time is not in question, but their role in forming and transforming social relations remains an assumption based on partial preservation of archaeological evidence.

Similarly, the ritual activities associated with the Neolithic temples and rock-cut tombs of Malta have provided both the basic evidence and the dynamic for changing social relations. The inference of a centrally organized, chiefdom society (Renfrew 1973b), based on population pressure in an isolated, island environment, has been criticized in recent years. With the notable exception of excavation and fieldwork on Gozo (e.g. Stoddart *et al.* 1993), changes in theoretical approach have played a greater role than new archaeological evidence in this critique. The architecture, scale and accessibility of the temples, coupled with the materials found inside them, have led to inferences of élites, ritual specialists, shamen, priests and competing factions (e.g. Bonanno *et al.* 1990; Stoddart *et al.* 1993). It was the ritual activities that led to the emergence of these social inequalities, whether through intra-island competition (Bonanno *et al.* 1990) or the creation of common identity (Robb 2001). But we still do not know the extent to which there was equal or unequal access to the means of production, both before and during the temple-building period *c.*3600–2500cal. BC. Was production centralized? Were the élites/priests, etc. removed from basic production? Although such 'individual agents' have been the focus of recent interpretations (e.g. Robb 2001), their study is currently divorced from an understanding of their place in the productive relations of Neolithic Maltese society. As elsewhere, we lack a materialist understanding of society and social change on these islands.

Concluding observations

Conceptions of society and particularly of the emergence of stratification and the state that are used in the Mediterranean are firmly rooted in neo-evolutionary concepts. For many this is no problem whatsoever! There is an established body of research, stretching back to the 1970s (see Chapter 3), with clear indicators in the archaeological record and an unproblematic 'Great Divide' between the early states of the east Mediterranean and Near East on the one side, and the stratified societies that emerged in some regions of the central and west Mediterranean during the Bronze Age. Mathers and Stoddart (1994) emphasize this contrast, especially with regard to features such as writing, institutionalized bureaucracy, élite iconography, professional standing armies, etc. In the same volume Mathers (1994: 57) states that the east Mediterranean showed an 'accelerated cultural development many orders of magnitude beyond contemporary Bronze Age societies in the west'. As was argued in Chapter 4, such a view of the state looks down from the first 'civilizations', which show all of these characteristics. It makes the identification of the state unproblematic. We *know* where all the early states were! All that there is left to do is rank the rest of the societies into a scale of more or less 'complex' societies, as we have seen for Iberia and the west Mediterranean in this chapter. However, this ranking is inconsistent, mostly undefined and lacking clear statements of the material evidence that would enable us to recognize such societies at different points along the evolutionary scale of complexity. This has become a rather fruitless and ambiguous exercise in classification.

The approach taken to social inequality in south-east Spain, as shown in Chapter 5, challenges us to rethink our approach to the study of social change in the west Mediterranean. While recent approaches to issues of gender, ideology and cultural identity take us in interesting directions, they are not yet 'rooted' in the material factors that determine social life. There are still large gaps in our basic knowledge of production and consumption in everyday social practices in just about every area of the west Mediterranean. There are also implications for our study of social change in other areas of Europe and the Mediterranean, as I will argue in the next chapter.

7

COMPLEX ARCHAEOLOGIES
AND ARCHAEOLOGIES OF
COMPLEXITY

It is now time to draw together the arguments proposed in this book. What are the main points and where do we go from here? What have we learnt about archaeology, archaeologists and the archaeology of what are called complex societies? I will begin by summarizing the argument chapter by chapter. Then I will make some further comments about archaeological theory and practice, the early state, and the pervasive nature of evolutionary thought in everyday Western discourse.

The argument

In Chapter 1, I began in the world in which we live, a world in which neo-liberal economics and globalization have driven the more marked development of social and economic inequalities within and between the First and Third Worlds. Politics and economics now operate at the global scale. This situation is neither inevitable nor natural, but a product of the past, whether over the last three decades or the last two million years of human history. Without the past we cannot understand the present. Within the social and historical sciences, this past has been studied since the eighteenth century through the use of the concept of social evolution, of change from simple to complex, whether this is of technologies, economies, art, ritual practices or entire societies. Archaeology owed its emergence as a discipline to the need to trace this social evolution in the Western world. It was a product of social evolutionary thought and became an essential source of evidence for the evolution of human societies. While speculation about the past permeates Western society, it is archaeology that has the conceptual and practical means to propose and evaluate such ideas with empirical evidence, thereby creating our current knowledge and understanding of how we came to be what we are.

However, modern archaeology is by no means unified in its theory and practice, as I have discussed in Chapter 2. The often bewildered student is presented with an array of different archaeologies, whether schools or 'isms', within the Anglo-American world. For some these different archaeologies are mutually exclusive: I was told recently of a colleague in another British university who announced to students at his first lecture on archaeological theory that they had to decide immediately whether they were processual or postprocessual archaeologists! For others there are areas of overlap, interaction, compatibility and knowledge of the past shared between the different archaeologies. Whether successful or not, there are attempts to build theoretical bridges between these approaches. Individual archaeologists do not get enough credit, as individual agents, for their creative input into the creation of archaeological knowledge, rather than being the passive absorbers of a limited number of theories as members of a small number of schools.

These different archaeologies are also viewed in evolutionary terms, from the simple, traditional archaeology to the more complex and more recent processual and postprocessual archaeologies. At the simpler end of the scale are the archaeologies of the non-English-speaking and non-Anglo-American worlds. And yet these archaeologies have vibrant, independent traditions of thought and are not waiting passively to absorb, and be integrated into, the more complex archaeologies. In spite of the best efforts of organizations such as the Association of European Archaeologists and the World Archaeological Congress, there remain structures of inequality between the archaeologies inside and outside the English-speaking world. These inequalities include, for example, access to published sources and translation into English, as well as lack of citation: one recent textbook on archaeological theory includes only minimal mention of any sources and thought outside the English-speaking world, and even then focuses almost exclusively on the typology of archaeologies given above (Johnson 1999). The critical question here is: What can we, with our structure of archaeological endogamy, learn from our colleagues in non-English-speaking countries? Using the example of such colleagues in Spain, I stressed the need for a materialist rather than idealist archaeology, a clearer focus on the relationship between theory and practice, and a shift of attention to issues of class, surplus, property, exploitation, production and consumption when studying inequalities in past societies.

In Chapter 3, I returned to the Anglo-American world and presented the main theoretical approaches used by archaeologists to think about society and social change. Essentially these are various shades of neo-evolutionism, historical materialism and practice theory. To what extent are they mutually exclusive? Are they successive bodies of thought? How have they been used? None of them can be argued to be unified bodies of thought and all are ongoing traditions. Neo-evolutionary approaches range from trait list studies based on comparative ethnography to the search for levels of decision-making as seen in settlement hierarchies and vary in their emphasis on political strategies or management theory, conflict or consensus, and resistance or control in social change. In all cases a limited number of social types or forms are arranged in a sequence from simple to complex, with clear theoretical and archaeological criteria marking out the change from one type/form to another. Concepts of power and ideology have been absorbed from historical materialism, mainly from continental neo-Marxist anthropology rather than classical Marxism, and the sources of these approaches are sometimes overt and sometimes hidden. This permeation, or suffusion, of historical materialism can be argued to have diluted its theoretical essence, especially when it is absorbed into idealist arguments, or when the concept of class is applied to all societies rather than just stratified ones. Practice theory can also be seen as an ongoing tradition, this time from the late 1950s, with an impact on archaeology over two decades later and differences of opinion over the meaning of concepts such as agency and the extent to which individual action can directly determine history. Once again there are examples of direct applications of this approach to archaeological data, as well as adoption without citation or any resulting analysis.

The examples cited in Chapter 3 show how these theoretical approaches have permeated archaeology, with neo-evolutionism dominating the literature. While each of the approaches has its purists, other archaeologists try to build theoretical bridges between them, although not always in an overt way. It is also apparent that the different theoretical approaches to society and social change do not necessarily lead to the use of different analytical units in archaeological practice (a criticism made by some Spanish archaeologists). Indeed the practice of archaeology can be seen here to be much more diverse and complicated than is normally assumed.

In addition to these theoretical approaches, there is a whole terminology of the study of past societies that is often used ambiguously, inconsistently or without definition, as was demonstrated in

Chapter 4. The classification of societies into opposites, such as equal/unequal, simple/complex, or egalitarian/stratified, ignores the subtlety of real situations: for example, there are so-called 'egalitarian' societies with unequal social relations in some aspects of everyday life, 'stratified' societies with egalitarian social relations in some areas or groups, and there may be egalitarian ideologies concealing inequalities. Hunter-gatherer societies with chiefs and other features of non-egalitarian societies are well known in the North American ethnographic literature and have been claimed (not always convincingly) for archaeological contexts. Not all stratified societies are centrally organized with a single decision-making hierarchy, as required by the information-processing model of neo-evolutionism, and may be organized as heterarchies, with, for example, centralized political power and decentralized economic production.

One of the biggest problems concerns the definition of the state and its recognition in the archaeological record. The 'top down' view from the Near East and Mesoamerica, based on information-processing and decision-making hierarchies, imposes clear, unambiguous criteria, but there is also heterogeneity in chiefdom and state societies, different kinds of state are defined (with the early bureaucratic state being but one example), and there is a tradition of thought that sees stratification as the beginning of state formation. While the ethnographic record of the Pacific defines chiefdoms, the archaeological record of the so-called 'early civilizations' defines states. Regional records, such as that of the African sub-continent, are still fitted into these guiding models based on other regions. Historical materialism has an alternative view of the state, based on qualitative change to class society, with producers and non-producers, the exploitation of the former by the latter and the appropriation of surplus production by the non-producers. It is these structural relations that are the important criteria in state definition, not the material form (e.g. pyramids, palaces, ziggurats) taken by individual states. This view of the state stems from a different body of theory and from the non-English-speaking world.

In Chapter 5, I used a materialist approach to social change and tried to avoid social dichotomies in a case study on the Vera basin and south-east Spain from the fifth to the second millennia cal. BC. This was based on individual and collective research on the period between the adoption of agriculture and the emergence of social stratification. Neolithic societies were small-scale, mobile communities, with domestic production, social distinctions based on age, gender and group affiliation and no permanent inequalities based on the control of production. During the Copper Age there was greater sedentism, increased population, a smaller number of larger settlements and possibly household rather than lineage control over production (in contrast to the ideological investment in lineages seen in collective tombs). Contrary to some arguments, there were no major capital investments in production or major changes in the means of production. There is evidence for social tensions, conflict and warfare. Further structural changes took place in the Argaric Bronze Age. A major disjunction in settlement marked the emergence of a regional political system with increased production based on monoculture and control over the instruments of production and surplus production. Political factors are proposed for all of these changes (for example, there is no evidence that the disjunction in settlement was caused by environmental factors). Coupled with the burial evidence, it is proposed that Argaric society was characterized by marked inequalities in access to production, by a class system and by exploitation. The homogeneity seen in material culture and the treatment of the dead across the region is argued to represent the imposition of a common ideological system. There were major costs to this system in terms of labour (hence the need for an increase in basic production, i.e. population), environmental stability and possibly diet. Once again the new evidence does not support the existence of capital intensification at this time. From a historical materialist perspective, the period of the Argaric, especially c.1700–1550cal. BC, was one of an early state system.

The use of terminology was criticized further in Chapter 6, this time in relation to the concept of social complexity. In both Iberia and the rest of the west Mediterranean archaeologists propose that there are relative levels of such complexity, often without defining what they mean by this concept or how it can be studied with material evidence. The kinds of evidence used, such as fortifications, are present in areas of different levels of complexity. As such, this concept has no analytical use and does not enable any kind of comparative study across the west Mediterranean basin. Following the approach adopted for south-east Spain, I argued that any such study should begin with factors of production and consumption to determine the nature of inequality and the existence or not of social classes. In areas such as the Guadalquivir valley and south-west Spain, this approach is under way, although subject to criticism, but it is poorly developed in large areas of the west Mediterranean (e.g. the Balearic Islands, Sardinia, Malta). Production and consumption are currently receiving less attention than ideological and agency approaches in areas such as the central Mediterranean. The potential for a more materialist approach is stressed throughout the region.

These case studies complete the argument presented in this book. They also highlight three issues that deserve further comment, as we look forward to further research and debate. I begin with archaeological theory and practice.

A more complex archaeology?

When archaeologists in the 1960s and 1970s wanted to learn about the processes by which knowledge, in this case of the past, was created, they turned to the philosophy of science for guidance. They were looking for models taken from other disciplines. While the search for such guidance remains a useful exercise, critical observation of our own practice also has enormous capacity for instruction. In this book I argue that the ideology of successive, mutually exclusive paradigms, or types, of archaeology conceals a more complicated reality. The division into three archaeologies, namely traditional, processual and postprocessual, has been perpetuated as the only typology of theory and practice in our discipline. But critical study of the history of Anglo-American archaeology since the 1960s reveals a more complicated picture of permeable boundaries between these archaeologies, internal dissension and debate, attempts to build bridges between different theories, arguments about the compatibility of different approaches and recognition that there is more than one typology of archaeology and archaeologists. We tend to forget that these typologies are historically situated and defined, and that archaeological practice plays a large part in determining their success in building knowledge of the past. This practice is the action of individual archaeologists, and we would do well to study this practice in relation to individual aims. Which theories are used, what are the key concepts, how far do these theories and concepts determine the units of analysis, and to what extent is the archaeological practice distinctive from that pursued by individuals from different archaeologies? There is greater potential for an understanding of how archaeology 'works' in pursuing such questions than in a retreat to the tired, old, simplistic typologies that have characterized archaeological debate in the late twentieth century.

We should also recognize that the world of archaeology is now one of world archaeology. Claims for a postprocessual 'era' are strictly limited to areas of the Anglo-American world. Rather than thinking of these 'other' archaeologies as being less 'developed', or 'not up to our level' (the simple–complex dichotomy we have seen applied to social evolution), we would do well to be more critical of what amounts to intellectual globalization. Rather than imposing our debates and our theoretical approaches on 'other' archaeologies, we should be asking what we might learn from them, especially if it is we who are conducting our research in their countries. We would also do well to instil into our students both knowledge and critical respect for these 'other' archaeologies and bring them in from the margins of archaeological visibility. Let us have more balanced debates with them and publication opportunities for them, given that the political and economic contexts of many countries make support of these activities difficult for their archaeologists. This requires a shift to a world archaeology characterized in both theory and practice by greater intellectual exogamy and less endogamy. One theme worthy of wider debate concerns the state, its definition and its recognition in the archaeological record.

Early states

It is an interesting observation that while the social sciences cannot agree on the definition of the state, archaeologists in the Anglo-American world have no such problem. As I have discussed in Chapters 3 and 4, they focus on characteristics such as legitimized force, bureaucratic government and centralized decision-making, with the key archaeological indicator being the presence of three or more levels of a settlement hierarchy. And yet there has been a strand of thought since Fried (1967) that has worried about the boundary between the chiefdom and the state, between non-class and class society, or between stratified societies and the state, depending on the terminology that is used. The model of 'state as manager' has been criticized in the context of Mesopotamian archae-ology, where more emphasis is now being placed on inequality and exploitation, and on the relationship between production and con-sumption, a more 'bottom up' than 'top down' approach (Pollock 1992; Stein 1994). There is greater emphasis on social, economic and political heterogeneity than on centralization. Stein argues that such early states were 'organizations operating within a social environment that, for a variety of reasons, they only partially con-trol' (1994: 13) and that the degree of centralization depended on the outcome of a struggle between the centripetal and centrifugal forces operating in these societies (the former being, more or less, the élites and the latter the producers). Even though the population was centralized in city states such as Uruk and Warka (for reasons of labour control and defence against raiding), the sizeable rural population enjoyed considerable autonomy in everyday life (Stein 1994: 15).

This shift from the 'state as manager' model, from the 'successes' of organization and management to oppression, exploitation, coercion and resistance, has not, however, led to any fundamental critique of the definition of the state and the archaeological criteria used to identify past states. Such a critique has come from historical materialism, which focuses attention on the change in structure from relations of kinship to those of class and emphasizes the role of the state in preserving class society. Non-producing classes may appropriate the land, labour or products of others, as well as the means of production. This focus on structure is distinct from that on material form (e.g. settlement hierarchies, bureaucracies) and recognizes that the early state may have many different forms.

Within the Mediterranean basin and temperate Europe, the orthodox view of the development of early states favours societies and regions that have a similar material form to that of the Near Eastern bureaucratic states. Cretan palace society of the third millennium cal. BC is closest both geographically and formally, with its evidence for centralized control of production, administrative control, theocratic government and craftsmen, followed by second millennium BC Mycenaean society and then the Etruscan society from c.700 BC in central Italy. The last has examples of princely tombs, monumental sculpture, a three-level settlement hierarchy, competing cities inhabited by up to 35,000 people, temples, craft production and planned settlement (Barker and Rasmussen 1998). As with the contemporary Greek city states, it is argued that these city states emerged out of competing chiefdoms during a period of a few generations. Using these formal criteria, it is argued that the early European state was an east and central Mediterranean development, until the Roman city expanded into empire across both the Mediterranean and temperate Europe.

However, if we adopt the historical materialist approach, a rather different scenario can be presented. In Chapter 5 the case was proposed for an early state society in south-east Spain during the Argaric Bronze Age. Using the same historical materialist approach, González Marcén et al. (1992: 141–5) have argued that state organization emerged in the Carpathian/North Pontic region during the early second millennium cal. BC, centred on cultural groups such as the Otomani and Madarovce. They cite examples of population nucleation in heavily fortified settlements with evidence for differences in access to production. For example, at the Otomani settlement of Spissky Stvrtok in Slovakia there were marked spatial distinctions between the population engaged in agricultural labour outside the fortifications, the area of craft production inside the fortifications and the acropolis area with larger and better constructed houses and hoards of gold and bronze ornaments on stands or in stone containers buried under the houses. The investment of labour in metal objects throughout the Otomani and its contemporary groups included weapons such as swords, daggers and axes. Although there was no evidence for centralized accumulation and storage of food, nor of any major long-distance trade relations, as occurs in the Cretan palaces, the authors argue that the evidence supports the inference of a social class exercising control over both craft and agricultural production, as well as the centralized accumulation of metal goods, and that these fortified centres dominated a landscape of smaller, unfortified and undifferentiated agricultural settlements. According to this argument, we are seeing the emergence of small-scale, inherently unstable, state societies that lasted only a few hundred years (most of the fortified settlements were destroyed or abandoned by *c*.1600 cal. BC). These societies had a different material form to those of the early Near Eastern and east Mediterranean states, and indeed to the later Etruscan and Roman states.

Elsewhere Kristiansen (1991, 1998) has argued for a major disjunction between kin-based and class societies and merges together what others would call stratified societies and the more complex chiefdoms as 'archaic states', which may be centralized or decentralized. He makes a distinction between these archaic states and the kinds of bureaucratic state societies that are seen in the Near East, the east Mediterranean and the central Italy of Etruria and Rome. For Europe north of the Alps, Kristiansen proposes the existence of decentralized archaic states from the Late Hallstatt period (1998: 250) and looks to extend them back to the Later Bronze Age Urnfield societies (1998: 122).

Now one reaction to these proposals for early state societies in south-east Spain, the Carpathians/north Pontic region and central Europe is completely predictable: in no way are they comparable in scale with the world's earliest 'civilizations' in areas such as Mesoamerica and Mesopotamia, so they cannot be described as states. Such a dismissal would go hand in hand with criticism of any claim to statehood for the Olmec and Cahokia, as was discussed in Chapter 4. These are all at best just complex chiefdoms. I have two problems with this criticism. The first is that it still confuses a structural model of the state with the various material forms it might take. Even the early city states of Mesopotamia were not as centralized as we once thought and current thinning considers centralization to be a variable characteristic of state societies. The degrees of bureaucracy, population nucleation and coercion seen in these states were not known from all early state societies. Second, there is the very real danger that we are trying to 'fit' our archaeological research on past societies into existing evolutionary typologies, rather than find out how far past social forms were similar or different from those known in the ethnographic record. I have already noted the distinctive nature of contemporary and past African societies and how they do not fit neatly into typologies of chiefdoms and states derived from the Pacific, the Near East and Mesoamerica. If nothing else, the historical materialist approach directs our attention to the kinds of data on production and consumption that are needed to evaluate the extent of social inequalities in different regions of the world at different times. How those inequalities were materialized is a matter for research, not assumption. This is not a question of changing the definition of the state so that we can all have early states! Rather, the separation of structural change from material representation enables us to look for 'other' kinds of society in the past. It is the search for the 'other' that is one of archaeology's greatest challenges.

Embedded thought

Notions of social evolution, of simple and complex societies and of levels of social complexity have been present in the social sciences since the Enlightenment and they are used throughout the Anglo-American world. Their use is not restricted to so-called processual or neo-evolutionary archaeologists: for example, Hodder claims that the archaeological evidence from Çatalhöyük, the testing ground for a postprocessual methodology, supports the inference of an 'apparently low degree of social complexity' (1996b: 363). This raises the question as to how far such notions of social evolution are embedded in everyday thought and action in Western society. I have noted in first year essays how often students use value judgements such as 'more advanced', 'more sophisticated' and 'more civilized' to describe past societies and they always seem keen to point out evidence of 'progress' in these societies. They want the archaeological evidence to document human achievement and interestingly it is the world's first civilizations that show them the best evidence of this. These are the past societies that are more like 'us', with their cities, their bureaucracies, their religions, their writing and their hereditary rulers. In this context it is interesting to note that one of George W. Bush's first responses to the events of 11 September 2001 was to condemn them as a 'barbarous' attack on 'civilization'; then others in the American administration distinguished 'civilized' as opposed to 'barbaric' societies. The intellectual legacy of Lewis Henry Morgan is clearly alive, well and embedded in Western thought.

And yet such dichotomies as equal/unequal or egalitarian/ stratified societies are simplifications of reality. Value judgements of progress and advance are of no use in our study of the past and our attempts to understand ourselves through history. Civilization, at the apex of complex societies, is one of the worst used and most abused of these value judgements, especially when it is opposed to 'uncivilized' or 'barbarous' societies. Terms such as these are of no analytical value in historical study and they too often embody idealist approaches, in which values or states of mind such as 'civility' or urbanism shape human action and operate at the level of whole societies. This is akin to notions of the 'personality' of cultures, and yet in this case the values of civilization have somehow survived for over 5,000 years and unite the West against the rest of the world (even though some early centres of 'civilization' were clearly present in Latin America, the Near East and the Far East!). Within the Western world these values are most often expressed in art, architecture and culture, as well as the ideology of democracy. But as any social or economic analysis shows us, there are gross inequalities and examples of exploitation that are conveniently overlooked by the leaders of Western democracies. The ideology does not necessarily conform to material reality.

Archaeology has made a major contribution to our knowledge of the history of human species during the last two centuries. As I argued in Chapter 1, we can develop our understanding of this history, as well as of our current situation, by the study of topics such as inequality, exploitation and ethnicity. We can show that they are not part of some 'natural order', that they have not simply evolved in some preordained manner, and that thinking in terms of dichotomies such as equal/unequal, simple/complex and civilized/ uncivilized societies fails to do justice to the complexities of history, let alone the world order of the present day. However, it is also clear that we have much to do to change the embedded nature of Western thought on progress, social evolution, advancement and civilization. In facing up to this challenge, as well as to the issues of theory and practice that have been discussed in this book, the discipline of archaeology now has a full agenda for the twenty-first century.

BIBLIOGRAPHY

Abercrombie, N., Hill, S. and Turner, B. (1980) *The Dominant Ideology Thesis*, London: Allen & Unwin.

Abrams, P. (1988) 'Notes on the difficulty of studying the state', *Journal of Historical Sociology*, 1: 58–89.

Alcina Franch, J. (1989) *Arqueología Antropológica*, Madrid: Akal.

Aldenderfer, M. (1993) 'Ritual, hierarchy and change in foraging societies', *Journal of Anthropological Archaeology*, 12: 1–40.

Almagro, M. and Arribas, A. (1963) *El poblado y la necrópolis megalíticos de Los Millares (Santa Fe de Mondújar, Almería)*, Madrid: Bibliotheca Praehistorica Hispana 3.

Andah, B. W. (1995) 'European encumbrances to the development of relevant theory in African archaeology', in P. J. Ucko (ed.) *Theory in Archaeology: A World Perspective*, London: Routledge, 96–109.

Aranda Jiménez, G. (2001) *El análisis de la relación forma-contenido de los conjuntos cerámicos del yacimiento arqueológico del Cerro de la Encina (Granada, España)*, Oxford: British Archaeological Reports International Series 927.

Araus, J. L., Buxó, R., Febrero, A., Camalich, M. D., Martín, D., Molina, F., Rodriguez Ariza, Ma. O. and Voltas, J. (1997a) 'Identification of ancient irrigation practices based on the carbon isotope discrimination of plant seeds: a case study from the south-east Iberian peninsula', *Journal of Archaeological Science*, 24: 729–40.

Araus, J. L., Febrero, A., Buxó, R., Camalich, M. D., Martín, D., Molina, F., Rodríguez Ariza, Ma. O. and Romagosa, I. (1997b) 'Changes in carbon isotope discrimination in cereal plants from different regions of the western Mediterranean Basin during the past seven millennia: palaeoenvironmental evidence of a differential change in aridity', *Global Change Biology*, 3: 107–18.

Arnold, J. E. (1992) 'Complex hunter-gatherer-fishers of prehistoric California: chiefs, specialists and maritime adaptations of the Channel Islands', *American Antiquity*, 57: 60–84.

—— (1993) 'Labor and the rise of complex hunter-gatherers', *Journal of Anthropological Archaeology*, 12: 75–119.

—— (1995) 'Social inequality, marginalization and economic process', in T. D.

Price and G. M. Feinman (eds) *Foundations of Social Inequality*, New York: Plenum, 87–103.

——(1996a) 'Organisational transformations: power and labor among complex hunter-gatherers and other intermediate societies', in J. E. Arnold (ed.) *Emergent Complexity: The Evolution of Intermediate Societies*, Ann Arbor, Mich.: International Monographs in Prehistory, 59–73.

——(1996b) 'The archaeology of complex hunter-gatherers', *Journal of Archaeological Method and Theory*, 3: 77–126.

——(ed.) (1996c) *Emergent Complexity: The Evolution of Intermediate Societies*, Ann Arbor, Mich.: International Monographs in Prehistory.

Arribas, A., Molina, F., Saéz, L., de la Torre, F., Aguayo, P. and Nájera, T. (1979) 'Excavaciones en Los Millares (Santa Fe, Almería). Campañas de 1978 y 1979', *Cuadernos de Prehistoria de la Universidad de Granada*, 4: 61–110.

Arribas, A., Molina, F., Saéz, L., de la Torre, F., Aguayo, P. and Nájera, T. (1981) 'Excavaciones en Los Millares (Santa Fe de Mondújar, Almería): campaña de 1981', *Cuadernos de Prehistoria de la Universidad de Granada*, 6: 91–121.

Arribas, A., Molina, F., Carrión, F., Contreras, F., Martínez, G., Ramos, A., Saéz, L., de la Torre, F., Blanco, I. and Martínez, J. (1985) 'Informe preliminar de los resultados obtenidos durante la VI campaña de excavaciones en la poblado de Los Millares (Santa Fe de Mondújar, Almería) 1985', *Anuario Arqueológico de Andalucía 1985*: 245–62.

Arteaga, O. (1992) 'Tribalización, jerarquización y estado en el territorio de El Argar', *Spal*, 1: 179–208.

Audouze, F. (1999) 'New advances in French prehistory', *Antiquity*, 73: 167–75.

Barker, G. and Rasmussen, T. (1998) *The Etruscans*, Oxford: Blackwell Publishers.

Barker, G. and Stoddart, S. (1994) 'The Bronze Age of Central Italy: *c*.2000–900 BC', in C. Mathers and S. Stoddart (eds) *Development and Decline in the Mediterranean Bronze Age*, Sheffield: J. R. Collis Publications, 145–65.

Barrera Morate, J. L., Martínez Navarrete, Ma. I., San Nicolas, M. and Vicent, J. M. (1987) 'El instrumental lítico pulimentado calcolítico de la comarca noroeste de Murcia: algunas implicaciones socio-económicas del estudio de su petrología y morfología', *Trabajos de Prehistoria*, 44: 87–146.

Barrett, J. C. (1988) 'Fields of discourse: reconstituting a social archaeology', *Critique of Anthropology*, 7: 5–16.

Barth, F. (1966) *Models of Social Organisation*, London: Royal Anthropological Institute Occasional Papers 23.

Bate, L. F. (1977) *Arqueología y materialismo histórico*, Mexico: Ediciones de Cultura Popular.

——(1978) *Sociedad, formación económico-social y cultura*, Mexico: Ediciones de Cultura Popular.

——(1984) 'Hipótesis sobre la sociedad clasista inicial', *Boletín de Antropología Americana*, 9: 47–86.

——(1998) *El Proceso de Investigación en arqueología*, Barcelona: Crítica.

Bawden, G. (1989) 'The Andean state as a state of mind', *Journal of Anthropological Research*, 45: 327–32.

Bender, B. (1978) 'Gatherer-hunter to farmer: a social perspective', *World Archaeology*, 10: 204–22.

—— (1985) 'Prehistoric developments in the American midcontinent and in Brittany, northwest France', in T. D. Price and J. A. Brown (eds) *Prehistoric Hunter-Gatherers*, Orlando, Fla.: Academic Press, 21–57.

—— (1989) 'The roots of inequality', in D. Miller, M. Rowlands and C. Tilley (eds) *Domination and Resistance*, London: Allen & Unwin, 83–95.

—— (1990) 'The dynamics of nonhierarchical societies', in S. Upham (ed.) *The Evolution of Political Systems: Sociopolitics in Small-scale Sedentary Societies*, Cambridge: Cambridge University Press, 247–63.

Bentley, G. R. (1991) 'A bioarchaeological reconstruction of the social and kinship systems at Early Bronze Age Bab edh-Dhra', Jordan', in S. A. Gregg (ed.) *Between Bands and States*, Carbondale: Center for Archaeological Investigations, Southern Illinois University, 5–34.

Berlin, I. (1939) *Karl Marx: His Life and Environment*, Oxford: Oxford University Press.

Bernbeck, R. (1995) 'Lasting alliances and economic competition: economic developments in early Mesopotamia', *Journal of Anthropological Archaeology*, 14: 1–25.

Berreman, G. D. (1981) 'Social inequality: a cross-cultural analysis', in G. D. Berreman (ed.) Social *Inequality: Comparative and Developmental Approaches*, New York: Academic Press, 3–40.

Binford, L. R. (1968) 'Archeological perspectives', in L. R. Binford and S. R. Binford (eds) *New Perspectives in Archeology*, New York and Chicago: Aldine, 5–32.

—— (1972) *An Archaeological Perspective*, New York: Academic Press.

—— (1977) 'General Introduction', in L. R. Binford (ed.) *For Theory Building in Archaeology*, New York: Academic Press, 1–10.

—— (1981) 'Behavioral archaeology and the "Pompeii Premise"', *Journal of Anthropological Research*, 37(3): 195–208.

—— (1989) *Debating Archaeology*, New York: Academic Press.

Binford, L. R. and Binford, S. R. (eds) (1968) *New Perspectives in Archaeology*, Chicago: Aldine.

Blanton, R. E., Feinman, G. M., Kowalewski, S. A. and Peregrine, P. N. (1996) 'A dual-processual theory for the evolution of Mesoamerican civilization', *Current Anthropology*, 37: 1–14.

Blanton, R.E., Kowalewski, S. A., Feinman, G. and Appel, J. (1981) *Ancient Mesoamerica*, Cambridge: Cambridge University Press.

Bloch, M. (1985) *Marxism and Anthropology*, Oxford: Oxford University Press.

Boissevain, J. (1964) 'Factions, parties and politics in a Maltese village', *American Anthropologist*, 66: 1275–87.

Bonanno, A., Gouder, T., Malone, C. and Stoddart, S. (1990) 'Monuments in an island society: the Maltese context', *World Archaeology*, 22: 190–205.

Boone, J. L. and Alden Smith, E. (1998) 'Is it evolution yet? A critique of evolutionary archaeology', *Current Anthropology*, 39, *Supplement*: 141–73.

Bourdieu, P. (1977) *Outline of a Theory of Practice*, Cambridge: Cambridge University Press.

Braun, D. P. (1991) 'Are there cross-cultural regularities in tribal social practices?', in S. A. Gregg (ed.) *Between Bands and States*, Carbondale: Centre for Archaeological Investigations, Southern Illinois University, 423–44.

Braun, D. P. and Plog, S. (1982) 'Evolution of "tribal" social networks: theory and prehistoric North American evidence', *American Antiquity*, 47: 504–25.

Brumfiel, E. (1995) 'Heterarchy and the analysis of complex societies: comments', in R. M. Ehrenreich, C. L. Crumley and J. E. Levy (eds) *Heterarchy and the Analysis of Complex Societies*, Arlington, Va.: American Anthropological Association, Archaeological Papers no. 6, 125–31.

Buchli, V. (1995) 'Interpreting material culture: the trouble with text', in I. Hodder, M. Shanks, A. Alexandri, V. Buchli, J. Carmen, J. Last and G. Lucas (eds) *Interpreting Archaeology*, London: Routledge, 181–93.

Buikstra, J. and Hoshower, L. (unpublished) 'Análisis de los restos humanos de la necrópolis de Gatas'.

Buikstra, J. E., Castro, P. V., Chapman, R. W., González Marcén, P., Hoshower, L. M., Lull, V., Picazo, M., Risch, R. and Sanahuja, Ma. E. (1995) 'Approaches to class inequalities in the later prehistory of south-east Iberia: the Gatas project', in K. Lillios (ed.) *The Origins of Complex Societies in Late Prehistoric Iberia*, Ann Arbor, Mich.: International Monographs in Prehistory, 153–86.

Bunge, M. (1996) *Finding Philosophy in Social Science*, New Haven and London: Yale University Press.

Burrow, J. W. (1968) *Evolution and Society: A Study in Victorian Social Theory*, Cambridge: Cambridge University Press.

Buxó, R. (1997) *Arqueología de Las Plantas*, Barcelona: Crítica.

Byrd, B. and Monahan, C. M. (1995) 'Death, mortuary ritual and Natufian social structure', *Journal of Anthropological Archaeology*, 14: 251–87.

Callinicos, A. (1987) *Making History: Agency, Structure and Change in Social Theory*, Cambridge: Polity Press.

—— (2000) *Equality*, Cambridge: Polity Press.

Cámalich, M. D. and Martín Socas, D. (1999) *El territorio almeriense desde los inicios de la producción hasta fines de la antigüedad. Un modelo: la depresión de Vera y Cuenca del río Almanzora*, Seville: Junta de Andalucía.

Cámalich, M. D., Martín Socas, D., González Quintero, P. and Mederos, A. (1987) 'Prospección arqueológica superficial en la cuenca del bajo Almanzora (Almería): informe provisional', *Anuario Arqueológico de Andalucía 1986*: 54–61.

Cámalich, M. D., Martín Socas, D., González Quintero, P., Mederos, A. and Meneses, M. D. (1990) 'Prospección arqueológica superficial en la cuenca del bajo Almanzora (Almería): informe provisional de la campaña de 1987', *Anuario Arqueológico de Andalucía 1987*: 33–6.

Cara, L. and Rodríguez, J. M. (1986) 'Prospección arqueológica superficial del Valle Medio del Río Andarax (Almería)', *Anuario Arqueológico de Andalucía 1986*: 58–61.

Carmichael, P. H. (1995) 'Nasca burial patterns: social structure and mortuary ideology', in T. Dillehay (ed.) *Tombs For The Living: Andean Mortuary Practices*, Washington DC: Dumbarton Oaks Research Library and Collection, 161–87.

Carneiro, R. L. (1998) 'What happened at the flashpoint? Conjectures on chiefdom formation at the very moment of conception', in E. M. Redmond (ed.) *Chiefdoms and Chieftaincy in the Americas*, Gainesville: University Press of Florida, 18–42.

Carrilero, M. and Suárez, A. (1989–90) 'Ciavieja (El Ejido, Almería): resultados obtenidos en las campañas de 1985 y 1986. El poblado de la Edad del Cobre', *Cuadernos de Prehistoria de la Universidad de Granada*, 14–15: 109–36.

Carrión, F. and Gómez, M. T. (1983) 'Análisis petroarqueológico de los artefactos de piedra trabajada durante la prehistoria reciente en la provincia de Granada', *Cuadernos de Prehistoria de la Universidad de Granada*, 8: 447–77.

Carrión, F., Alonso, J. M., Rull, E., Castilla, J., Ceprián, B., Martínez, J. L., Haro, M. and Manzano, A. (1993) 'Los recursos abióticos y los sistemas de aprovisionamiento de rocas por las comunidades prehistóricas del S.E. de la península ibérica durante la prehistoria reciente', in *Investigaciones Arqueológicas en Andalucía 1985–92: Proyectos*: Huelva: Junta de Andalucía, 295–309,

Castro, P. V., Chapman, R. W., González Marcén, P., Lull, V., Micó, R., Picazo, M., Risch, R. and Sanahuja, Ma. E. (1991) 'Informe preliminar de la tercera campaña de excavaciones en el yacimiento de Gatas (Turre, Almería), Septiembre 1989', *Anuario Arqueológico de Andalucía 1989*: 219–26.

Castro, P. V., Chapman, R. W., González Marcén, P., Lull, V., Micó, R., Picazo, M., Risch, R. and Sanahuja, Ma. E. (1993) '4ª campaña de excavaciones en el yacimiento de Gatas (Turre, Almería). Septiembre 1991', *Anuario Arqueológico de Andalucía 1991*: 17–23.

Castro, P. V., Lull, V. and Micó, R. (1993) 'Arqueología: algo más que tafonomía', *Arqueología Espacial*, 16–17: 19–28.

Castro, P. V., Chapman, R. W., Gili, S., Lull, V., Micó, R., Rihuete, C., Risch, R. and Sanahuja, Ma. E. (1993–4) 'Tiempos sociales de los contextos funerarios argáricos', *Anales de Prehistoria de la Universidad de Murcia*, 9–10: 77–107.

Castro, P. V., Colomer, E., Courty, M. A., Federoff, N., Gili, S., González Marcén, P., Jones, M. K., Lull, V., McGlade, J., Micó, R., Montón, S., Rihuete, C., Risch, R., Ruiz Parra, M., Sanahuja Yll, Ma. E. and Tenas, M. (eds) (1994) *Temporalities and Desertification in the Vera Basin, South-east Spain*, Brussels: Archaeomedes Project vol. 2.

Castro, P. V., Chapman, R. W., Gili, S., Lull, V., Micó, R., Rihuete, C., Risch, R. and Sanahuja, Ma. E. (1996a) 'Teoría de las prácticas sociales', *Complutum, Extra 6, Vol II. Homenaje al Profesor Manuel Fernández-Miranda*, 35–48.

Castro, P. V., Lull, V. and Micó, R. (1996b) *Cronología de la prehistoria reciente de la península ibérica y Baleares (c.2800–900 cal a.n.e)*, Oxford: BAR International Series 652.

Castro, P. V., Gili, S., Lull, V., Micó, R., Rihuete, C., Risch, R. and Sanahuja Yll, Ma. E. (1998a) 'Teoría de la producción de la vida social: Mecanismos de explotación en el sudeste ibérico', *Boletín de Antropología Americana*, 33: 25-77.

Castro, P. V., Chapman, R. W., Gili, S., Lull, V., Micó, R., Rihuete, C., Risch, R. and Sanahuja, Ma. E. (1998b) *Aguas Project: Palaeoclimatic Reconstruction and the Dynamics of Human Settlement and Land Use in the Area of the Middle Aguas (Almería) in the South-east of the Iberian Peninsula*, Luxembourg: European Commission.

Castro, P. V., Chapman, R. W., Gili, S., Lull, V., Micó, R., Rihuete, C., Risch, R. and Sanahuja, Ma. E. (1999a) *Proyecto Gatas 2: la dinámica arqueoecológica de la ocupación prehistórica*, Seville: Junta de Andalucía.

Castro, P. V., Chapman, R. W., Gili, S., Lull, V., Micó, R., Rihuete, C., Risch, R. and Sanahuja, Ma. E. (1999b) 'Agricultural production and social change in the Bronze Age of south-east Spain: the Gatas Project', *Antiquity*, 73: 846–56.

Castro, P. V., Chapman, R. W., Gili, S., Lull, V., Micó, R., Rihuete, C., Risch, R. and Sanahuja, Ma. E. (2000) 'Archaeology and desertification in the Vera Basin (Almería, South-east Spain)', *European Journal of Archaeology*, 3(2): 147–66.

Castro, P. V., Chapman, R. W., Gili, S., Lull, V., Micó, R., Rihuete, C., Risch, R. and Sanahuja, Ma. E. (in press) '5ª campaña de excavaciones en el yacimiento de Gatas (Turre, Almería) 1995', *Anuario Arqueológico de Andalucía.*

Cazzella, A. and Moscoloni, M. (1999) 'The walled Bronze Age settlement of Coppa Nevigata, Manfredonia and the development of craft specialisation in south-eastern Italy', in R. H. Tykot, J. Morter and J. E. Robb (eds) *Social Dynamics of the Prehistoric Central Mediterranean*, London: Accordia Specialist Studies on the Mediterranean 3, 205–16.

Chapman, R. (1978) 'The evidence for prehistoric water control in south-east Spain', *Journal of Arid Environments*, 1: 261–74.

—— (1981) 'Archaeological theory and communal burial in prehistoric Europe', in I. Hodder, G. Isaac and N. Hammond (eds) *Pattern of the Past: Studies in Honour of David Clarke*, Cambridge: Cambridge University Press, 387–411.

—— (1982) 'Autonomy, ranking and resources in Iberian prehistory', in C. Renfrew and S. Shennan (eds) *Ranking, Resource and Exchange*, Cambridge: Cambridge University Press, 46–51.

—— (1990) *Emerging Complexity*, Cambridge: Cambridge University Press.

Chapman, R. and Grant, A. (1997) 'Prehistoric subsistence and monuments in Mallorca', in M. S. Balmuth, A. Gilman and L. Prados-Torreira (eds) *Encounters and Transformations: The Archaeology of Iberia in Transition*, Sheffield: Sheffield Academic Press, 69–87.

Chapman, R., Lull, V., Picazo, M. and Sanahuja, Ma. E. (eds) (1987) *Proyecto Gatas: sociedad y economía en el sudeste de España c.2500–800 a.n.e. 1. La prospección arqueoecológica*, Oxford: British Archaeological Report International Series 348.

Cherry, J. F. (1978) 'Generalization and the archaeology of the state', in M. Green, C. Haselgrove and M. Spriggs (eds) *Social Organisation and Settlement*, Oxford: British Archaeological Reports 47, 411–37.

Childe, V. G. (1936) *Man Makes Himself*, London: Watts.

—— (1942) *What Happened in History*, Harmondsworth: Penguin.

—— (1951) *Social Evolution*, London: Fontana.

Chowning, A. (1979) 'Leadership in Melanesia', *Journal of Pacific History*, 14: 66-84.

Claessen, H. J. M. and Skalnik, P. (eds) (1978) *The Early State*, The Hague: Mouton.

Clapham, A. J., Jones, M. K., Reed, J. and Tenas, M. (1999) 'Análisis carpológico del proyecto Gatas', in P. V. Castro, R. W. Chapman, S. Gili, V. Lull, R. Micó, C. Rihuete, R. Risch and Ma. E. Sanahuja, *Proyecto Gatas 2: la dinámica arqueoecológica de la ocupación prehistórica*, Seville: Junta de Andalucía, 311–19.

Clark, J. E. (1993) 'Una reevaluación de la entidad política olmeca: imperio, estado o cacicazgo', *Segundo y Tercer Foro de Arqueología de Chiapas*: 159–69, Chiapas: Instituto Chiapaneco de Cultura.

—— (1997) 'The arts of government in early Mesoamerica', *Annual Review of Anthropology*, 26: 211–34.

Clark, J. E. and Blake, M. (1994) 'The power of prestige: competitive generosity and the emergence of rank societies in lowland Mesoamerica', in E. M. Brumfiel and J.W.Fox (eds) *Factional Competition and Political Development in the New World*, Cambridge: Cambridge University Press, 17–30.

Clarke, D. L. (1968) *Analytical Archaeology*, London: Methuen.

—— (ed.) (1972) *Models in Archaeology*, London: Methuen.

—— (1973) 'Archaeology: the loss of innocence', *Antiquity*, 47: 6–18.

Clemente, I., Gibaja, J. F. and Vila, A. (1999) 'Análisis funcional de la industria lítica tallada procedente de los sondeos de Gatas', in P. V. Castro *et al.*, *Proyecto Gatas 2: la dinámica arqueoecológica de la ocupación prehistórica*, Seville: Junta de Andalucía, 341–47.

Cohen, A. P. (1974) *Two-Dimensional Man: An Essay on the Anthropology of Power and Symbolism in Complex Societies*, London: Routledge & Kegan Paul.

Contreras, F. (2000) *Proyecto Peñalosa: análisis histórico de las comunidades de la Edad del Bronce del piedemonte meridional de Sierra Morena y depresión Linares-Bailén*, Seville: Junta de Andalucía.

Contreras, F., Capel, J., Esquivel, J. A., Molina, F. and de la Torre, F. (1987–8) 'Las ajuares cerámicas de la necrópolis argárica de la Cuesta del Negro (Purullena, Granada): avance al estudio analítica y estadístico', *Cuadernos de Prehistoria de la Universidad de Granada*, 12–13: 135–55.

Contreras, F., Cámara, J. A., Lizcano, R., Pérez, C., Robledo, B. and Trancho, G. (1995) 'Enterramientos y diferenciación social 1: El registro funerario del yacimiento de la Edad del Bronce de Peñalosa (Baños de la Encina, Jaén)', *Trabajos de Prehistoria*, 52(1): 87–108.

Cordy, R. H. (1974) 'Complex rank cultural systems in the Hawaiian Islands: suggested explanations for their origins', *Archaeology and Physical Anthropology in Oceania*, 10: 89–109.

—— (1981) *A Study of Prehistoric Social Change: The Development of Complex Societies in the Hawaiian Islands*, New York: Academic Press.

Coudart, A. (1999) 'Is post-processualism bound to happen everywhere? The French case', *Antiquity*, 73: 161–7.

Courty, M. A. and Fedoroff, N. (1999) 'Análisis de micromorfología de suelos del yacimiento de Gatas (España): resultados preliminares', in P. V. Castro *et al.*, *Proyecto Gatas 2: la dinámica arqueoecológica de la ocupación prehistórica*, Seville: Junta de Andalucía, 291–6.

Creamer, W. and Haas, J. (1985) 'Tribe versus chiefdom in lower central America', *American Antiquity*, 50: 738–54.

Crumley, C. L. (1979) 'Three locational models: an epistemological assessment for anthropology and archaeology', in M. B. Schiffer (ed.) *Advances in Archaeological Method and Theory*, 2, New York: Academic Press, 141–73.

Cruz-Auñon, R. and Arteaga, O. (1995) 'Acerca de un campo de silos y un foso de cierre prehistóricos ubicados en "La Estacada Larga" (Valencina de la Concepción, Sevilla): excavación de urgencia de 1995', *Anuario Arqueológico de Andalucía 1995*: 600–7.

Delibes, G., Fernández-Miranda, M., Fernández-Posse, Ma. D. and Martín Morales, C. (1986) 'El poblado de Almizaraque', in *Homenaje a Luis Siret 1934–84*, Seville: Junta de Andalucía, 165–77.

Delibes, G., Fernández-Miranda, M., Fernández-Posse, Ma. D., Martín, C., Rovira, S. and Sanz, M. (1989) 'Almizaraque (Almería): minería y metalurgia calcolíticas en el sureste de la península ibérica', in *Minería y Metalurgia en las Antiguas Civilizaciones Mediterráneas y Europeas*, 1: 81–94.

Delibes, G., Herrán Martínez, J. I., Santiago Pardo, J. de and Val Recio, J. del (1995) 'Evidence for social complexity in the Copper Age of the Northern Meseta', in K. T. Lillios (ed.) *The Origins of Complex Societies in Late Prehistoric Iberia*, Ann Arbor, Mich.: International Monographs in Prehistory, 44–63.

Delibes, G., Díaz-Andreu, M., Fernández-Posse, Ma. D. Martín, C., Montero, I., Muñoz, I. and Ruiz, A. (1996) 'Poblamiento y desarrollo cultural en la cuenca de Vera durante la prehistoria reciente', in *Homenaje al Profesor Manuel Fernández-Miranda Vol. I. Complutum Extra*: 153–70.

DeMarrais, E., Castillo, L. J. and Earle, T. (1996) 'Ideology, materialization and power strategies', *Current Anthropology*, 37: 15–32.

Dever, L. (1998) 'Isotopic studies of secondary carbonates', in P. V. Castro *et al.*, *Aguas Project: Palaeoclimatic Reconstruction and the Dynamics of Human Settlement and Land-use in the Area of the Middle Aguas (Almería), in the south-east of the Iberian Peninsula*, Luxembourg: European Commission, 42–3.

Díaz-Andreu, M. (1993) 'Las sociedades complejas del Calcolítico y Edad del Bronce en la península ibérica', *I Congresso de Arqueologia Peninsular: Actas 1*: 245–63.

—— (1995) 'Complex societies in Copper and Bronze Age Iberia: a reappraisal', *Oxford Journal of Archaeology*, 14: 23–39.

Dobres, M-A. and Robb, J. E. (2000) *Agency in Archaeology*, London: Routledge.

Dolukhanov, P. M. (1995) 'Archaeology in Russia and its impact on archaeological theory', in P. J. Ucko (ed.) *Theory in Archaeology: A World Perspective*, London: Routledge, 327–42.

Donner, W. (1988) 'Context and community: equality and social change in a Polynesian outlier', in J. G. Flanagan and S. Rayner (eds) *Rules, Decisions and Inequality in Egalitarian Societies*, Aldershot: Avebury, 145–63.

Douglas, B. (1979) 'Rank, power and authority: a reassessment of traditional leadership in South Pacific societies', *Journal of Pacific History*, 14: 2–27.

Drennan, R. D. (1987) 'Regional demography in chiefdoms', in R. D. Drennan and C. Uribe (eds) *Chiefdoms in the Americas*, Lanham, Md: University Press of America, 307–23.

—— (1991) 'Pre-Hispanic chiefdom trajectories in Mesoamerica, Central America and northern South America', in T. Earle (ed.) *Chiefdoms: Power, Economy and Ideology*, Cambridge: Cambridge University Press, 263–87.

—— (1992) 'What is the archaeology of chiefdoms about?', in L. Embree (ed.) *Metaarchaeology*, Dordrecht: Kluwer Academic, 53–74.

Drennan, R. D. and Uribe, C. (eds) (1987) *Chiefdoms in the Americas*, Lanham, Md: University Press of America.

Driesch, A. von den (1972) *Osteoarchäologische Untersuchungen auf der Iberischen Halbinsel*, Munich: Studien über frühe Tierknochenfunde von der Iberischen Halbinsel 3.

Driesch, A. von den and Morales, A. (1977) 'Los restos animales del yacimiento de Terrera Ventura (Tabernas, Almería)', *Cuadernos de Prehistoria y Arqueología de la Universidad Autónoma de Madrid*, 4: 15–34.

Dunnell, R. C. (1980) 'Evolutionary theory and archaeology', *Advances in Archaeological Method and Theory*, 3: 35–99.

Earle, T. (1978) *Economic and Social Organization of a Complex Chiefdom: The Halelea District, Kaua'I, Hawaii*, Anthropological Papers of the Museum of Anthropology 63. Ann Arbor: University of Michigan.

—— (1987) 'Chiefdoms in archaeological and ethnohistorical perspective', *Annual Review of Anthropology*, 16: 279–308.

—— (1991a) 'Toward a behavioral archaeology', in R. W. Preucel (ed.) *Processual and Postprocessual Archaeologies: Multiple Ways of Knowing the Past*, Carbondale: Southern Illinois University, 83- 95.

—— (ed.) (1991b) *Chiefdoms: Power, Economy and Ideology*, Cambridge: Cambridge University Press.

—— (1991c) 'The evolution of chiefdoms', in T. Earle (ed.) *Chiefdoms: Power, Economy and Ideology*, Cambridge: Cambridge University Press, 1–15.

—— (1997) *How Chiefs Came to Power: The Political Economy in Prehistory*, Stanford: Stanford University Press.

Emerson, T. E. (1997) *Cahokia and the Archaeology of Power*, Tuscaloosa: University of Alabama Press.

Engels, F. (1972) *The Origins of the Family, Private Property and the State*, London: Lawrence & Wishart.

Estévez, J., Gasull, P., Lull, V., Sanahuja, Ma. E. and Vila, A. (1984) 'Arqueología como arqueología. Propuesta para una terminología operativa', in *Primeras Jornadas de Metodología de Investigación Prehistórica, Soria 1981*, Madrid: Ministerio de Cultura, 21–8.

Feinman, G. M. (1991) 'Demography, surplus and inequality: early political formations in highland Mesoamerica', in T. Earle (ed.) *Chiefdoms: Power, Economy and Ideology*, Cambridge: Cambridge University Press, 229–62.

—— (1998) 'Scale and social organization: perspectives on the Archaic State', in G. M. Feinman and J. Marcus (eds) *Archaic States*, Santa Fe, NM: School of American Research Press, 95–133.

Feinman, G. M. and Neitzel, J. (1984) 'Too many types: an overview of sedentary prestate societies in the Americas', *Advances in Archaeological Method and Theory*, 7: 39–102.

Fernández-Miranda, M., Fernández-Posse, Ma. D., Gilman, A. and Martín, C. (1993) 'El sustrato neolítico en la cuenca de Vera (Almería)', *Trabajos de Prehistoria*, 50: 57–85.

Flanagan, J. G. (1988) 'The cultural construction of equality in the New Guinea Highlands', in J. G. Flanagan and S. Rayner (eds) *Rules, Decisions and Inequality in Egalitarian Societies*, Aldershot: Avebury, 164–80.

—— (1989) 'Hierarchy in simple "egalitarian" societies', *Annual Review of Anthropology*, 18: 245–66.

Flanagan, J. G. and Rayner, S. (1988)' Introduction', in J. G. Flanagan and S. Rayner (eds) *Rules, Decisions and Inequality in Egalitarian Societies*, Aldershot: Avebury, 1–19

Flannery, K. V. (1972) 'The cultural evolution of civilisations', *Annual Review of Ecology and Systematics*, 3: 339–426.

—— (1973) 'Archaeology with a capital "S"', in C. L. Redman (ed.) *Research and Theory in Current Archaeology*, New York: John Wiley & Sons, 47–53.

—— (1999) 'The ground plans of archaic states', in G. M. Feinman and J. Marcus (eds) *Archaic States*, Santa Fe, NM: School of American Research Press, 15–57.

Flannery, K. V. and Marcus, J. (2000) 'Formative Mexican chiefdoms and the myth of the "Mother Culture"', *Journal of Anthropological Archaeology*, 19: 1–37.

Forenbaher, S. (1998) 'Production and exchange during the Portuguese Chalcolithic: the case of bifacial flaked stone industries', *Trabajos de Prehistoria*, 55(2): 1–17.

Fortes, M. and Evans-Pritchard, E. E. (eds) (1940) *African Political Systems*, London: Oxford University Press.

French, C., Passmore, D. and Schülte, L. (1998) 'Geomorphological, erosion and edaphic processes', In P. V. Castro *et al.*, *Aguas Project: Palaeoclimatic Reconstruction and the Dynamics of Human Settlement and Land-use in the Area of the Middle Aguas (Almería), in the south-east of the Iberian Peninsula*, Luxembourg: European Commission, 45–52.

Fried, M. H. (1967) *The Evolution of Political Society*, New York: Random House.

Friedman, J. (1975) 'Tribes, states and transformations', in M. Bloch (ed.) *Marxist Analyses and Social Anthropology*, London: Malaby Press, 161–202.

Friedman, J. and Rowlands, M. J. (1978) 'Notes towards an epigenetic model of the evolution of "civilisation"', in J. Friedman and M. J. Rowlands (eds) *The Evolution of Social Systems*, London: Duckworth, 201–76.

Funari, P. P. A. (1995) 'Mixed features of archaeological theory in Brazil', in P. J. Ucko (ed.) *Theory in Archaeology: A World Perspective*, London: Routledge, 236–50.

—— (1999) 'Brazilian archaeology: a reappraisal', in G. G. Politis and B. Alberti (eds) *Archaeology in Latin America*, London: Routledge, 17–37.

Gailey, C. W. (1987) *Kinship to Kingship: Gender Hierarchy and State Formation in the Tongan Islands*, Austin: University of Texas Press.

Gailey, C. W. and Patterson, T. C. (1987) 'Power relations and state formation', in T. C. Patterson and C. W. Gailey (eds) *Power Relations and State Formation*, Washington DC: American Anthropological Association, 1–26.

—— (1988) 'State formation and uneven development', in J. Gledhill, B. Bender and M. T. Larsen (eds) *State and Society: The Emergence and Development of Social Hierarchy and Political Centralisation*, London: Unwin & Hyman, 77–90.

Gall, P. L. and Saxe, A. A. (1977) 'The ecological evolution of culture: the state as

BIBLIOGRAPHY

predator in succession theory', in T. K. Earle and T. K. Ericson (eds) *Exchange Systems in Prehistory*, New York: Academic Press, 255–68.

Gándara, M. (1982) 'La "vieja" nueva arqueología', in *Teorías, métodos y técnicas en arqueología*, Mexico: Reimpresiones del Boletín de Antropología Americana, 59–159.

García Sanjuán, L. (1999) 'Expressions of inequality: settlement patterns, economy and social organization in the southwest Iberian Bronze Age (*c.*1700–1100 BC)', *Antiquity*, 73: 337–51.

Gasull, P., Lull, V. and Sanahuja, Ma. E. (1984) *Son Fornés 1: La fase Talayótica: ensayo de reconstrucción socio-económico de una comunidad prehistórica de la isla de Mallorca*, Oxford: British Archaeological Reports 209.

Gerlach, L. P. and Gerlach, U. M. (1988) 'Egalitarianism, collectivism and individualism: the Digo of Kenya', in J. G. Flanagan and S. Rayner (eds) *Rules, Decisions and Inequality in Egalitarian Societies*, Aldershot: Avebury, 113–44.

Gero, J. M. (2000) 'Troubled travels in agency and feminism', in M-A. Dobres and J. E. Robb (eds) *Agency in Archaeology*, London: Routledge, 34–9.

Giddens, A. (1979) *Central Problems in Social Theory*, London: Macmillan.

—— (1982) *Profiles and Critiques in Social Theory*, London; Macmillan.

Gilman, A. (1976) 'Bronze Age dynamics in south-east Spain', *Dialectical Anthropology*, 1: 307–19.

—— (1981) 'The development of social stratification in Bronze Age Europe', *Current Anthropology*, 22: 1–23.

—— (1987a) 'Regadío y conflicto en sociedades acefalas', *Boletín del Seminario de Estudios de Arte y Arqueología*, liii: 59–72.

—— (1987b) 'Unequal developments in Copper Age Iberia', in E. M. Brumfiel and T. K. Earle (eds) *Specialization, Exchange and Complex Societies*, Cambridge: Cambridge University Press, 22–9.

—— (1989) 'Marxism in American archaeology', in C. C. Lamberg-Karlovsky (ed.) *Archaeological Thought in America*, Cambridge: Cambridge University Press, 63–73.

—— (1991) 'Trajectories towards social complexity in the later prehistory of the Mediterranean', in T. Earle (ed.) *Chiefdoms: Power, Economy and Ideology*, Cambridge: Cambridge University Press, 146–68.

—— (1995) 'Prehistoric European chiefdoms: rethinking "Germanic" societies', in T. D. Price and G. M. Feinman (eds) *Foundations of Social Inequality*, New York: Plenum Press, 235–51.

—— (1997) 'Cómo valorar los sistemas de propiedad a partir de datos arqueológicos', *Trabajos de Prehistoria*, 54(2): 81–92.

—— (1998) 'The Communist manifesto, 150 years later', *Antiquity*, 72: 910–13.

Gilman, A. and Thornes, J. B. (1985) *Land-use and Prehistory in South-east Spain*, London: George Allen & Unwin.

Gledhill, J. (1988) 'Introduction: the comparative analysis of social and political transitions', in J. Gledhill, B. Bender and M. Trolle Larsen (eds) *State and Society: The Emergence and Development of Social Hierarchy and Political Centralisation*, London: Unwin Hyman, 1–29.

Godelier, M. (1982) 'Social hierarchies among the Baruya of New Guinea', in A. Strathern (ed.) *Inequality in New Guinea Highlands Societies*, Cambridge: Cambridge University Press, 3–34.

Goñi Quintero, A., Rodríguez, A., Camalich, Ma. D., Martín, D. and Francisco, Ma. I. (1999) 'La tecnología de los elementos de adorno personal en materias minerales durante el Neolítico Medio: El ejemplo del poblado de Cabecicos Negros (Almería)', *Saguntum Extra*, 2: 163–70.

González Marcén, P. and Risch, R. (1990) 'Archaeology and historical materialism: outsider's reflections on theoretical discussion in British archaeology', in F. Baker and J. Thomas (eds) *Writing the Past in the Present*, Lampeter: St David's University College, 94–104.

González Marcén, P., Lull, V. and Risch, R. (1992) *Arqueología de Europa, 2250–1200 AC: una introducción a la 'Edad del Bronce*, Madrid: Editorial Síntesis.

Goody, J. (1977) 'Population and polity in the Voltaic region', in J. Friedman and M. J. Rowlands (eds) *The Evolution of Social Systems*, London: Duckworth, 535–46.

Gosden, C. (1999) *Anthropology and Archaeology: A Changing Relationship*, London: Routledge.

Gossé, G. (1941) 'Aljoroque, estación neolítica inicial de la provincia de Almería', *Ampurias*, 3: 63–84.

Greenwood, D. (1988) 'Egalitarianism or solidarity in Basque industrial cooperatives: the FAGOR Group of Mondragón', in J. G. Flanagan and S. Rayner (eds) *Rules, Decisions and Inequality in Egalitarian Societies*, Aldershot: Avebury, 43–69.

Gregg, S. A. (ed.) (1991) *Between Bands and States*, Carbondale: Center for Archaeological Investigations, Southern Illinois University.

Grove, D. C. (1997) 'Olmec archaeology: a half century of research and its accomplishments', *Journal of World Prehistory*, 11: 51–101.

Guidi, A. (1988) 'The development of prehistoric archaeology in Italy: a short review', *Acta Archaeologica*, 58: 237–47.

—— (1996) 'Processual and postprocessual trends in Italian archaeology', in A. Bietti, A. Cazzella, I. Johnson and A. Voorips (eds) *Theoretical and Methodological Problems*, Forli: ABACO, 29–36.

Gusi, F. and Olaria, C. (1991) *El poblado neoeneolítico de Terrera Ventura (Tabernas, Almería)*, Madrid: Excavaciones Arqueológicas en España 160.

Haas, J., Pozorski, S. and Pozorski, T. (eds) (1987) *The Origins and Development of the Andean State*, Cambridge: Cambridge University Press.

Hall, R. L. (1991) 'Cahokia identity and interaction models of Cahokia Mississippian', in T. E. Emerson and R. B. Lewis (eds) *Cahokia and the Hinterlands: Middle Mississippian Cultures of the Midwest*, Urbana and Chicago: University of Illinois Press, 3–34.

Halstead, P. and O'Shea, J. (1982) '"A friend in need is a friend indeed": social storage and the origins of ranking', in C. Renfrew and S. Shennan (eds) *Ranking, Resource and Exchange*, Cambridge: Cambridge University Press, 92–9.

Harris, E. C. (1989) *Principles of Archaeological Stratigraphy*, London: Academic Press.

Harris, M. (1968) *The Rise of Anthropological Theory*, New York: Crowell.

Harrison, R. J. and Gilman, A. (1977)' Trade in the second and third millennia BC between the Maghreb and Iberia', in V. Markotic (ed.) *Ancient Europe and the Mediterranean*, Warminster: Aris and Phillips, 89–104.

Harrison, R. J. and Orozco-Köhler, T. (2001) 'Beyond characterisation: polished stone exchange in the Western Mediterranean 5500–2000 BC', *Oxford Journal of Archaeology*, 20(2): 107–27.

Harvey, D. (1989) *The Condition of Postmodernity: An Enquiry into the Origins of Cultural Change*, Oxford: Blackwell.

Hastorf, C. A. (1990) 'One path to the heights: negotiating political inequality in the Sausa of Peru', in S.Upham (ed.) *The Evolution of Political Systems: Sociopolitics in Small-scale Sedentary Societies*, Cambridge: Cambridge University Press, 146–76.

Hawkes, C. (1954) 'Archaeological theory and method', *American Anthropologist*, 56: 155–68.

Headland, T. N. and Reid, L. A. (1989) 'Hunter gatherers and their neighbours from prehistory to the present', *Current Anthropology*, 30: 43–66.

Helms, M. W. (1979) *Ancient Panama: Chiefs in Search of Power*, Austin: University of Texas Press.

Hernando, A. (1987) 'Evolución cultural differencial del calcolítico entre las zonas áridas y húmedas del sureste español', *Trabajos de Prehistoria*, 44: 171–200.

—— (1997) 'The funerary world and the dynamics of change in south-east Spain (fourth–second millennia BC)', in M. Díaz-Andreu and S. Keay (eds) *The Archaeology of Iberia: The Dynamics of Change*, London: Routledge, 85–97.

Hertz, N. (2001) *The Silent Takeover: Global Capitalism and the Death of Democracy*, London: William Heinemann.

Hodder, I. (1982a) *Symbols in Action*, Cambridge: Cambridge University Press.

—— (ed.) (1982b) *Symbolic and Structural Archaeology*, Cambridge: Cambridge University Press.

—— (1986) *Reading the Past*, Cambridge: Cambridge University Press.

—— (1988) 'Material culture texts and social change: a theoretical discussion and some archaeological examples', *Proceedings of the Prehistoric Society*, 54: 67–76.

—— (ed.) (1991a) *Archaeological Theory in Europe*, London: Routledge.

—— (1991b) 'Postprocessual archaeology and the current debate', in R. W. Preucel (ed.) *Processual and Postprocessual Archaeologies: Multiple Ways of Knowing the Past*, Carbondale: Southern Illinois University, 30–41.

—— (1996a) 'Comments on "Agency, Ideology and Power in Archaeological Theory"', *Current Anthropology*, 37: 57–9.

—— (ed.) (1996b) *On The Surface: Çatalhöyük 1993–95*, Cambridge: McDonald Institute for Archaeological Research.

—— (1997) '"Always momentary, fluid and flexible": towards a reflexive excavation methodology', *Antiquity*, 71: 691–700.

—— (1999) *The Archaeological Process*, Oxford: Blackwell.

—— (2000) 'Agency and individuals in long-term process', in M-A. Dobres and J. E. Robb (eds) *Agency in Archaeology*, London: Routledge, 21–33.

—— (2001) 'Introduction: a review of contemporary theoretical debates in archaeology', in I. Hodder (ed.) *Archaeological Theory Today*, Cambridge: Polity Press, 1–13.

Hoffmann, G. (1988) *Holozänstratigraphie und Küstenlinienverlagerung an der Andalusischen Mittelmeerküste*, Bremen: Universität Bremen.

Holtorf, C. and Karlsson, H. (2000) 'Changing configurations of archaeological theory: an introduction', in C. Holtorf and H. Karlsson (eds) *Philosophy and Archaeological Practice. Perspectives for the 21st Century*, Göteborg: Bricoleur Press, 1–11.

Hopf, M. (1991) 'Kulturpflanzenreste aus der Sammlung Siret in Brüssel', in H. Schubart and H. Ulreich, *Die Funde der südostspanischen Bronzezeit aus der Sammlung Siret*, Madrider Beitrage 17, Mainz: Philipp von Zabern, 397–431.

Hunt, R. C. and Gilman, A. (eds) (1998) *Property in Economic Context*, Lanham, Md: University Press of America.

Hurtado, V. (1997) 'The dynamics of the occupation of the middle basin of the river Guadiana between the fourth and second millennia BC', in M. Díaz-Andreu and S. Keay (eds) *The Archaeology of Iberia. The Dynamics of Change*, London: Routledge, 98–127.

Hutterer, K. L. (1991) 'Losing track of the tribes: evolutionary sequences in southeast Asia', in A. T. Rambo and K. Gillogly (eds) *Profiles in Cultural Evolution*, Ann Arbor, Mich.: Museum of Anthropology, 219–46.

Isbell, W. H. and Schreiber, K. J. (1978) 'Was Huari a state?', *American Antiquity*, 43: 372–89.

Jiménez Brobeil, S. A. and García Sánchez, M. (1989–90) 'Estudio de los restos humanos de la Edad del Bronce del Cerro de la Encina (Monachil, Granada)', *Cuadernos de Prehistoria de la Universidad de Granada*, 14–15: 157–80.

Johnson, G. A. (1978) 'Information sources and the development of decision-making organisations', in C. Redman *et al.* (eds) *Social Archaeology: Beyond Subsistence and Dating*, New York: Academic Press, 87–112.

—— (1982) 'Organizational structure and scalar stress', in C. Renfrew, M. J. Rowlands and B. A. Segraves (eds) *Theory and Explanation in Archaeology*, New York: Academic Press, 389–421.

Johnson, M. (1989) 'Conceptions of agency in archaeological interpretation', *Journal of Anthropological Archaeology*, 8: 189–211.

—— (1999) *Archaeological Theory: An Introduction*, Oxford: Blackwell.

Jones, S. (1981) 'Institutionalised inequalities in Nuristan', in G. D. Berreman (ed.) *Social Inequality: Comparative and Developmental Approaches*, New York: Academic Press, 151–62.

Jorge, V. and Oliveira Jorge, S. (1995) 'Theoretical underpinnings of Portuguese archaeology in the twentieth century', in P. J. Ucko (ed.) *Theory in Archaeology: A World Perspective*, London: Routledge, 251–62.

Kalb, P. and Höck, M. (1997) 'O povoado fortificado calcolítico do Monte da Ponte, Évora', *II Congresso de Arqueología Peninsular, vol. II*, Zamora: Fundación Rey Afonso Henriques, 417–23.

Kaplan, H. and Hill, K. (1985) 'Hunting ability and reproductive success among male Ache foragers: Preliminary results', *Current Anthropology*, 26(1): 131–3.

Keech McIntosh, S. (1999a) 'Pathways to complexity: an African perspective', in S. Keech McIntosh (ed.) *Beyond Chiefdoms: Pathways to Complexity in Africa*, Cambridge: Cambridge University Press, 1–30.

—— (ed.) (1999b) *Beyond Chiefdoms: Pathways to Complexity in Africa*, Cambridge: Cambridge University Press.

—— (1999c) 'Modeling political organization in large-scale settlement clusters: a case study from the Inland Niger Delta', in S. Keech McIntosh (ed.) *Beyond Chiefdoms: Pathways to Complexity in Africa*, Cambridge: Cambridge University Press, 66–79.

Keene, A. S. (1991) 'Cohesion and contradiction in the communal mode of production: the lessons of the kibbutz', in S. A. Gregg (ed.) *Between Bands and States*, Carbondale: Center for Archaeological Investigations, Southern Illinois University, 376–94.

Keesing, R. M. (1987) 'Ta'a geni: women's perspectives on Kwaio society', in M. Strathern (ed.) *Dealing with Inequality: Analysing Gender Relations in Melanesia and Beyond*, Cambridge: Cambridge University Press, 33–62.

Kehoe, A. B. (1998) *The Land of Prehistory: A Critical History of American Archaeology*, London: Routledge.

Kinehan, J. (1995) 'Theory, practice and criticism in the history of Namibian archaeology', in P. J. Ucko (ed.) *Theory in Archaeology: A World Perspective*, London: Routledge, 76–95.

Kirch, P. (1991) 'Chiefship and competitive involution: the Marquesas Islands of eastern Polynesia', in T. Earle (ed.) *Chiefdoms: Power, Economy and Ideology*, Cambridge: Cambridge University Press, 119–45.

Kirk, T. (1991) 'Structure, agency and power relations "chez les derniers chasseurs-cueilleurs" of northwestern France', in R. W. Preucel (ed.) *Processual and Postprocessual Archaeologies: Multiple Ways of Knowing the Past*, Carbondale: Southern Illinois University, 108–25.

—— (1993) 'Space, subjectivity, power and hegemony: megaliths and long mounds in earlier Neolithic Brittany', in C. Tilley (ed.) *Interpretative Archaeology*, Oxford: Berg, 181–223.

Klein, N. (2000) *No Logo*, London: Flamingo.

Klejn, L. S. (1977) 'A panorama of theoretical archaeology', *Current Anthropology*, 18: 1–42.

Kobylinski, Z. (1991) 'Theory in Polish archaeology 1960–90: searching for paradigms', in I. Hodder (ed.) *Archaeological Theory in Europe*, London: Routledge, 223–47.

Kohl, P. (1984) 'Force, history and the evolutionist paradigm', in M. Spriggs (ed.) *Marxist Perspectives in Archaeology*, Cambridge: Cambridge University Press, 127–34.

—— (1987) 'State formation: useful concept or idée fixe?', in T. C. Patterson and C. W. Gailey (eds) *Power Relations and State Formation*, Washington DC: American Anthropological Association, 27–34.

Kosse, K. (1990) 'Group size and societal complexity: thresholds in the long-term memory', *Journal of Anthropological Archaeology*, 9: 275–303.

Kotsakis, K. (1991) 'The powerful past: theoretical trends in Greek archaeology', in I. Hodder (ed.) *Archaeological Theory in Europe*, London: Routledge, 65–90.

Kristiansen, K. (1982) 'The formation of tribal systems in later European prehistory: Northern Europe, 4000–500 BC', in C. Renfrew, M. J. Rowlands and B. A. Segraves (eds) *Theory and Explanation in Archaeology*, New York: Academic Press, 241–80.

—— (1991) 'Chiefdoms, states and systems of social evolution', in T. Earle (ed.) *Chiefdoms: Power, Economy and Ideology*, Cambridge: Cambridge University Press, 16–43.

—— (1998) *Europe Before History*, Cambridge: Cambridge University Press.

Kuhn, T. S. (1962) *The Structure of Scientific Revolutions*, Chicago, Ill.: University of Chicago Press.

Kuijt, I. (1996) 'Negotiating equality through ritual: a consideration of late Natufian and prepottery Neolithic A period mortuary practices', *Journal of Anthropological Archaeology*, 15: 313–36.

Kunst, M. (1995) 'Central places and social complexity in the Iberian Copper Age', in K. T. Lillios (ed.) *The Origins of Complex Societies in Late Prehistoric Iberia*, Ann Arbor, Mich.: International Monographs in Prehistory, 32–43.

Kunter, M. (1990) *Menschliche Skelettreste aus Siedlungen del El Argar-Kultur: Ein Bietrag der Prähistorischen Anthropologie zur Kenntnis bronzezeitlicher Bevölkerungen Südostspaniens*, Madrider Beitrage 18, Mainz: Philipp von Zabern.

—— (2001) 'Los restos de esqueletos humanos hallados en Fuente Álamo durante las campañas de 1985, 1988 y 1991', in H. Schubart, V. Pingel and O. Arteaga, *Fuente Álamo: las excavaciones arqueológicas 1977–1991 en el poblado de la Edad del Bronce*, Seville: Junta de Andalucía, 265–82.

Last, J. (1995) 'The nature of history', in I. Hodder, M. Shanks, A. Alexandri, V. Buchli, J. Carmen, J. Last and G. Lucas (eds) *Interpreting Archaeology*, London: Routledge, 141–57.

Laudan, L. (1990) *Science and Relativism*, Chicago, Ill.: University of Chicago Press.

Leacock, E. (1983) 'Interpreting the origins of gender inequality: conceptual and historical problems', *Dialectical Anthropology*, 7: 263–83.

Lee, R. (1982) 'Politics, sexual and non-sexual, in an egalitarian society', in E. Leacock and R. Lee (eds) *Politics and History in Band Societies*, Cambridge: Cambridge University Press, Editions de la Maison des Sciences de l'Homme, 37–59.

—— (1990) 'Primitive communism and the origin of social inequality', in S. Upham (ed.) *The Evolution of Political Systems: Sociopolitics in Small-scale Sedentary Societies*, Cambridge: Cambridge University Press, 225–46.

Lee, R. B. and Devore, I. (1968) 'Problems in the study of hunters and gatherers', in R. B. Lee and I. Devore (eds) *Man The Hunter*, Chicago: Aldine, 3–12.

Leisner, G. and Leisner, V. (1943) *Die Megalithgräber der Iberischen Halbinsel: Der Süden*, Berlin: Walter de Gruyter.

Lemonnier, P. (1991) 'From great men to big men: peace, substitution and competition in the Highlands of New Guinea', In M. Godelier and M. Strathern (eds) *Big*

Men and Great Men. Personifications of Power in Melanesia, Cambridge: Cambridge University Press, 7–27.

Lenin, V. I. (1969) *The State and Revolution*, London: Central Books.

Leonard, R. D. and Jones, G. T. (1987) 'Elements of an inclusive evolutionary model for archaeology', *Journal of Anthropological Archaeology*, 6: 199–219.

Levy, J. E. (1995) 'Heterarchy in Bronze Age Denmark: settlement pattern, gender and ritual', in R. M. Ehrenreich, C. L. Crumley and J. E. Levy (eds) *Heterarchy and the Analysis of Complex Societies*, Archaeological Papers of the American Anthropological Association no. 6, 41–53.

Lewin, R. (1993) *Complexity: Life on the Edge of Chaos*, London: Phoenix.

Liep, J. (1991) 'Great Man, Big Man, Chief: a triangulation of the Massim', in M. Godelier and M. Strathern (eds) *Big Men and Great Men: Personifications of Power in Melanesia*, Cambridge: Cambridge University Press, 28–47.

Lightfoot, K. G. (1993) 'Long-term developments in complex hunter-gatherer societies: recent perspectives from the Pacific Coast of North America', *Journal of Archaeological Research*, 1: 167–201.

Lillios, K. (1993) 'Regional settlement abandonment at the end of the Copper Age in the lowlands of west-central Portugal', in C. Cameron and S. Tomka (eds) *Abandonment of Settlements and Regions: Ethnoarchaeological and Archaeological Approaches*, Cambridge: Cambridge University Press, 110–20.

—— (1997) 'Amphibolite tools of the Portuguese Copper Age (3000–2000 BC): a geoarchaeological approach to prehistoric economics and symbolism', *Geoarchaeology*, 12: 137–63.

López Mazz, J. M. (1999) 'Some aspects of the French influence upon Uruguayan and Brazilian archaeology', in G. G. Politis and B. Alberti (eds) *Archaeology in Latin America*, London: Routledge, 38–58.

Lull, V. (1983) *La 'cultura' de El Argar. Un modelo para el estudio de las formaciones económico-sociales prehistóricas*, Madrid: Akal.

—— (1984) 'A new assessment of Argaric society and economy', in W. H. Waldren, R. W. Chapman, J. Lewthwaite and R. C. Kennard (eds) *The Deya Conference of Prehistory*, Oxford: British Archaeological Reports International Series 229, 1197–238.

—— (1988) 'Hacia una teoría de la representación en arqueología', *Revista de Occidente*, 81: 62–76.

—— (1991) 'La prehistoria de la teoría arqueológica en el estado español', in A. Vila (ed.) *Arqueología*, Madrid: Consejo Superior de Investigaciones Científicas, 231–50.

—— (2000) 'Argaric society: death at home', *Antiquity*, 74: 581–90.

Lull, V. and Estévez, J. (1986) 'Propuesta metodológica para el estudio de las necrópolis argáricas', in *Homenaje a Luis Siret 1934–84*, Seville: Junta de Andalucía, 441–52.

Lull, V., Micó, R., Montón, S. and Picazo, M. (1990) 'La arqueología entre la insoportable levedad y la voluntad de poder' *Archivo de Prehistoria Levantina*, xx: 461–74.

Lull, V., Micó, R., Rihuete, C. and Risch, R. (1999) *La Cova des Cárritx y la Cova des*

Mussol. ideología y sociedad en la prehistoria de Menorca, Barcelona: Consell Insular de Menorca.

Lull, V. and Risch, R. (1996) 'El estado argárico', *Verdolay*, 7: 97–109.

Lumbreras, L. G. (1974) *La arqueología como ciencia social*, Lima: Histar.

—— (1994) 'Acerca de la aparición del estado', *Boletín de Antropología Americana*, 29: 5–33.

Maicas Ramos, R. (1999) 'La industria ósea neolítica del sureste: avance preliminar', *Saguntum Extra*, 2: 151–6.

Malone, C., Stoddart, S. and Trump, D. (1988) 'A house for the temple builders: recent investigations on Gozo, Malta', *Antiquity*, 62: 297–301.

Malone, C., Stoddart, S. and Whitehouse, R. (1994) 'The Bronze Age of southern Italy, Sicily and Malta *c*.2000–800 BC', in C. Mathers and S. Stoddart (eds) *Development and Decline in the Mediterranean Bronze Age*, Sheffield: J. R. Collis Publications, 167–94.

Marcus, J. and Feinman, G. M. (1999) 'Introduction', in G. M. Feinman and J. Marcus (eds) *Archaic States*, Santa Fe, NM: School of American Research Press, 3–13.

Mars, G. (1988) 'Hidden hierarchies in Israeli Kibbutzim', in J. G. Flanagan and S. Rayner (eds) *Rules, Decisions and Inequality in Egalitarian Societies*, Aldershot: Avebury, 98–112.

Martín Socas, D., Camalich, Ma. D., Tejedor, Ma. L., Rodríguez, A. and González, P. (1985) 'Composición mineralógica y evaluación de las temperaturas de cocción de la cerámica de Campos (Cuevas del Almanzora, Almería). Estudio preliminar', *Cuadernos de Prehistoria de la Universidad de Granada*, 10: 131–85.

Martín Socas, D., Camalich, Ma. D., Mederos, A., González Quintero, P., Díaz Cantón, A. and López Salmeron, J. (1992–3) 'Análisis de la problemática de los inicios de la prehistoria reciente en la cuenca baja del río Almanzora (Almería)', *Tabona*, viii: 493–506.

Martínez Navarrete, Ma.1. (1989) *Una revisión crítica de la prehistoria española: la Edad del Bronce como paradigma*, Madrid: Siglo Veintiuno Editores.

Martínez Santa Olalla, J. (1946) 'Cereales y plantas en al cultura ibero-sahariana en Almizaraque (Almería)', *Cuadernos de Historia Primitiva*, 1: 35–45.

Marx, K. (1973) *Grundrisse. Foundations of the Critique of Political Economy*, London: Penguin Books.

Marx, K. and Engels, F. (1970) *The German Ideology*, London: Lawrence & Wishart.

—— (1998) *The Communist Manifesto: A Modern Edition* (with an introduction by Eric Hobsbawn), London: Verso.

Maschner, H. D. G. (1991) 'The emergence of cultural complexity on the northern Northwest Coast', *Antiquity*, 65: 924–34.

Mathers, C. (1984a) 'Beyond the grave: the context and wider implications of mortuary practices in south-east Spain', in T. F. C. Blagg, R. F. J. Jones and S. J. Keay (eds) *Papers in Iberian Archaeology*, Oxford: BAR International Series 193, 13–46.

—— (1984b) '"Linear regression", inflation and prestige competition: second millennium transformations in south-east Spain', in W. H. Waldren, R. Chapman,

J. Lewthwaite and R. C. Kennard (eds) *The Deya Conference of Prehistory*, Oxford: British Archaeological Report International Series 229, 1167–96.

—— (1994) 'Goodbye to all that?: contrasting patterns of change in the south-east Iberian Bronze Age *c*.24/2200–600 BC', in C. Mathers and S. Stoddart (eds) *Development and Decline in the Mediterranean Bronze Age*, Sheffield: J. R. Collis Publications, 21–71.

Mathers, C. and Stoddart, S. (1994) 'Introduction', in C. Mathers and S. Stoddart (eds) *Development and Decline in the Mediterranean Bronze Age*, Sheffield: J. R. Collis Publications, 13–20.

Mays, S. (1988) 'Marxist perspectives on social organisation in the central European Early Bronze Age', in D. Miller, M. Rowlands and C. Tilley (eds) *Domination and Resistance*, London: Allen & Unwin, 215–26.

McGlade, J. and van der Leeuw, S. (eds) (1997) *Time, Process and Structured Transformation in Archaeology*, London: Routledge.

McGuire, R. H. (1983) 'Breaking down cultural complexity: inequality and heterogeneity', *Advances in Archaeological Method and Theory*, 6: 91–142.

—— (1992) *A Marxist Archaeology*, New York: Academic Press.

—— (1993) 'Archaeology and Marxism', *Archaeological Method and Theory*, 5: 110–57.

McGuire, R. H. and Saitta, D. J. (1996) 'Although they have petty captains, they obey them badly: the dialectics of prehispanic western pueblo social organisation', *American Antiquity*, 61: 197–216.

McLellan, D. (1973) *Karl Marx: His Life and Thought*, London: Macmillan.

—— (1975) *Marx*, London: Fontana.

Meskell, L. M. (1998) 'Oh my goddesses: archaeology, sexuality and ecofeminism', *Archaeological Dialogues*, 5 (2): 126–42.

—— (1999) *Archaeologies of Social Life*, London: Routledge.

Michels, J. and Webster, G. (eds) (1987) *Studies in Nuragic Archaeology: Village Excavations at Nuraghe Urpes and Nuraghe Toscano*, Oxford: British Archaeological Reports International Series 373.

Micó, R. (1990) 'La elaboración de modelos explicativos en arqueología. el ejemplo del Calcolítico del sudeste de la península ibérica', unpublished manuscript, Autonomous University of Barcelona.

—— (1991) 'Objeto y discurso arqueológico: el Calcolítico del sudeste peninsular', *Revista d'Arqueologia de Ponent*, 1: 51–70.

—— (1993) 'Pensamientos y prácticas en las arqueologías contemporáneas: normatividad y exclusión en los grupos arqueológicos del III y II milenios cal a.n.e en el sudeste de la península ibérica', unpublished PhD thesis, Autonomous University of Barcelona.

Miller, D. and Tilley, C. (eds) (1984) *Ideology, Power and Prehistory*, Cambridge: Cambridge University Press.

Milner, G. (1998) *The Cahokia Chiefdom: The Archaeology of a Mississippian Society*, Washington DC: Smithsonian Institution Press.

Minnegal, M. and Dwyer, P. P. (1998) 'Intensification and social complexity in the interior lowlands of Papua New Guinea: a comparison of Bedamuni and Kubo', *Journal of Anthropological Archaeology*, 17: 375–400.

Modjeska, N. (1982) 'Production and inequality: perspectives from central New Guinea', in A. Strathern (ed.) *Inequality in New Guinea Highlands Societies*, Cambridge: Cambridge University Press, 50–108.

Molina, F. (1983) *Prehistoria de Granada*, Granada: Editorial Don Quijote.

—— (1989) 'Proyecto Millares (los inicios de la metalurgia y el desarollo de las comunidades del sudeste de la península ibérica durante la Edad del Cobre)', *Anuario Arqueológico de Andalucía 1989*: 211–13.

Molina, F. and Arribas, A. (1993) 'Millares: Los Inicios de la metalurgia y el desarollo de las comunidades del sudeste de la península ibérica durante la Edad del Cobre', *Investigaciones Arqueológicas en Andalucía (1985–1992): Proyectos*, Huelva: Junta de Andalucía, 311–15.

Molina, F., Contreras, F., Ramos, A., Merida, V., Ortiz, F. and Ruiz, V. (1986) 'Programa de recuperación del registro arqueológico del Fortín de Los Millares: Análisis preliminar de la organización del espacio', *Arqueología Espacial* 8, 175–201. Teruel: Colegio Universitario de Teruel.

Monks, S. J. (1997) 'Conflict and competition in Spanish prehistory: the role of warfare in societal development from the late fourth to third millennium BC', *Journal of Mediterranean Archaeology*, 10: 3–32.

Montané, J. (1980) *Marxismo y Arqueología*, Mexico: Ediciones de Cultura Popular.

Montero, I. (1992) 'La actividad metalúrgica en la Edad del Bronce del sudeste de la península ibérica', *Trabajos de Prehistoria*, 49: 189–215.

—— (1993) 'Bronze Age metallurgy in south-east Spain', *Antiquity*, 67: 46–57.

—— (1994) *El origen de la metalurgia en el sudeste de la península ibérica*, Almería: Instituto de Estudios Almerienses.

—— (1999) 'Sureste', in G. Delibes and I. Montero (eds) *Las primeras etapas metalúrgicas en la península ibérica ii. estudios regionales*, Madrid: Instituto Universitario Ortega y Gasset, 333–57.

Montero, I. and Ruiz Taboada, A. (1996) 'Enterramiento colectivo y metalurgia en el yacimiento neolítico de Cerro Virtud (Cuevas de Almanzora, Almería)', *Trabajos de Prehistoria*, 53(2): 55–75.

Montero, I., Rihuete, C. and Ruiz Taboada, A. (1999) 'Precisiones sobre el enterramiento colectivo neolítico de Cerro Virtud (Cuevas de Almanzora, Almería)', *Trabajos de Prehistoria*, 56(1): 119–30.

Motos, F. de (1918) 'La edad neolítica en Vélez Blanco', *Comisión de Investigaciones Palaeontológicas y Prehistóricas, Memoria*, 19: 1–81.

Navarrete, Ma. S., Capel, J., Linares, J., Huertas, F. and Reyes, E. (1991) *Cerámicas neolíticas de la provincia de Granada: materias primas y técnicas de manufacturación*, Granada: Universidad de Granada.

Nelson, B. A. (1995) 'Complexity, hierarchy and scale: a controlled comparison between Chaco Canyon, New Mexico and La Quemada, Zacatecas', *American Antiquity*, 60: 597–618.

Nelson, S. M. (1998) 'Gender hierarchy and the queens of Silla', in K. Hays-Gilpin and D. S. Whitley (eds) *Reader in Gender Archaeology*, London: Routledge, 319–35.

Netting, R. McC. (1990) 'Population, permanent agriculture and polities: unpacking the evolutionary portmanteau', in S. Upham (ed.) *The Evolution of Political Systems: Sociopolitics in Small-scale Sedentary Societies*, Cambridge: Cambridge University Press, 21–61.

Nocete, F. (1994) 'Space as coercion: the transition to the state in the social formations of La Campiña, upper Guadalquivir valley, Spain *c.* 1900–1600 BC', *Journal of Anthropological Archaeology*, 13: 171–200.

—— (2001) *Tercer milenio antes de nuestra era: relaciones y contradicciones centro/periferia en el Valle del Guadalquivir*, Barcelona: Bellaterra.

Oberg, K. (1955) 'Types of social structure among the lowland tribes of South and Central America', *American Anthropologist*, 57: 472–87.

Oliveira Jorge, S. (1994) 'Colónias, fortificações, lugares monumentalizados: trajectória das concepções sobre um tema do Calcolítico peninsular', *Revista da Faculdade de Letras*, xi: 447–546.

—— (2000) 'Domesticating the land: the first agricultural communities in Portugal', *Journal of Iberian Archaeology*, 2: 43–98.

Oliveira Jorge, S. and Jorge, V. (1997) 'The Neolithic/Chalcolithic transition in Portugal: the dynamics of change in the third millennium BC', in M. Díaz-Andreu and S. Keay (eds) *The Archaeology of Iberia: The Dynamics of Change*, London: Routledge, 128–42.

Olivier, L. (1999) 'The origins of French archaeology', *Antiquity*, 73: 176–83.

Olivier, L. and Coudart, A. (1995) 'French tradition and the central place of history in the human sciences: preamble to a dialogue between Robinson Crusoe and his Man Friday', in P. J. Ucko (ed.) *Theory in Archaeology. A World Perspective*, London: Routledge, 363–81.

Olsen, B. J. (1991) 'Metropolises and satellites in archaeology: on power and asymmetry in global archaeological discourse', in R. W. Preucel (ed.) *Processual and Postprocessual Archaeologies: Multiple Ways of Knowing the Past*, Carbondale: Southern Illinois University, 211–24.

Orozco-Köhler, T. (2000) *Aprovisionamiento e intercambio: análisis petrológico del utillaje pulimentado en la prehistoria reciente del país valenciano (España)*, Oxford: British Archaeological Report International Series 867.

Ortner, S. B. (1984) 'Theory in anthropology since the sixties', *Comparative Studies in Society and History*, 26: 126–66.

Pascual-Benito, J. Ll. (1995.) 'Origen y significado del marfil durante el horizonte campaniforme y los inicios de la Edad del Bronce en el país valenciano', *Saguntum*, 29: 19–31.

Pätzold, J., Hagedorn, C. and Wefer, G. (1998) 'O18 and O16 isotopes in Glycimeris shells', In P. V. Castro *et al.*, *Aguas Project: Palaeoclimatic Reconstruction and the Dynamics of Human Settlement and Land-use in the Area of the Middle Aguas (Almería), in the South-east of the Iberian Peninsula*, Luxembourg: European Commission, 43.

Pauketat, T. R. (1998) 'Refiguring the archaeology of greater Cahokia', *Journal of Archaeological Research*, 6: 45–89.

—— (2000) 'The tragedy of the commoners', in M-A. Dobres and J. E. Robb (eds) *Agency in Archaeology*, London: Routledge, 113–29.

Pauketat, T. R. and Emerson, T. E. (eds) (1997) *Cahokia: Domination and Ideology in the Mississippian World*, Lincoln: University of Nebraska Press.

Pauketat, T. R. and Lopinot, N. H. (1997) 'Cahokian population dynamics', in T. R. Pauketat and T. E. Emerson (eds) *Cahokia: Domination and Ideology in the Mississippian World*, Lincoln: University of Nebraska Press, 103–23.

Paynter, R. (1989) 'The archaeology of equality and inequality', *Annual Review of Anthropology*, 18: 369–99.

Paynter, R. and McGuire, R. H. (1991) 'The archaeology of inequality: material culture, domination and resistance', in R. Paynter and R. H. McGuire (eds) *The Archaeology of Inequality*, Oxford: Blackwell, 1–27.

Peebles, C. S. and Kus, S. M. (1977) 'Some archaeological correlates of ranked societies', *American Antiquity*, 42: 421–48.

Peña-Chocarro, L. (1999) *Prehistoric Agriculture in Southern Spain during the Neolithic and the Bronze Age: The Application of Ethnographic Models*, Oxford: British Archaeological Reports International Series 818.

Peregrine, P. N. (2001) 'Matrilocality, corporate strategy and the organisation of production in the Chacoan world', *American Antiquity*, 66: 36–46.

Pérez Bareas, C. and Cámara, J. A. (1995) 'Intervención arqueológica en Marroquíes Bajos (Jaén): sector urbanistico RP-4, Parcela G-3', *Anuario Arqueológico de Andalucía 1995*: 256–70.

Perra, M. (1997) 'From deserted ruins: an interpretation of Nuragic Sardinia', *Europeae*, iii–2: 49–76.

Persson, P. and Sjogren, K.-G. (1995) 'Radiocarbon and the chronology of the Scandinavian megalithic graves', *Journal of European Archaeology*, 3: 59–88.

Peters, J. and Driesch, A. von den (1990) *Neolithische und Kupferzeitliche Tierknochenfunde aus Südspanien: Los Castillejos. Los Millares*, Munich: Studien über frühe Tierknochenfunde von der Iberischen Halbinsel 12.

Plog, S. (1995) 'Equality and hierarchy: holistic approaches to understanding social dynamics in the Pueblo Southwest', in T. D. Price and G. M. Feinman (eds) *Foundations of Social Inequality*, New York: Plenum Press, 189–206.

Plog, S. and Braun, D. P. (1984) 'Some issues in the archaeology of "tribal" social systems', *American Antiquity*, 49: 619–25.

Pluciennik, M. (1999) 'Archaeological narratives and other ways of telling', *Current Anthropology*, 40: 653–78.

Politis, G. (1995) 'The socio-politics of the development of archaeology in Hispanic South America', in P. J. Ucko (ed.) *Theory in Archaeology: A World Perspective*, London: Routledge, 197–235.

Pollock, S. (1992) 'Bureaucrats and managers, peasants and pastoralists, imperialists and traders: research on the Uruk and Jemdet Nasr periods in Mesopotamia', *Journal of World Prehistory*, 6: 297–336.

Possehl, G. L. (1999) 'Sociocultural complexity without the state', in G. M. Feinman and J. Marcus (eds) *Archaic States*, Santa Fe, NM: School of American Research Press, 261–309.

Potter, D. R. and King, E. M. (1995) 'A heterarchical approach to lowland Maya socioeconomics', in R. M. Ehrenreich, C. L. Crumley and J. E. Levy (eds) *Heterar-*

chy and the Analysis of Complex Societies, Archaeological Papers of the American Anthropological Association no. 6, 17–32.

Preucel, R. W. (1991a) 'Introduction', in R. W. Preucel (ed.) *Processual and Post-processual Archaeologies: Multiple Ways of Knowing the Past*, Carbondale: Southern Illinois University, 1–14.

—— (1991b) 'The philosophy of archaeology', in R. W. Preucel (ed.) *Processual and Postprocessual Archaeologies: Multiple Ways of Knowing the Past*, Carbondale: Southern Illinois University, 17–29.

—— (1995) 'The postprocessual condition', *Journal of Archaeological Research*, 3: 147–75.

Price, T. D. (1995) 'Social inequality at the origins of agriculture', in T. D. Price and G. M. Feinman (eds) *Foundations of Social Complexity*, New York: Plenum Press, 129–51.

Price, T. D. and Brown, J. A. (eds) (1985) *Prehistoric Hunter-Gatherers: The Emergence of Cultural Complexity*, New York: Academic Press.

Price, T. D. and Feinman, G. M. (eds) (1995) *Foundations of Social Complexity*, New York: Plenum Press.

Raab, L. M. and Goodyear, A. C. (1984) 'Middle-range theory in archaeology: a critical review of origins and applications', *American Antiquity*, 49: 255–68.

Ramos, A. (1981) 'Interpretaciones secuenciales y culturales de la Edad del Cobre en la zone meridional de la península ibérica: la alternativa de materialismo cultural', *Cuadernos de Prehistoria de la Universidad de Granada*, 6: 242–56.

—— (1998) 'La minería, la artesanía y el intercambio de sílex durante la Edad del Cobre en el sudeste de la península ibérica', in G. Delibes de Castro (ed.) *Minerales y metales en la prehistoria reciente. algunos testimonios de su explotación y laboreo en la península ibérica*, Valladolid: Universidad de Valladolid, 13–40.

—— (1999) 'Culturas neolíticas, sociedades tribales: economía política y proceso histórico en la península ibérica', *Saguntum Extra, 2*: 597–608.

Rayner, S. (1988) 'The rules that keep us equal: complexity and costs of egalitarian organization', in J. G. Flanagan and S. Rayner (eds) *Rules, Decisions and Inequality in Egalitarian Societies*, Aldershot: Avebury, 20–42.

Redmond, E. M. (ed.) (1998) *Chiefdoms and Chieftaincy in the Americas*, Gainesville: University Press of Florida.

Renfrew, C. (1967) 'Colonialism and megalithismus', *Antiquity*, 41: 276–88.

—— (1972) *The Emergence of Civilisation*, London: Methuen.

—— (1973a) 'Monuments, mobilisation and social organisation in Neolithic Wessex', in C. Renfrew (ed.) *The Explanation of Culture Change: Models in Prehistory*, London: Duckworth, 539–58.

—— (1973b) *Before Civilisation: The Radiocarbon Revolution and Prehistoric Europe*, London: Jonathan Cape.

—— (1974) 'Beyond a subsistence economy: the evolution of social organisation in prehistoric Europe', in C. B. Moore (ed.) *Reconstructing Complex Societies: An Archaeological Colloquium*, Supplement to the Bulletin of the American Schools of Oriental Research no. 20, 69–95.

—— (1975) 'Trade as action at a distance: questions of integration and communication', in J. A. Sabloff and C. C. Lamberg-Karlovsky (eds) *Ancient Civilization and Trade*, Albuquerque, NM: School of American Research Press, 3–59.

Reynolds, R. G. (1984) 'A computational model of hierarchical decision systems', *Journal of Anthropological Archaeology*, 3: 159–89.

Richards, C. (1995) 'Knowing about the past', in I. Hodder, M. Shanks, A. Alexandri, V. Buchli, J. Carmen, J. Last and G. Lucas (eds) *Interpreting Archaeology*, London: Routledge, 216–19.

Risch, R. (1995) 'Recursos naturales y sistemas de producción en el sudeste de la península ibérica entre 3000 y 1000 a.n.e', unpublished PhD thesis, Autonomous University of Barcelona.

—— (1998) 'Análisis paleoeconómico y medios de producción líticos: el caso de Fuente Álamo', in G. Delibes de Castro (ed.) *Minerales y metales en la prehistoria reciente. Algunos testimonios de su explotación y laboreo en la península ibérica*, Valladolid: Universidad de Valladolid, 105–54.

Risch, R. and Ruiz, M. (1994) 'Distribución y control territorial en el sudeste de la península ibérica durante el tercer y segundo milenios a.n.e.', *Verdolay*, 5: 77–87.

Robb, J. (1994) 'Gender contradictions, moral coalitions and inequality in prehistoric Italy', *Journal of European Archaeology*, 2(1): 20–49.

—— (1999) 'Great Persons and Big Men in the Italian Neolithic', in R. H. Tykot, J. Morter and J. E. Robb (eds) *Social Dynamics of the Prehistoric Central Mediterranean*, London: Accordia Specialist Studies on the Mediterranean 3, 111–21.

—— (2001) 'Island identities: ritual, travel and the creation of difference in Neolithic Malta', *European Journal of Archaeology*, 4(2): 175–202.

Rodríguez Ariza, Ma. O. (2000) 'El paisaje vegetal de la depresión de Vera durante la prehistoria reciente: una aproximación desde la antracología', *Trabajos de Prehistoria*, 57(1): 145–56.

Rodríguez Ariza, Ma. O. and Ruíz Sánchez, V. (1995) 'Antracología y palinología del yacimiento argárico de Castellón Alto (Galera, Granada)', *Anuario Arqueológico de Andalucía 1992*: 169–76.

Rodríguez Ariza, Ma. O. and Stevenson, A. C. (1998) 'Vegetation and its exploitation', in P. V. Castro, R. W. Chapman, S. Gili, V. Lull, R. Micó, C. Rihuete, R. Risch and Ma. E. Sanahuja, *Aguas Project: Palaeoclimatic Reconstruction and the Dynamics of Human Settlement and Land Use in the Area of the Middle Aguas (Almería) in the South-east of the Iberian Peninsula*, Luxembourg: European Commission, 62–8.

Rodríguez Ariza, Ma. O. and Vernet, J-L. (1991) 'Premiers résultats paléoécologiques de l'établissement chalcolithique de Los Millares (Santa Fe de Mondújar, Almería, Espagne) d'après l'analyse anthracologique de l'établissement', in W. Waldren, J-A. Ensenyat and R. C. Kennard (eds) *II Deya Conference of Prehistory*, Oxford: British Archaeological Reports International Series 573, 1–16.

Román Díaz, Ma. P. (1999) 'Primeras aldeas con almacenamiento en el sureste de la península ibérica', *Saguntum Extra*, 2: 199–206.

Román Díaz, Ma. P. and Martínez Padilla, C. (1998) 'Aproximación al estudio de las transformaciones históricas en las sociedades del VI al III milenio AC en el sureste peninsular', *Trabajos de Prehistoria*, 55(2): 35–54.

Roscoe, P. B. (1993) 'Practice and political centralisation', *Current Anthropology*, 34: 111–40.

Rovira, N. (2000) 'Semillas y frutos arqueológicos del yacimiento calcolítico de Las Pilas (Mojácar, Almería)', *Complutum*, 11: 191–208.

Rowlands, M. J. (1988) 'A question of complexity', in D. Miller, M. Rowlands and C. Tilley (eds) *Domination and Resistance*, London: Allen & Unwin, 29–40.

Ruiz, A., Chapa, T. and Ruiz, G. (1988) 'La arqueología contextual: una revisión crítica', *Trabajos de Prehistoria*, 45: 11–17.

Ruiz, A., Molinos, M. and Hornos, F. (1986) *Arqueología en Jaén*, Jaén: Diputación Provincial de Jaén.

Ruiz, A. and Nocete, F. (1990) 'The dialectic of the past and the present in the construction of a scientific archaeology', in F. Baker and J. Thomas (eds) *Writing the Past in the Present*, Lampeter: St David's University College, 105–11.

Ruiz Gálvez, M., Leira, R. and Berzosa, L. (1987) 'Primera campaña de excavaciones sistemáticas en el yacimiento de Lugarico Viejo (Antas, Almería)', *Anuario Arqueológico de Andalucía 1987*: 232–42.

Ruiz Mata, D. (1983) 'El yacimiento de la Edad del Bronce de Valencina de la Concepción (Sevilla) en el marco cultural del bajo Guadalquivir', *Actas del I Congreso de Historia de Andalucía: Prehistoria y Arqueología*, 183–208. Córdoba: Publicaciones del Monte de Piedad y Caja de Ahorros de Córdoba.

Ruiz Taboada, A. and Montero Ruiz, I. (1999a) 'Ocupaciones neolíticas en Cerro Virtud: estratigrafía y dataciones', *Saguntum Extra*, 2: 207–11.

—— (1999b) 'The oldest metallurgy in western Europe', *Antiquity*, 73: 897–903.

Sahlins, M. (1958) *Social Stratification in Polynesia*, Seattle: University of Washington Press.

—— (1968) *Tribesmen*, Englewood Cliffs, NJ: Prentice-Hall.

—— (1972) *Stone Age Economics*, London: Tavistock Publications.

Sahlins, M. and Service, E. R. (eds) (1960) *Evolution and Culture*, Ann Arbor: University of Michigan Press.

Saitta, D. J. (1988) 'Marxism, prehistory and primitive communism', *Rethinking Marxism*, 1: 145–68.

—— (1992) 'Radical archaeology and middle-range methodology', *Antiquity*, 66: 886–97.

Saitta, D. J. and Keene, A. S. (1990) 'Politics and surplus flow in prehistoric communal societies', in S. Upham (ed.) *The Evolution of Political Systems: Sociopolitics in Small-scale Sedentary Societies*, Cambridge: Cambridge University Press, 203–24.

Salzman, P. C. (1999) 'Is inequality universal?', *Current Anthropology*, 40: 31–61.

Sánchez Romero, M. (2000) *Espacios de producción y uso de los útiles de piedra tallada del Neolítico: el poblado de 'Los Castillejos de las Peñas de Los Gitanos' (Granada, España)*, Oxford: British Archaeological Reports International Series 874.

Savory, H. N. (1968) *Spain and Portugal*, London: Thames & Hudson.

Saxe, A. A. (1970.) 'Social dimensions of mortuary practices', unpublished PhD thesis, University of Michigan.

Scarre, C. (1999) 'Archaeological theory in France and Britain', *Antiquity*, 73: 155–61.

Schmidt, P. (1983) 'An alternative to the strictly materialist perspective: a review of historical archaeology, ethnoarchaeology and symbolic approaches in African archaeology', *American Antiquity*, 48: 62–79.

Schrire, C. (ed.) (1984) *Past and Present in Hunter-Gatherer Studies*, London: Academic Press.

Schubart, H. (1993) 'El Argar: Vorbericht über probegrabung 1991', *Madrider Mitteilungen*, 34: 13–21.

Schubart, H. and Arteaga, O. (1978) 'Fuente Álamo: Vorbericht über die Grabung 1977 in der bronzezeitlichen Höhensiedlung', *Madrider Mitteilungen*, 19: 23–51.

——(1980) 'Fuente Álamo: Vorbericht über die Grabung 1979 in der bronzezeitlichen Höhensiedlung', *Madrider Mitteilungen*, 21: 45–61.

——(1986) 'Fundamentos arqueológicos para el estudio socio-económico y cultural del area de El Argar', in *Homenaje a Luis Siret 1934–84*, Seville: Junta de Andalucía, 298–307.

Schubart, H. and Pingel, V. (1995) 'Fuente Álamo: eine bronzezeitliche Höhensiedlung in Andalusien', *Madrider Mitteilungen*, 36: 150–65.

Schubart, H., Pingel, V. and Arteaga, O. (2001) *Fuente Álamo: las excavaciones arqueológicas 1977–1991 en el poblado de la Edad del Bronce*, Seville: Junta de Andalucía.

Schüle. W. (1980) *Orce und Galera: Zwei Siedlungen aus dem 3 bis 1 Jahrtausend v. chr. im Südosten der Iberischen Halbinsel I*, Mainz am Rhein: Philipp von Zabern.

Service, E. R. (1962) *Primitive Social Organisation: An Evolutionary Perspective*, New York: Random House.

——(1967) 'Our contemporary ancestors: extant stages and extinct ages', in M. Fried, M. Harris and R. Murphy (eds) *War: The Anthropology of Armed Conflict and Aggression*, Chicago, Ill.: American Museum of Natural History, 160–7.

——(1975) *Origins of the State and Civilisation: The Process of Cultural Evolution*, New York: Norton.

Shanks, M. and Tilley, C. (1987a) *Social Theory and Archaeology*, Cambridge: Polity Press.

——(1987b) *Reconstructing Archaeology*, Cambridge: Cambridge University Press.

Shennan, S. (1989) 'Cultural transmission and cultural change', in S. E. van der Leeuw and R. Torrence (eds) *What's New? A Closer Look at the Process of Innovation*, London: Unwin Hyman, 330–46.

——(1991) 'Tradition, rationality and cultural transmission', in R. W. Preucel (ed.) *Processual and Postprocessual Archaeologies: Multiple Ways of Knowing the Past*, Carbondale: Southern Illinois University, 197–208.

——(1993) 'After social evolution: a new archaeological agenda?', in N. Yoffee and A. Sherratt (eds) *Archaeological Theory: Who Sets the Agenda?*, Cambridge: Cambridge University Press, 53–9.

Silverblatt, I. (1988) 'Women in states', *Annual Review of Anthropology*, 17: 427–60.

Siret, H. and Siret, L. (1887) *Les Premiers âges du métal dans le sud-est de l'Espagne*, Anvers.

Siret, L. (1913) *Questions de chronologie et d'ethnographie ibériques I*, Paris: Paul Geuthner.

—— (1948) 'El tell de Almizaraque y sus problemas', *Cuadernos de Historia Primitiva*, 3: 117–24.

Skeates, R. (1994) 'Ritual, context and gender in Neolithic south-eastern Italy', *Journal of European Archaeology*, 2(2): 199–214

—— (1995) 'Transformations in mortuary practice and meaning in the Neolithic and Copper Age of lowland east-central Italy', in W. H .Waldren, J. A. Ensenyat and R. C. Kennard (eds) *Ritual, Rites and Religion in Prehistory*, Oxford: British Archaeological Reports International Series 611, 212–38.

—— (1999) 'Unveiling inequality: social life and social change in the Mesolithic and Early Neolithic of East-Central Italy', in R. H. Tykot, J. Morter and J. E. Robb (eds) *Social Dynamics of the Prehistoric Central Mediterranean*, London: Accordia Specialist Studies on the Mediterranean 3, 15–45.

—— (2000) 'The social dynamics of enclosure in the Neolithic of the Tavoliere, south-east Italy', *Journal of Mediterranean Archaeology*, 13(2): 155–88.

Soffer, O. (1985) 'Patterns of intensification as seen from the Upper Palaeolithic of the Central Russian Plain', in T. D. Price and J. A. Brown (eds) *Prehistoric Hunter-Gatherers: The Emergence of Cultural Complexity*, New York: Academic Press, 235–70.

Sollas, W. J. (1911) *Ancient Hunters and Their Modern Representatives*, London: Macmillan.

Spencer, C. S. (1987) 'Rethinking the chiefdom', in R. D. Drennan and C. Uribe (eds) *Chiefdoms in the Americas*, Lanham, Md: University Press of America, 369–89.

—— (1993) 'Human agency, biased transmission and the cultural evolution of chiefly authority', *Journal of Anthropological Archaeology*, 12: 41–74.

—— (1997) 'Evolutionary approaches in archaeology', *Journal of Archaeological Research*, 5: 209–64.

Speth, J. D. (1990) 'Seasonality, resource stress and food sharing in so-called "Egalitarian" foraging societies', *Journal of Anthropological Archaeology*, 9: 148–88.

Spriggs, M. (ed.) (1984) *Marxist Perspectives in Archaeology*, Cambridge: Cambridge University Press.

Stein, G. J. (1994) 'The organizational dynamics of complexity in Greater Mesopotamia', in G. Stein and M. S. Rothman (eds) *Chiefdoms and Early States in the Near East: The Organizational Dynamics of Complexity*, Madison, Wis.: Prehistory Press, 11–22.

—— (1998) 'Heterogeneity, power and political economy: some current research issues in the archaeology of Old World complex societies', *Journal of Archaeological Research*, 6: 1–44.

Steponaitis, V. P. (1978) 'Location theory and complex chiefdoms: a Mississippian example', in B. D. Smith (ed.) *Mississippian Settlement Patterns*, New York: Academic Press, 417–53.

—— (1991) 'Contrasting patterns of Mississippian development', in T. Earle (ed.) *Chiefdoms: Power, Economy and Ideology*, Cambridge: Cambridge University Press, 193–228.

Sterud, G. (1973) 'A paradigmatic view of prehistory', in C. Renfrew (ed.) *The Explanation of Culture Change: Models in Prehistory*, London: Duckworth, 3–17.

Stika, H-P. (1988) 'Botanische Untersuchungen in der bronzezeitlichen Höhensiedlung Fuente Alamo', *Madrider Mitteilungen*, 29: 21–76.

—— (2000) 'Resultados arqueobotánicos de la campaña de 1988 en Fuente Álamo', in H. Schubart, V. Pingel and O. Arteaga *Fuente Álamo: las excavaciones arqueológicas 1977–1991 en el poblado de la Edad del Bronce*, Seville: Junta de Andalućia, 183–221.

Stika, H-P. and Jurich, B. (1998) 'Pflanzenreste aus der Probegrabung 1991 im bronzezeitlichen Siedlungsplatz el Argar, prov. Almería, südostspanien', *Madrider Mitteilungen*, 39: 35–48.

Stoddart, S., Bonanno, A., Gouder, T., Malone, C. and Trump, D. (1993) 'Cult in an island society: prehistoric Malta in the Tarxien period', *Cambridge Archaeological Journal*, 3: 3–19.

Stos-Gale, S. (2000) 'Trade in metals in the Bronze Age Mediterranean: an overview of lead isotope data for provenance studies', in C. F. E. Pare (ed.) *Metals Make The World Go Round: The Supply and Circulation of Metals in Bronze Age Europe*, Oxford: Oxbow Books, 56–69.

Stos-Gale, S., Hunt-Ortiz, M. and Gale, N. H. (1999) 'Análisis elemental y de isótopos de plomo de objetos metálicos de Gatas', in P. V. Castro *et al.*, *Proyecto Gatas 2: la dinámica arqueoecológica de la ocupación prehistórica*, Seville: Junta de Andalucía, 347–58.

Strathern, M. (1987) 'Introduction', in M. Strathern (ed.) *Dealing with Inequality: Analysing Gender Relations in Melanesia and Beyond*, Cambridge: Cambridge University Press, 1–32.

Suárez, A., Bravo, A., Cara, L., Martínez, J., Ortiz, D., Ramos, R. and Rodríguez, J. Ma. (1986) 'Aportaciones al estudio de la Edad del Cobre en la provincia de Almería: Análisis de la distribución de yacimientos', in *Homenaje a Luis Siret 1934–84*, Seville: Junta de Andalucía, 196–207.

Taylor, D. (1975) 'Some locational aspects of middle-range hierarchical societies', unpublished PhD dissertation, City University of New York.

Téllez, R. and Ciferri, F. (1954) *Trigos arqueológicos de España 1*, Madrid: Instituto Nacional de Investigaciones Agronómicas.

Terral, J-F. (1996) 'Wild and cultivated olive (*Olea europaea L.*): a new approach to an old problem using inorganic analyses of modern wood and archaeological charcoal', *Review of Palaeobotany and Palynology*, 91: 383–97.

—— (2000) 'Exploitation and management of the olive tree during prehistoric times in Mediterranean France and Spain', *Journal of Archaeological Science*, 27: 127–33.

Thomas, J. (1995) 'Where are we now? Archaeological theory in the 1990s', in P. J. Ucko (ed.) *Theory in Archaeology: A World Perspective*, London: Routledge, 343–62.

—— (2000) 'Introduction: The polarities of post-processual archaeology', in J. Thomas (ed.) *Interpretive Archaeology: A Reader*, Leicester: Leicester University Press, 1–18.

Thomas, J. and Tilley, C. (1993) 'The axe and the torso: symbolic structures in the Neolithic of Brittany', in C. Tilley (ed.) *Interpretative Archaeology*, Oxford: Berg, 225–324.

Tilley, C. (2000) 'Materialism and an archaeology of dissonance', in J. Thomas (ed.) *Interpretive Archaeology: A Reader*, Leicester: Leicester University Press, 71–80.

Trigger, B. G. (1989) *A History of Archaeological Thought*, Cambridge: Cambridge University Press.

—— (1990) 'Maintaining economic equality in opposition to complexity: an Iroquoian case study', in S. Upham (ed.) *The Evolution of Political Systems: Sociopolitics in small-Scale Sedentary Societies*, Cambridge: Cambridge University Press, 119–45.

—— (1993) 'Marxism in contemporary western archaeology', *Archaeological Method and Theory*, 5: 159–200.

—— (1998a) *Sociocultural Evolution*, Oxford: Blackwell.

—— (1998b) 'Archaeology and epistemology: dialoguing across the Darwinian chasm', *American Journal of Archaeology*, 102: 1–34.

Tschauner, H. (1996) 'Middle-range theory, behavioral archaeology and post-empiricist philosophy of science in archaeology, *Journal of Archaeological Method and Theory*, 3: 1–30.

Turner, B. S. (1994) *Orientalism, Postmodernism and Globalism*, London: Routledge.

Turner, V. W. (1957) *Schism and Continuity in an African Society*, Manchester: Manchester University Press.

Tusa, S. (1996) 'From hunter-gatherers to farmers in western Sicily', in R. Leighton (ed.) *Early Societies in Sicily: New Developments in Archaeological Research*, London: University of London, Accordia Specialist Studies in Italy 5, 41–55.

Tykot, R. (1994) 'Radiocarbon dating and absolute chronology in Sardinia and Corsica', in R. Skeates and R. Whitehouse (eds) *Radiocarbon Dating and Italian Prehistory*, London: British School at Rome and Accordia Research Centre, 115–45.

Ucko, P. J. (ed.) (1995) *Theory in Archaeology: A World Perspective*, London: Routledge.

Upham, S. (1987) 'A theoretical consideration of middle range societies', in R. D. Drennan and C. Uribe (eds) *Chiefdoms in the Americas*, Lanham, Md: University Press of America, 345–67.

—— (1990a) 'Decoupling the processes of political evolution', in S. Upham (ed.) *The Evolution of Political Systems: Sociopolitics in Small-scale Sedentary Societies*, Cambridge: Cambridge University Press, 1–17.

—— (ed.) (1990b) *The Evolution of Political Systems: Sociopolitics in Small-scale Sedentary Societies*, Cambridge: Cambridge University Press.

—— (1990c) 'Analog or digital?: toward a generic framework for explaining the development of emergent political systems', in S. Upham (ed.) *The Evolution of Political Systems: Sociopolitics in Small-Scale Sedentary Societies*, Cambridge: Cambridge University Press, 87–115.

VanPool, C. S. and VanPool, T. L. (1999) 'The scientific nature of postprocessualism', *American Antiquity*, 64: 33–53.

Vargas Arenas, I. and Sanoja, M. (1999) 'Archaeology as a social science: its expression in Latin America', in G. G. Politis and B. Alberti (eds) *Archaeology in Latin America*, London: Routledge, 59–75.

Vázquez Varela, J. M. and Risch, R. (1991) 'Theory in Spanish archaeology since 1960', in I. Hodder (ed.) *Archaeological Theory in Europe*, London: Routledge, 25–51.

Vicent, J. M. (1991) 'Arqueología y filosofía: la teoría crítica', *Trabajos de Prehistoria*, 48: 29–76.

Vigne, J.-D. (1988) *Les Mammifères post-glaciaires de Corse: Étude Archéozoologique*, Paris: Editions du Centre National de la Recherche Scientifique.

Vincent, J. (1978) 'Political anthropology: manipulative strategies', *Annual Review of Anthropology*, 7: 175–94.

Wailes, B. (1995) 'A case study of heterarchy in complex societies: early medieval Ireland and its archaeological implications', in R. M. Ehrenreich, C. L. Crumley and J. E. Levy (eds) *Heterarchy and the Analysis of Complex Societies*, Archaeological Papers of the American Anthropological Association no. 6, 55–69.

Waldren, W. (2001) 'A new megalithic dolmen from the Balearic island of Mallorca: Its radiocarbon dating and artefacts', *Oxford Journal of Archaeology*, 20: 241–62.

Webster, G. S. (1990) 'Labor control and emergent stratification in prehistoric Europe', *Current Anthropology*, 31: 337–66.

—— (1991a) 'Monuments, mobilization and Nuragic organization', *Antiquity*, 65: 840–56.

—— (1991b) 'The functions and social significance of nuraghi', in B. Santillo Frizell (ed.) *Arte Militare e Architettura Nuragica*, Stockholm: Acta Instituti Regni Sueciae, Series 4, xlviii, 169–85.

—— (1996) *A Prehistory of Sardinia 2300–500* BC, Sheffield: Sheffield Academic Press.

Webster, G. S. and Michels, J. W. (1986) 'Palaeoeconomy in west-central Sardinia', *Antiquity*, 60: 226–9.

Wenke, R. J. (1981) 'Explaining the evolution of cultural complexity: a review', *Advances in Archaeological Method and Theory*, 4: 79–127.

Whallon, R. (1982) 'Comments on "explanation"', in C. Renfrew and S. Shennan (eds) *Ranking, Resource and Exchange*, Cambridge: Cambridge University Press, 155–8.

White, J. C. (1995) 'Incorporating heterarchy into theory on socio-political development: the case for South-east Asia', in R. M. Ehrenreich, C. L. Crumley and J. E. Levy (eds) *Heterarchy and the Analysis of Complex Societies*, Archaeological Papers of the American Anthropological Association no. 6, 101–23.

White, J. P. (1985) 'Digging out Big Men?', *Archaeology in Oceania*, 20: 57–60.

Wolf, E. R. (1982) *Europe and the People Without History*, Berkeley: University of California Press.

Wright, H. T. (1977) 'Recent research on the origins of the state', *Annual Review of Anthropology*, 6: 379–97.

—— (1984) 'Prestate political formations', in T. Earle (ed.) *On the Evolution of*

Complex Societies: Essays in Honor of Harry Hoijer 1982, Malibu, Cal.: Undena Publications, 41–77.

—— (1986) 'The evolution of civilisations', in D. J. Meltzer, D. D. Fowler and J. A. Sabloff (eds) *American Archaeology Past and Future: A Celebration of the Society for American Archaeology 1935–85*, Washington DC: Smithsonian Institution Press, 323–65.

Wright, H. T. and Johnson, G. A. (1975) 'Population, exchange and early state formation in southwestern Iran', *American Anthropologist*, 77: 267–89.

Wylie, A. (1982) 'Epistemological issues raised by a structuralist archaeology', in I. Hodder (ed.) *Symbolic and Structural Archaeology*, Cambridge: Cambridge University Press, 39–46.

—— (1989) 'The interpretive dilemma', in V. Pinsky and A. Wylie (eds) *Critical Traditions in Contemporary Archaeology*, Cambridge: Cambridge University Press, 18–27.

—— (1992) 'On "heavily decomposing red herrings": scientific method in archaeology and the ladening of evidence with theory', in L. Embree (ed.) *Metaarchaeology*, Dordrecht: Kluwer Academic Publishers, 269–88.

—— (2000) 'Questions of evidence, legitimacy and the disunity of science', *American Antiquity*, 69: 227–37.

Yates, T. (1989) 'Habitus and social space: some suggestions about meaning in the Saami (Lapp) tent ca. 1700–1900', in I. Hodder (ed.) *The Meaning of Things. Material Culture and Symbolic Expression*, London: Unwin Hyman, 249–62.

Yengoyan, A. A. (1991) 'Evolutionary theory in ethnological perspectives', in A. T. Rambo and K. Gillogly (eds) *Profiles in Cultural Evolution*, Ann Arbor, Mich.: Museum of Anthropology, 3–21.

Zafra de la Torre, N., Hornos, F. and Castro, M. (1999) 'Una macro-aldea en el origen del modo de vida campesino: Marroqíes Bajos (Jaén) *c.* 2500–2000 cal a.n.e', *Trabajos de Prehistoria*, 56(1): 77–102.

Zeidler, J. A. (1987) 'The evolution of prehistoric "tribal" systems as historical process: archaeological indicators of social reproduction', in R. D. Drennan and C. Uribe (eds) *Chiefdoms in the America*: Lanham, Md: University Press of America, 325–43.

Zilhão, J. (2000) 'From the Mesolithic to the Neolithic in the Iberian peninsula', in T. D. Price (ed.) *Europe's First Farmers*, Cambridge: Cambridge University Press, 144–82.

INDEX

Numbers in bold indicate figures in the text.

Cahokia 88–90, 93, 94, 160, 195
Callinicos, A. 3, 4, 68
Cámalich, M. D. 109, 110, 114,
   118, 123, 125
Cámara, J. C. 169
Campos 104, 108, 109, 122, 123,
   125, 126, 130, 132
capital investment 155–8, 183
capitalism 1, 2, 3, 8, 30, 59
Cara, L. 110
Carigüela de Piñar 103, 104
Carmichael, P. H. 91
Carneiro, R. L. 43
Carrilero, M. 109, 118, 155
Carrión, F. 118, 124
Castro, P. V. 24, 25, 97, 110, 111,
   112, 113, 114, 115, 116, 117,
   121, 122, 123, 126, 130, 131,
   132, 133, 135, 136, 138, 143,
   144, 146, 151, 153, 154, 156
Çatalhöyük 196
Cazzella, A. 177
centralization 83, 94, 95, 161, 193
Cerro del Real 103
Cerro de la Encina, Monachil 103,
   105, 133, 162, 175
Cerro de la Virgen 103, 104, 105,
   122, 123, 125, 130, 133, 155,
   169
Cerro de las Canteras 103, 126
Cerro de los Castellones, Laborcillas
   103, 108
Cerro Virtud 104, 114, 117, 118,
   119, 120, 155
Chapman, R. 104, 106, 109, 110,
   111, 114, 121, 122, 123, 129,
   130, 133, 144, 151, 152, 155,
   159, 160, 164–5, 174, 178, 179
Cherry, J. F. 43, 95
chiefdoms 35–6, 37, 38, 39–41, 44,
   45, 47–8, 50–6, 58, 66–7, 86,
   93, 94–5, 159, 162, 177, 180,
   182, 185; coercive 42, 84;
   collaborative 42, 84; complex 42,
   48, 49, 52, 90, 161, 180; group-
   oriented 39, 40, 42;
   individualizing 41, 42; simple
   42, 91, 180
Childe, V. G. 19, 22, 30, 33, 60
Chowning, A. 42

Ciavieja, El Éjido 103, 109, 118,
   124, 155
Ciferri, F. 122
civilization 5, 43, 197
Claessen, H. J. M. 88, 93
Clapham, A. J. 133
Clark, J. E. 67, 91, 93
Clarke, D. L. 13,
class 24, 37, 60, 63, 64, 68, 96–9
class societies 5, 173, 174–5, 181
Clemente, I. 139
coercion 96–7, 98
Cohen, A. P. 64
complexity 4–5, 6, 7, 8, 9, 10, 11,
   24, 82–4; horizontal 83;
   organizational 54, 55; social 66;
   vertical 83
complex societies 5, 7, 10, 72;
   Iberia 164–7; West
   Mediterranean 176–85
conjunto 25, 26
Contreras, F. 109, 142, 163, 174,
   175
Coppa Nevigata 177
Cordy, R. H. 42, 45, 49, 52, 94
Coudart, A. 14, 16
Courty, M. A. 135
Creamer, W. 41
Cretan palace society 194, 195
Crumley, C. L. 81
Cruz-Auñón, R. 171, 172, 173
Cuartillas 104, 114, 118, 119
Cuesta del Negro, Purullena 103,
   105, 133, 163
Cueva de los Murciélagos, Zuheros
   103, 104, 118
Cueva de los Toyos 103, 119
Cueva de Nerja 103, 104
cultural ecology 27, 28, 45, 46, 50,
   58
cultural evolution 38, 50, 55, 58
cultural materialism 28

Delibes, G. 110, 117, 118, 119,
   120, 122, 126, 131, 166
DeMarrais, E. 62, 63
Dever, L. 154
Devore, I. 84
Díaz-Andreu, M. 166–7
Dobres, M-A. 66